Many Unhappy Returns

LEADERSHIP FOR THE COMMON GOOD

HARVARD BUSINESS SCHOOL PRESS

CENTER FOR PUBLIC LEADERSHIP
JOHN F. KENNEDY SCHOOL OF GOVERNMENT
HARVARD UNIVERSITY

The Leadership for the Common Good series represents a partnership between Harvard Business School Press and the Center for Public Leadership at Harvard University's John F. Kennedy School of Government. Books in the series aim to provoke conversations about the role of leaders in business, government, and society, to enrich leadership theory and enhance leadership practice, and to set the agenda for defining effective leadership in the future.

OTHER BOOKS IN THE SERIES

Predictable Surprises
by Max H. Bazerman and
Michael D. Watkins

Changing Minds
by Howard Gardner

Bad Leadership
by Barbara Kellerman

Many Unhappy Returns

One Man's Quest to Turn Around the Most Unpopular Organization in America

Charles O. Rossotti

Commissioner of the IRS, 1997–2002

HARVARD BUSINESS SCHOOL PRESS
BOSTON, MASSACHUSETTS

Printed in the United States of America
09 08 07 06 05 5 4 3 2 1

Library of Congress Cataloging-in-Publication Data

Rossotti, Charles O., 1941–
Many unhappy returns : one man's quest to turn around the most unpopular organization in America / Charles O. Rossotti.
p. cm.
Includes bibliographical references.
ISBN 1-59139-441-4
1. United States. Internal Revenue Service. 2. Tax administration and procedure—United States. I. Title.
HJ2361.R667 2005
352.4'4—dc22 2004023103

The paper used in this publication meets the minimum requirements of the American National Standard for Information Sciences—Permanence of Paper for Printed Library Materials, ANSI Z39.48-1992.

To my wife, Barbara,

who supported my decision to throw our plans

to the winds so I could take a job, of all things,

as IRS Commissioner.

Contents

Acknowledgments

I was able to mention in this book only a few of the many people who played important roles during my tenure at the IRS. If I had written about all of them, the book would rival the tax code in length. I extend my thanks here to each and every person in the Treasury Department, the IRS, the Congress, the tax professional associations, the vendors, and the numerous other groups who worked with me to make the IRS work better for taxpayers.

A few people in the IRS bore an even heavier burden than the rest. They worked in my own office and put up with me every day. Adrienne Griffen, Vicki Fiore, and Joanne Sullivan were successively my special assistants, a job that I described as making sure we did whatever most needed to be done every day. They saw to it that every meeting, trip, and event was carefully prepared and then followed up to achieve its purpose. Belinda Smith, ably assisted by Carol Peterson, accomplished the impossible by managing my ever changing schedule, while treating every caller and visitor with the utmost courtesy. Joann Buck, Linda Hurd, and their small staff handled with great skill the avalanche of mail and requests that poured into my office, somehow making sure that every request received a response and that I saw what I needed to, when I needed to.

When I started thinking about writing a book, the first person I turned to was Father Bill Byron, S.J. Having written many books himself, he knew the ropes, and I knew he would give me honest advice. With his encouragement, I looked for an agent and was lucky enough to find William Janklow and Tina Bennett, of Janklow and Nesbit Associates. Though I was a novice author, they thought my topic was important enough to take me on and to guide me through the process. They in turn led me to the Harvard Business School Press, where director Carol Franco agreed to publish the book and assigned me to work with editor Jeff Kehoe. For nineteen months, Jeff, assisted by Julia Ely, provided me great advice and support while I was writing. Adrienne Griffen agreed to research the vast amount of material I had accumulated. She unerringly came up with the right items for me to review in preparation for writing each chapter. Tony Dresden, a talented writer, agreed to read a rough draft of the whole manuscript, and gave me invaluable recommendations for what to keep and what to trim. Aileen Sullivan put my rough manuscript into finished form. Finally, Connie Hale, a remarkably insightful editor, showed me how to make very significant improvements in the final manuscript.

The people who were most important to me in writing this book, as well as in the rest of my life, were my family. My wife, Barbara, after reading the first draft of my book proposal, surprised me by advising me to go ahead with the project. As the drafts poured out, she read them and helped me keep the right focus. While I was writing, my son and daughter-in-law, Edward and Lynn Rossotti, and my daughter, Allegra Rossotti Rich, talked to me almost weekly and gave me encouragement and suggestions. At the end, the whole family joined in a round-robin debate to come up with a title.

The customary statement by an author that he or she alone is responsible for any deficiencies in a book is entirely applicable in this case. I wrote it. I'm responsible for it.

PROLOGUE

Why I Wrote This Story

WHEN MY NOMINATION as IRS commissioner was announced on June 3, 1997, one newspaper reporter asked me, "Were you ever in the military, and if you were, did you volunteer for a suicide mission?"

Although this reporter's question was snide, his point of view was widely held: The mess at the IRS was hopeless. That bureaucracy could never be changed.

Years later, one person who learned that I was writing this book snapped, "The IRS. *Ugh.* I'd rather read about gum disease."

But just as I didn't see the commissioner's job as a suicide mission, I didn't see this book as an IRS book. This is a story about how a huge and seriously out-of-date institution actually changed to begin running like a twenty-first-century business. It is a story that is relevant for any leader trying to turn around the performance of an organization for its customers and owners. The IRS made fundamental changes in the way it did business while continuing to collect $2 trillion per year—all in the glare of extraordinary public scrutiny.

Under attack from all sides, by 1997 the IRS seemed to be in an impossible situation. It had the largest number of customers and the lowest approval rating of any institution in America.

An unrelenting drumbeat of press stories and congressional hearings reported on poor service, alleged mistreatment of taxpayers, billions wasted on failed computer projects, and bad management of the agency. Taxpayers were in tears on live television, and a *Newsweek* cover story said, "The IRS itself has become a rogue organization wielding its awesome power under a cloak of secrecy."[1]

The public and Congress were demanding major reform, but most informed observers of the IRS questioned whether real change for the better would ever happen. Not only was the agency big—serving 132 million individual and 6 million business taxpayers and employing 100,000 people—but it was essential, collecting 95 percent of the government's revenue.[2]

Could such a disliked, but huge and entrenched, agency be changed to one that operated more like a well-run business? Could the IRS treat taxpayers like valued customers and still collect the taxes? After previous failures, could the agency manage one of the world's largest and most complex technology modernization programs? Would the intense political controversies about the IRS and the tax system defeat the goal of making the agency work better?

While these criticisms raged and the questions mounted, I was asked by Treasury Secretary Robert Rubin to become the first businessperson to be commissioner of the Internal Revenue Service, an agency that had been run by tax experts for fifty years. I decided to take a chance that the extreme pressures on the agency could be turned from creating a political storm into a force for real progress.

My first challenge, before I was even confirmed as commissioner, was to convince the administration I had just joined that the IRS's problems could not be solved by public relations maneuvers, and that fundamental changes in the IRS were truly necessary. Once I took office in November 1997, I had to rebuild relationships with members of Congress and representatives of the many other groups that deal with the IRS, while setting strict priorities to stop the IRS from its self-defeating practice of promising everything and delivering nothing in reaction to complaints. At the same time, I had to regain the initiative by winning acceptance of a comprehensive plan to modernize the whole agency, not just the technology.

To have any chance of implementing my plan I had to work with Congress on its IRS reform bill, to put into the bill the authority I needed to change the agency, while trying—unsuccessfully as it turned out—to keep destructive micromandates out. By July 1998, the reform bill was passed and my plan to modernize the agency was launched.

For the rest of my term, I worked on changing the culture and measurement systems of the agency to focus on improving performance across the board—on providing better service to taxpayers *and* on becoming more effective at enforcing compliance with the tax law. But the changes needed went much beyond setting new direction.

The agency needed to be reorganized from top to bottom—for a clearer emphasis externally on understanding taxpayers' specific characteristics, and a greater emphasis internally on accountability of management for quality performance. This huge reorganization required eliminating and refilling more than two thousand executive and senior management jobs and cutting management layers and several hundred of these jobs along the way.

The agency's ancient technology—it was still using software written in the 1960s to make weekly updates of taxpayer records kept on tape files—locked in obsolete ways for everything the IRS did, from processing returns to auditing businesses. Once the modernized organization structure was in place, we began the high-stakes process of replacing the IRS's vast suite of business systems.

With my new senior leadership team—for the first time comprising executives from inside and outside the IRS—we implemented new strategies for service to taxpayers and for enforcing compliance. We upgraded traditional services, on the telephones and in local offices, and offered new electronic services for filing, paying, and getting information. We created initiatives for combating the epidemic of tax shelters and other tax schemes that emerged in the 1990s, and updated long-out-of-date methods of collecting and auditing.

While making these changes, we dealt daily with mistakes, setbacks, crises, and potential disasters, which ranged from demands for the firing of employees who allegedly abused taxpayers, to delays in computer systems projects, to threats to IRS operations from terrorist attacks. These incidents were well explored in public, in the forty-eight congressional hearings at which I testified, and the 850 audit reports and thousands of press stories published about IRS failings. We coped by acknowledging problems forthrightly and engaging our stakeholders in helping us solve our problems.

As I left office after five years one big change was evident: most informed observers no longer believed that the IRS could not change. Because they knew it had.

USA Today reported in 2001 that customers surveyed said they were "more satisfied with service from the Internal Revenue Service than with service from McDonald's."[3] This amusing report did not come about because people now enjoyed paying taxes more than eating hamburgers. People rate service relative to their expectations, and the IRS was doing much better in providing taxpayers what they expected when they dealt with the agency.

Service to taxpayers doing business with the IRS has in fact become measurably better. But the purpose of the change was never just to make things seem easier for taxpayers by easing off on those who don't pay what they owe. As a result of the changes, the IRS has started to become more effective in enforcing compliance with the tax law than it used to be.

By no means are all the IRS's problems solved. Years of work remain before the IRS will reach fully acceptable levels of performance. But now people inside and outside the agency believe it can increasingly improve the way it does its job on behalf of taxpayers.

The story does not have an entirely happy ending. No matter how much the IRS improves, an ever expanding tax code and ever shrinking resources to administer it are making the whole tax system more and more unfair to the vast majority of taxpayers, who diligently pay what they owe no matter what their tax bracket. At the end of my term, and since then, I have spoken out about this critical situation, which unnecessarily threatens one of the foundations of our economy. Every honest taxpayer has a stake in demanding that the president and Congress fix this broader problem—just as in 1997 citizens demanded that the IRS be changed to better serve the public.

I was privileged to have led the IRS during a period that started with a crisis but that precipitated badly needed change. From this experience, I learned much that I think is relevant to people in many organizations, public or private. This book is a way for me to share my insights with readers, but it is also more than that. It is a way for me to state my deep conviction that any organization, even a tax collection agency, can serve its stakeholders at higher levels than it ever imagined—if its leaders resolutely and passionately set out to do so.

PART I

From a Political Storm to a Practical Plan

CHAPTER 1

The IRS Is Out of Control

A Growing Crisis

I'LL NEVER FORGET the day *CBS News* correspondent Bob Schieffer interviewed Internal Revenue Service employee Jennifer Long on *Face the Nation*:

> *Schieffer:* And how many people do you know of that did commit suicide or . . . or threatened suicide because of troubles with the IRS? Do you know of specific cases?
>
> *Long:* I . . . I know of at least five cases.
>
> *Schieffer:* You know of five specific cases where people committed suicide because they were being hounded by the IRS?
>
> *Long:* Right.[1]

It was Sunday morning, September 28, 1997. Schieffer spent the rest of the show that day discussing the previous week's Senate hearings, where charges had been made against the IRS by Long and other witnesses. Republican Senator William Roth of Delaware, the chairman of the powerful Senate Finance Committee that oversees the IRS, had used

FIGURE 1-1

Herblock made a gripping image out of the theme of the Senate hearings: IRS employees abusing taxpayers and getting away with it.

Source: From *Herblock: A Cartoonist's Life* (Times Books, 1998)

the hearings to dramatize his contention that the IRS was an out-of-control agency systematically abusing taxpayers.

Senator Roth was a soft-spoken, immaculately dressed, and impeccably courteous lawyer who kept pictures of his Saint Bernard dogs in his office. Occupying the same seat as that of a 1950s Republican senator from Delaware who had become famous by exposing scandals in the IRS, Roth was convinced that it was now his job to expose what he believed were widespread abuses of taxpayers by IRS employees. His gentle demeanor notwithstanding, Roth was relentless in pursuing this agenda.

For six months, Roth's investigators had been combing through IRS files, interviewing employees and taxpayers, and planning hearings. To maximize the impact of the charges, he had revealed little about his plans. The hearings were given the bland title *Practices and Procedures of the IRS,* and the witness list was kept secret even from other members of the committee.

Meanwhile, IRS Acting Commissioner Michael Dolan had his staff working feverishly to prepare for whatever charges might be made. Press and political agents in both the White House and the Treasury Department were working overtime to portray the hearings as a politically motivated trick to undermine the tax system.

The setting for Senator Roth's hearings intensified the drama. The front of the Senate Finance Committee hearing room, dominated by a horseshoe-shaped table set on a dais, put the committee chairman at the top of the horseshoe, flanked by the nineteen members around the horseshoe. The senators looked down from their platform at the witness table. A dozen or more television cameramen and press photographers crouched on the floor inside the horseshoe, training their cameras and bright lights on the witness. Behind the witness table were rows of chairs for the public, completing the image that the witness was the object of a public spectacle controlled by the senators. The people crowded in, and cameras jostled for position.

But the most telling detail was the large screens set up to hide the identity of six IRS employees who were to testify. Hiding the identity of congressional witnesses is a technique normally limited to intelligence agents or Mafia informers, but Senator Roth said this was necessary to protect IRS employees from "retaliation" by the agency. For those watching on television, and especially for those viewing the short clips shown on the evening network news shows, the screen visually conveyed the theme of the hearings: that the IRS was a bureaucracy that wielded fear and intimidation to get its way—even with its own employees.

"There is no other agency in this country that directly touches the lives of more Americans, nor is there any agency which strikes more fear into their hearts," Senator Roth intoned to open the hearing. "We are going to see a picture of a troubled agency, one that is losing the

FIGURE 1-2

IRS employees testified behind screens to hide their identity, dramatizing the charge that the IRS used fear to intimidate anyone who defied it.

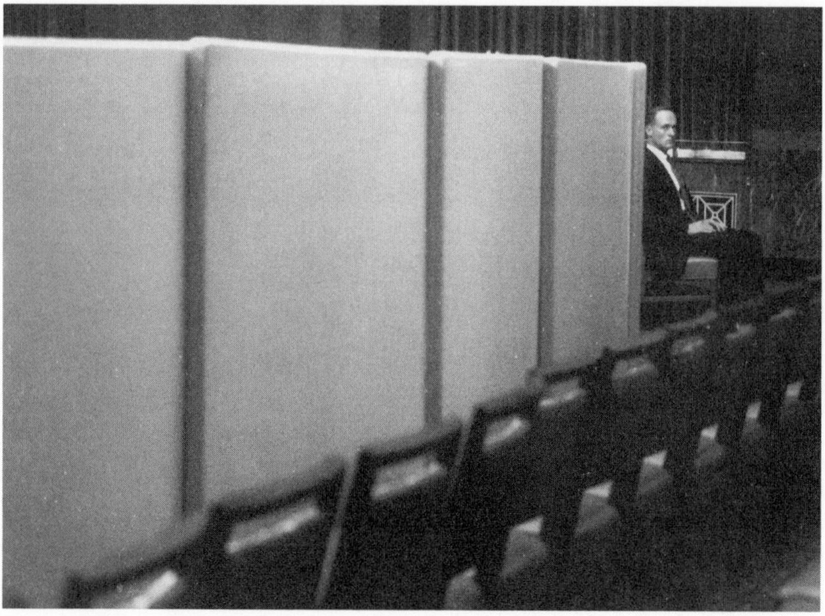

Source: Stephen Crowley / *New York Times*

confidence of the American people, and one that all too frequently acts as if it were above the law."[2]

Taxpayers were the star witnesses, telling stories of how their lives were ruined by the IRS's abuse of its authority, its inability to explain its own procedures, and its indifference to the plight of ordinary taxpayers who were victims of IRS mistakes. Employees told of how they were goaded by IRS managers to meet statistical collection goals, even when it meant disregarding taxpayer rights.

The first taxpayer to tell her story was Katherine Lund Hicks of Apple Valley, California.

Looking calmly into the cameras, Hicks carefully recounted her story. For fourteen years she tried to pay off a $2,709 tax debt incurred by her first husband prior to their divorce in 1983. Kafka himself could not have invented this real-life tale of an ordinary person caught in a maddening bureaucratic maze with no maps, no exits, and no explanations. Hicks described the absurd twists:

- Her husband had gotten all the notices, but she alone had gotten the bill for the interest on the unpaid balance.
- She tried to pay what she owed, but the IRS repeatedly refused to accept payment, telling her that she didn't owe anything and even sending her refunds.
- Years after she thought she was in the clear, her new husband was threatened with the loss of his home as a result of a lien filed by the IRS because of her prior debt.
- She paid the debt a second time to release the lien, but five years later, her second husband's salary was levied by the IRS for payment of the same debt again, which left the couple with $18 per week to live on.
- The collection agent acknowledged that the only way to get rid of the tax lien was to pay the $8,000, whether she owed it or not.
- Her second husband filed for divorce to protect his property.
- She filed for bankruptcy, only to receive additional notices from the IRS the very next day.

In case anyone missed the depiction of a confused and inept IRS, Senator Roth's follow-up questions complete the picture:

Roth: How many IRS employees and offices do you think you dealt with over the years that your problem lingered on? . . .

Hicks: The list is, like, three pages of different individuals that I dealt with.

Roth: How many times did you try to pay the taxes owed? . . .

Hicks: Three.

Roth: How many times did the IRS tell you that you owed no tax?

Hicks: About six.

"The IRS is judge, jury and executioner—answerable to none," Hicks said, concluding her testimony.[3]

If one such story was not infuriating enough, more taxpayers recounted their horror stories on the same afternoon.

Nancy Jacobs told of a fifteen-year-old problem and how it wore her down: "When you have someone come to you from the IRS and tell you they're going to take your home, your vehicles, whatever you own, close your business so you have no way of making a living, you do what they tell you to do."[4]

Tom Savage, a construction contractor from Delaware, claimed he paid $50,000 he didn't owe because of a "zealous, unrelenting and abusive pursuit by an IRS revenue officer." Echoing Jacobs's feeling of resignation, he added, "Believe me, when the resources of the government are unleashed on you, you are in trouble, no matter how good your case."[5]

Monsignor Lawrence Ballweg, a kindly gentleman who had been a priest for fifty-seven years, recounted living with "this constant worry, if not fear, that the trust that my dear mother had established to help the poor would be penalized because of what I can only call the unprofessional, [callous], and indifferent behavior of IRS employees."[6]

Throughout the morning, anger built among the onlookers. Jennifer Long's afternoon testimony stoked the fury to the boiling point. An IRS agent in the Houston office, she was the only current employee of the IRS willing to testify without concealing her identity.

Long claimed that it was an intentional policy of IRS management to pick on weak taxpayers to make the IRS's statistics look better—and that the more the taxpayers suffered, the better the IRS liked it. She told of "egregious tactics used by IRS revenue agents with the encouragement of IRS management. These tactics, which appear nowhere in the IRS manual, are used to extract unfairly assessed taxes from taxpayers, literally ruining families, lives, and businesses—all unnecessarily and sometimes illegally."[7]

She testified that the IRS often pursued taxpayers believed to be vulnerable. "To the IRS, vulnerabilities can be based on a perception that the taxpayer has limited formal education, has suffered a personal tragedy, is having a financial crisis, or may not necessarily have a solid grasp of their legal rights." She said that managers pushed employees to pursue tax assessments from individuals who could not fight back, claiming that "if that taxpayer does object or complain, every effort will be made by the IRS to run up their tax assessment, deplete their financial resources, and force them to capitulate to IRS demands."[8]

Press coverage of the IRS hearings was unprecedented. Stories of IRS abuse were recounted in evening and early morning news shows and in newspapers around the country. Typical was the lead story on *ABC World News Tonight*. "In Washington today, there was some stunning testimony at the second day of Senate hearings on the Internal Revenue Service," it reported. "An IRS employee testified that agents would make up false accusations against taxpayers just to raise extra money. And . . . there are others who say the IRS goes out of its way to ruin people's lives."[9]

The day's coverage only increased interest in the next day's hearings, which opened with the arresting scene of six more IRS employees testifying behind screens to hide their identity.

Acting Commissioner Mike Dolan, a career IRS executive who looked like the former Notre Dame football player that he was, testified at the end of the third day. He could only apologize to the taxpayers for "disrupting their lives."[10]

The sensational charges and the solid week of intense news coverage outraged the public and whipped up demands in Congress for major IRS reform. But that week's events, devastating as they were for the IRS, were only the latest and most dramatic reports of failures by the IRS that, after years of relative quiet for the agency, had seen crises growing for the two years before the Senate hearings.

1985 to 1995: Occasional Attacks, Then Business As Usual

In its long history, the IRS had periodically come under attack for one particular failure or another. The attacks would invariably be calmed with a commitment by IRS management to fix the problem. Then, years of relative quiet would pass as the IRS went about its business of collecting the ever growing stream of federal tax revenues. The sheer enormity of the agency's job, and the clear understanding that any interruption of the tax revenue stream would be disastrous for the economy, made it hard for anyone to propose changes that might seriously disturb the agency's work. The IRS, after all, dealt directly with more people than did any other organization in America, and it financed 95 percent of the government's activities.[11]

In 1985, when the IRS fell behind in processing tax returns during the peak season, a scandal broke after some employees tried to cover up the problem by stuffing tax returns into ceiling spaces. This incident brought to light the IRS's difficulties in updating the computer systems that were essential to handle the agency's ever increasing workload. As a response to these problems, Congress eventually approved a major IRS investment program to develop new systems that were intended to improve the agency's service to taxpayers while increasing its ability to collect taxes efficiently.

Meanwhile, complaints from taxpayers would occasionally arouse Congress. In 1988, Congress passed the first taxpayer bill of rights to rein in what some lawmakers viewed as an overly aggressive IRS. This law specified new procedures to protect taxpayers who, the IRS believed, owed money, and specifically forbade the IRS from using collection quotas to rate agents.

In congressional hearings the following year, the IRS was accused of tolerating unethical conduct, such as abuse of expense accounts and rogue enforcement operations.

With many other high-profile problems dominating the news and demanding attention, these periodic reports of IRS failures soon dropped off Congress's priority list and failed to engage top officials in each presidential administration. Most of the pressure on the agency from the Treasury Department and the White House was to increase enforcement revenue so as to reduce the federal government deficit. For the first half of the 1990s, changes in the way the agency operated were modest and incremental. Congress did provide money to update IRS computer systems and to build the staff to enforce compliance with the increasingly complex tax code.

1995 to 1997: A Growing Crisis

Despite this relatively placid situation, signs of trouble began to emerge. In 1995, taxpayers received four hundred million busy signals when trying to call the IRS, more busy signals than there were people in the United States.[12] Taxpayers called over and over again when they could not get through. And frequently, when they did get through, IRS employees could not resolve the taxpayers' issues. Resolution of these questions thus required additional calls and letters.

Most of these taxpayers were calling the IRS in the first place because they received letters from the IRS claiming that additional money was owed. The letters made clear that failure to respond carried serious consequences, including levying wages or seizing properties. Millions of taxpayers were caught in this stressful Catch-22. They were required under threat of serious penalty to conduct business with the IRS, but when they tried to complete seemingly routine transactions they found it hard or impossible to do so.

Complaints began to pour into congressional offices. Some members of Congress paid a full-time staff person just to handle taxpayer complaints about the IRS. During the Senate hearings in 1997, Senator Carol Moseley-Braun of Illinois summed up the conclusions that members of Congress had drawn from their experience in dealing with the IRS over the previous few years: "If there is one level of objection that we hear the most about, it is that nobody can figure out how to get through the maze of procedures or how to get through to where they need to go to get an answer."[13]

At the same time that taxpayers were having more and more trouble conducting business with the IRS, the service provided by private banking and credit card and mail-order businesses was getting better and better. In the late 1980s and early 1990s, many firms serving consumers upgraded their services, especially telephone service. The quality movement in private industry spread to service industries, as did an emphasis on courteous and quick response to customer inquiries. But the same person who called L.L. Bean in the morning to place an order might call the IRS in the afternoon and then compare the drastically less favorable results.

Senator Bob Kerrey of Nebraska studied the IRS for a year and summed up his conclusion in a hearing in 1997: "In the area of services being performed, there is a breathtaking gap between what the IRS can do and what the private sector can do. Taxpayers do not compare the IRS with a tax collection agency in Australia or the Federal Republic of Germany, they compare it to what they can get with their ATM card."[14]

While millions of taxpayers were experiencing frustration in doing business with the IRS, other agency failures were coming to the public's attention. The General Accounting Office (GAO), Congress's investigative arm, uncovered repeated incidents of unauthorized browsing through taxpayer records by IRS employees.

The idea that strangers might be poking around in one's personal finances just for fun produced feelings of outrage akin to finding a peeping Tom lurking outside the bedroom window. The *Washington Post* reported that "thousands of IRS employees have been caught or suspected of browsing through taxpayer records they were not authorized to see. . . . They snooped through the returns of celebrities, friends, and relatives, raising questions about security and taxpayer privacy."[15] For six months in 1997, the public heard repeatedly that the personal financial details they sent every year to the IRS might be misused, as the press continued to report on audit findings, and Congress acted to make it a crime to indulge in unauthorized access of taxpayer data.

During the same period, still another IRS problem added to the impression that the agency was failing in the immense responsibilities it was assigned to carry out in trust for the public. The GAO reported in March 1995 that the agency that scrutinized taxpayers' finances could not properly keep track of the $1.4 trillion of taxpayer money it was collecting each year. This situation seemed to most people like an obvious case of watching your doctor chain-smoking Marlboro cigarettes while advising you on how to stop smoking. But it was more than that. You could always change doctors, but you could not change your tax collector. The IRS had the power to audit taxpayers' personal financial records and even assess penalties if the documentation was inadequate.

The IRS's own accounting problems created more fodder for the ever-growing numbers of critics of the agency. "The agency that is so strict on the way Americans keep their books cannot itself pass a financial audit," said Senator Ted Stevens of Alaska. He even suggested that Congress might appoint an outside control board to run the IRS, similar to the board that at the time oversaw the District of Columbia government.[16] The senator's comment revealed the depths to which confidence in the IRS was sinking during this period of building crisis. The IRS, for years viewed as perhaps fearsome but at least efficient, was being equated to the inept D.C. government.

1996: Congress Creates a Commission to Study What to Do About the IRS

As dissatisfaction with the IRS grew, the failure of the program that the agency touted as the solution to many of its problems—its technology modernization program—led to an unprecedented action. In 1996, Congress passed legislation forming a commission whose sole job was to study what should be done with the IRS. This action led to far more intense scrutiny of the IRS than had been sustained in the past two decades.

In 1989, the IRS had launched a sweeping program to replace its obsolete technology. In the early 1990s, Congress began to provide hundreds of millions of dollars per year for this program, and by 1996 the tab had run to nearly $4 billion, with additional expenses projected to reach $20 billion.

While there was little doubt in any quarter that the ever growing tax system could not continue to depend on computer systems developed in the 1960s and 1970s, there was also increasing concern about the IRS's ability to manage its technology program. As early as 1990—shortly after the program effort got under way—the GAO began sounding alarms about ineffective management. As time went on, the tone of GAO audit reports became stronger, repeatedly identifying pervasive management and technical risks.

By early 1996, it was clear that the entire program was in serious trouble. Congressman Jim Lightfoot of Iowa erupted at reports of failures of the IRS program to modernize its computer systems. Calling the program a "$4 billion fiasco," Lightfoot compared the IRS system to a house project gone haywire. "They're probably out there building the roof right now [but] nobody's dug the foundation anywhere yet. The plumbing's probably going to end up in the living room, and when you flush the commodes the lights come on in the garage."[17]

Even as the Treasury and the IRS announced steps to fix the problems, the bad news was unrelenting. A particularly visible fiasco was the collapse of a project called Cyberfile, which was designed to let taxpayers file returns directly over the newly popular Internet. In September 1996, the GAO concluded that Cyberfile was plagued by mismanagement, shoddy contracting practices, and numerous security problems. Rona Stillman, then chief scientist at the GAO's Office of Computers and Telecommunications, said: "When IRS developed Cyberfile, they did it ass-backwards. There was no security policy. This was intended to go out over the Internet, which is a very dangerous environment."[18]

The sinking of Cyberfile drew an angry rebuke from Congress. "It's an absolute fiasco!" shouted Senator Stevens, after learning that the IRS violated a host of federal laws and regulations. "There is a lack of confidence here in terms of the management of the IRS," Stevens added, pointing his finger at IRS officials in the room. "We have been going at this for twelve years, and every year we get the same reports. Are we going to go another twelve years before you figure out how to put together these systems?"[19]

These failures, after billions had been spent, led Congress to be receptive to a new proposal for dealing with IRS problems. Senator Bob Kerrey of Nebraska was the prime proponent of legislation to establish a bipartisan commission, officially called the National Commission on Restructuring the Internal Revenue Service, comprising politicians and private citizens. A war hero and an energetic and outspoken maverick who had run for president in the 1992 Democratic primaries, Kerrey set up the legislation in such a way that he would be designated cochairman. Starting work in the fall of 1996, he intended to use the commission to conduct a top-to-bottom review of every aspect of the IRS management, including its oversight by the Treasury Department—a prospect not welcomed either by the department or by the Clinton White House.

Largely because few Republican members of Congress wanted to be involved in a time-consuming study of the IRS, a relatively junior congressman, Rob Portman of Ohio, was designated by Republican leader Newt Gingrich to be commission cochairman. Highly intelligent and far more interested in management than most politicians, Portman formed an unexpectedly close alliance with Kerrey. They set out to make the commission much more than the usual talkfest. Prominent businesspeople and tax professionals joined the commission, promising to lend more credibility to its work. The commission began holding interviews and hearings with hundreds of people who worked with or interacted with the IRS all around the country. As the seriousness of the commission's efforts became evident, the commission created even more nervousness in the Treasury Department.

One of the commission's first conclusions dealt, not surprisingly, with the failure of the IRS to modernize technology, charging that "the IRS has failed to enter the Information Age." The technology program, it added, "has been a complete disaster."[20]

By this time, even the Treasury Department acknowledged that the decade-long, multibillion-dollar effort needed to be rethought from top to bottom. The department began to take steps to correct the perceived problems. In March 1997, Deputy Treasury Secretary Lawrence Summers said that the IRS's modernization project had gone badly off track. He announced several steps to correct the problems, including hiring a chief information officer from outside the agency and more use of private contractors to manage the program.

Undeterred by these reactions from the Treasury Department, the commission stepped up its work. Its focus began to shift from weaknesses in managing technology toward weaknesses in managing the agency as a whole. In particular, the commission began to focus on the top leadership of the agency and on the lack of effective oversight by the Treasury Department, even suggesting that the IRS be removed from the Treasury Department completely.

Commission member Ernest J. Dronenburg Jr. stated the problem most colorfully: "When faced with the continuing enslavement of his people's minds and bodies, Moses said to Pharaoh, 'Let my people go.' In order for the Internal Revenue Service to reach its potential and be successful in meeting the challenges that it faces, IRS must be released from the bondage of the Treasury Department and the conflicting policy-making functions that are necessarily its highest priority."[21]

This idea was greeted by the Treasury Department much as IBM might have reacted to a proposal that it could continue doing business as usual as long as it stopped selling computers. Wary of the restructuring commission from the beginning, the Treasury Department began a public dispute about the commission's proposal for how the IRS should be governed. This dispute escalated throughout the spring and summer of 1997. Senator Kerrey, along with nearly all the Republicans in Congress, strongly endorsed the commission's recommendation of an outside board of directors. The Clinton administration fought publicly against this and other commission proposals to reform the IRS, seeing it as little more than a publicity stunt by Kerry, the Clinton rival, and a free chance for Republicans to bash the administration. From the White House point of view, fixing the IRS was not the main issue. Defending the administration was.

White House Economic Adviser Gene Sperling said the White House would "vigorously oppose the efforts to turn over the IRS management to part-time, outside private people." Sperling added that this "would lead to a recipe for conflicts of interest, less accountability, and less trust."[22]

Meanwhile, the fiery Republican House Speaker, Newt Gingrich of Georgia, warned that President Clinton was about to ally himself "with the IRS's bureaucratic machine and turn [his] back on the millions of Americans who have been pulled through its gears."[23]

In June 1997, the National Commission on Restructuring the Internal Revenue Service issued its report, proposing more than fifty reforms to transform the IRS into a more "efficient, modern and responsive agency" and to help "restore the public faith in the American tax system."[24] Congress embraced the work of the commission, with the House of Representatives quickly passing a bill incorporating most of its recommendations.

At the opposite end of Pennsylvania Avenue, the Treasury Department and White House continued to oppose many recommendations of the report. In fact, the Clinton administration launched a competing program to show that it was already solving the problem without the need for help from Congress. Vice President Al Gore announced the administration's own ninety-day task force of White House, Treasury, and IRS employees to improve customer service in the agency.

When there is a political storm brewing in Washington, reporters and television cameras will show up. While the details of the disputes over IRS governance were of little interest to most of the public, it was clear that a lot of important people in Washington were spending a lot of their time arguing about how to fix problems at the IRS. This noisy debate could only reinforce the public's already deteriorating view of the agency.

The Storm Peaks

The public's opinion of the IRS, as measured in independent surveys, had already been on a long-term decline. In the early 1980s, the public had rated the IRS about the same as other federal agencies and only slightly lower than many large, private companies. By 1996, however, surveys were showing that the IRS was rated far lower than any other institution measured. In December of that year, an annual survey by the University of Michigan reported that taxpayers gave the IRS the lowest satisfaction rating among two hundred private-sector companies and government agencies.[25] By July 1997, the Roper opinion research organization recorded the lowest rating ever given to an institution, private or public, in the previous fifteen years. Only 34 percent of the public gave a positive rating to the IRS, ten percentage points lower than the next lowest organization rated.[26]

By the summer of 1997—two months *before* the devastating Senate hearings—it had come to this: The IRS had the largest number of customers and the lowest approval rating of any institution in America.

Where there is a failure of any kind in government, some politicians will try to win points for their side by exploiting it. As the public's view of the IRS sunk lower and lower, and the press reported more and more failures, political pollsters saw an opportunity for their clients. Republican pollster Frank Luntz advised his Republican clients to feature the failures of the IRS in fund-raising letters for Republican congressional candidates. One Republican group sent out a fund-raising letter called

"The *People v. the IRS* Survey." It shouted its point out in the first line of the letter. "With your immediate help today, we can virtually abolish the IRS as you know it! That's right—abolish the IRS! But I repeat, your help now is vitally needed."[27]

These mailings only made the political storm around the IRS bigger and nastier. Then the storm peaked—at an unprecedented level.

In September 1997, the Senate began its sensational hearings. Arriving on top of the personal frustrations of millions of taxpayers, the years of audit reports of IRS failures, and the conclusions of the year-long study by the restructuring commission, these IRS hearings achieved a rare impact. The debate in Congress and the press was no longer about whether the IRS needed major fixing; the debate was on how drastic the fixing needed to be and whether it could be fixed at all.

Unlike the aftermath of so many other congressional hearings that highlight a problem, the spotlight on the IRS did not fade. After seeing taxpayers tell of mistreatment by the IRS on television, taxpayers across the country began writing and calling Congress and the press with even more stories.

A week after the hearings, *Newsweek* reported that "more than 2,000 calls, faxes, and e-mails had poured into the committee, most from taxpayers alleging wrongs. Many sobbed into the phone." According to a Senate Finance Committee spokesperson, "people are just venting."[28]

Investigative reporters picked up leads from the hearings and made their own reports. Among the most prominent of these was a cover story in *Newsweek* on October 13, 1997, which said: "Victimization of taxpayers isn't just the isolated deviltry of a few agents."[29] On the front cover of this national magazine was a picture of an Oklahoma-based IRS collection manager whom the story called King James: "In the spare, cloistered world of the Internal Revenue Service, Ronald James lived like a prince of the church."[30]

The key point of the *Newsweek* story seemed to validate one of the underlying accusations of the Senate hearings—that abuses were not accidental but rather were caused by managers trying to inflate their enforcement statistics. "According to more than a dozen agents interviewed by *Newsweek,* whose charges are corroborated by documents—[management] pushed for ever more property seizures from delinquent taxpayers, even though the IRS manual says such moves should be a final resort, riding roughshod in some cases over their rights to appeal. They closed cases and sometimes slapped on levies and liens prematurely—which boosted the enforcement stats that the IRS rewards with cash awards for top officers," the story continued.[31]

As the new year began in 1998, taxpayers and the press kept the IRS in their sights. Another stream of horror stories about people with IRS problems filled the press. One newspaper cartoon showed an executioner in a black hood carrying a large ax, with the letters "IRS" on his shirt.

In April 1998, Senator Roth convened another round of dramatic televised IRS hearings. This time, the hearings featured taxpayers alleging that rogue IRS criminal investigators were conducting massive and unnecessary raids on taxpayer businesses, and that IRS executives were allowed to get away with violations of rules for which ordinary employees were disciplined or fired.

Even more startling was testimony alleging a bizarre plot by rogue agents in Tennessee to try to create false tax charges to frame former Senate Majority Leader Howard Baker, a respected moderate Republican who had also served as the White House chief of staff.

"The Criminal Investigative Division is out of control," Senator Don Nickles of Oklahoma said after hearing the testimony. "The IRS is out of control."[32]

On the last day, the IRS commissioner was invited to testify to comment on the charges made in the previous days' hearings. But this time I was not watching on television. I was the commissioner.

CHAPTER 2

Operating on Good, Sound Business Principles

A Family Tradition

IF SOMEONE HAD SAID to me on the morning of February 5, 1997, that a phone call later in the day would lead to my becoming the IRS commissioner, I might have said that there would be more chance of my taking over at third base for the Baltimore Orioles when Cal Ripken retired. I was literally minding my own business in my office at American Management Systems, the company I helped found and manage for twenty-eight years. I was doing what I had always wanted to do.

From the time I was a young boy, I had wanted to run my own business. This was not surprising. Both my grandfathers had owned and run businesses. So had my mother and father.

My mother's father, known as Jack Ossola, came to America as a teenager, from the Piedmont region of Italy in the 1890s, to work in the coal mines in Western Pennsylvania. He got out of the mines by opening a grocery store catering to other miners from Italy. His store carried imported food products like olives, olive oil, cheese, and canned tomatoes.

As the business prospered, he expanded from retailing to wholesaling, and then importing, the same line of products. In the 1930s, Jack

Ossola moved his family from Pittsburgh to New York to be near the import district in lower Manhattan. He established his own brand—Torino—complete with labels the color of the Italian flag. He sold the brand through small neighborhood grocery stores up and down the East Coast.

My mother, Betty, was Jack Ossola's only child. After attending the University of Pittsburgh, she began working in the business, too. As my grandfather began traveling more to buy goods in Europe, she began to take over running the Torino business back home.

My father's father, Edward Rossotti, had attended high school in Milan, where he learned a technique called lithography, which was especially useful for high-quality color printing. As a young man, he moved to New York and soon established a small lithography shop.

FIGURE 2-1

My grandfather, Edward Rossotti (far right), with his employees in his lithography business in lower Manhattan.

Rossotti Lithograph prospered in the early 1900s. After attending Columbia University, my father, Charles Rossotti, and his brother came to work in the business. Then, big trouble struck in the form of the Eighteenth Amendment to the Constitution. Prohibition wiped out the company's specialty of making fancy labels for wine bottles, almost sending the business into bankruptcy and making my father a fervent lifelong opponent of government regulations.

Shortly after the passage of the Eighteenth Amendment, my grandfather died, leaving his two sons, still in their twenties, to take over the struggling business. They regained prosperity by developing a method for using their lithography technique to print high-quality designs and colors on paperboard that could be used to make boxes for solid products like pasta and rice. As packaged goods became more popular, Rossotti Lithograph printed more and more boxes.

My father met my mother when he went to call on Jack Ossola to sell him labels for his jars of imported olives, but found that Betty Ossola was making a lot of the decisions in the business. They married in 1939, and Charlie and Betty, as their many friends called them, both continued to run their respective businesses. That same year, my father moved Rossotti Lithograph to an industrial section in New Jersey and settled the family in Englewood, a bedroom community a few miles north of the George Washington Bridge. I was born two years later, and my brother, Jack, named after my grandfather, was born three years after that.

We grew up in Englewood, both attending grade school and high school at Saint Cecilia's, the local Catholic school whose main claim to fame was that Vince Lombardi had once been its high school football coach.

In the 1940s and 1950s, my mother continued to run the Torino importing business, commuting daily to lower Manhattan. It was so unusual then for a woman to run a business that newspapers occasionally ran feature stories about her. Meanwhile, my father was busy expanding Rossotti Lithograph in the postwar economy.

I remember as a teenager thinking that my mother was a more hardheaded, pragmatic businessperson than my father. A beautiful woman who loved to dress up in the latest fashions, she was also good with numbers and often did her own financial projections. When something didn't work, she'd stop and try something else. When her food import business started to fall off because of competition from large chain stores, she started importing household products from Japan, even traveling there in the early 1950s to find goods to buy. She took money out of the business and invested some in the stock market, a move my father thought not much different from gambling.

My father was more of a dreamer. Gregarious and outgoing, he loved nothing more than a good meal with his friends, who were also often his customers. He thought that numbers were for accountants and that his job was to expand the business by reinvesting every available cent in new projects. Unfortunately, a lot of this money was lost on ill-fated ventures like buying a factory in California and a paper mill in Massachusetts.

In summers and whenever else I could, I worked in one or the other of these businesses doing odd jobs in the office and picking up the daily rhythm of doing business. I could not miss that my mother and father spent more of their time on people than on products. Both my parents had a wide circle of friends, many connected to their businesses as customers, suppliers, employees, or competitors. In 1950, we moved to a larger house in Englewood. Almost every day, friends and business associates would come over to visit. Business was a favorite topic at dinner since most of the guests had been doing some kind of business together for many years.

Everything in my parents' businesses was based on relationships with people who did business together for a long time. I learned that, even if you wanted to, you couldn't fool people whom you dealt with for decades.

Entrepreneurial Ambitions

As I entered adulthood, my mother was happy to have me pursue whatever interests I had, but my father assumed that I would come into Rossotti Lithograph and continue to build it. Having been living my whole life with parents and family friends who loved running their own businesses, I was sure I wanted to be in business, too. My first venture was in high school, when I promoted some rock-and-roll concerts to raise money for the school's dances.

Harvard Business School, I heard, was considered the best business school, but it only accepted people after they had finished college. So I realized I would have to go to college first. The Sisters of Charity, who ran Saint Cecilia's, worked hard to steer their good students to Georgetown University in Washington, which they considered the premier Catholic college. They were not reluctant to tell us that if we went to an Ivy League school, we would risk losing the faith. Without much thought, I decided to go to Georgetown, enrolling as a freshman in the liberal arts school in the fall of 1958.

I majored in economics, working in my father's business in the summer and trying a few business ventures on the side. I successfully promoted a Dave Brubeck concert to fund some school activities. But when I tried to promote my first concert outside the school as a profit-making venture, I lost money and had to sheepishly ask my father for a loan to finance the loss. Looking back, I realize this might have been a lucky break for me, not only because it steered me away from the concert-promotion business, but because it taught me in a painfully personal way the basic point that you could lose as well as make money in business.

At Georgetown I also developed a friendship with a colorful, cigar-smoking professor named Lev Dobriansky. Although an economics professor, Dobriansky was legendary for his lobbying on behalf of the "Captive Nations" of the Soviet Union, especially Ukraine. In the face of opposition by the State Department and vitriolic objections by the Soviet Union, he single-handedly got Congress to pass an annual resolution calling for the liberation of these Captive Nations. His stories of how he maneuvered around Washington to get this done fascinated me. It was my first exposure to politics. Still, I thought that my graduation from Georgetown marked the last I would ever see of Washington except for an occasional alumni weekend.

By then, I had even more reason to want to go to Harvard Business School, since Barbara, the woman I had courted since high school, was enrolled at Harvard Law School. The business school wanted its students to have a few years of work experience before they entered, but I was able to talk up my years of working in the family businesses, and in the fall of 1962, I started the two-year M.B.A. program.

After my first year at Harvard, Barbara and I made two decisions. One, we decided to get married. Two, we decided we didn't want to go back to Englewood for me to work at Rossotti Lithograph. My dad was very disappointed, but he treated it as a temporary setback, figuring that I would get some experience and then come home.

I still had the desire to run my own business as soon as possible, and I found several similarly driven second-year students. We formed an informal group and decided that we would each take a job that could give us some experience for a year or two while we researched businesses that we might start or buy.

When an impressive man named Bruce Henderson showed up on campus and said he had just started a new consulting firm in Boston, I decided that his new firm would a good place to go for some more experience before starting a business of my own. When I arrived in May 1964, Henderson's firm had one client and four professional employees, including me, the firm's first new M.B.A. (Henderson's start-up firm has since developed into a major international strategic consulting firm, the Boston Consulting Group.)

While working at Boston Consulting, I spent as much spare time as possible working with my business school friends, who were now spread out in jobs around the country. We were still trying to find a business that we could go into on our own. After about six months, we all agreed with the conclusion that one of our members, Ed Hajim, had reached after extensive market research. The way we could all make a fortune was to go into the business of making mobile homes.

We decided that one of us would have to gain practical experience in the industry by taking a job at a factory in Indiana, the center of the mobile home manufacturing industry. None of us relished this prospect. Business school theories began clashing with practical realities. But we agreed to do more research on the industry while mulling over the sending of one of us to work in a mobile home factory.

An Unexpected Detour: Government

In May 1965, about a year after starting at Boston Consulting, I got a phone call from a man I had met while still at Harvard interviewing for jobs. Robert Valtz said he had left his job at Arthur D. Little in Boston to join the systems analysis office at the Pentagon. This small office, headed by a brilliant young economist named Alain Enthoven, was working directly for Robert McNamara, the secretary of defense. The group was out recruiting M.B.A.'s and economists who would spend a few years figuring out how to make the Defense Department use its vast resources more effectively. I knew nothing about defense, and working for the government would be a total detour from all my plans. But Valtz was a fast-rising M.B.A. I figured if he was there, something unusual must be going on.

After I visited the office, Enthoven offered me a job. His pitch was simple: You'll never get a better chance to work with bright people on important problems for the country. You can do other things later. This idea was far removed from my goal to go into business. To my own surprise, I found Enthoven's offer appealing. I agreed to think it over.

I thought about going to Indiana to work in a mobile home factory and decided that doing that really wouldn't be much fun. There were news reports of the possibility of a big buildup of troops in Vietnam. I thought that if there was a war, I'd be better off working as an M.B.A. analyst than as a twenty-four-year-old enlisted man. And I really liked Enthoven. So I threw away all my plans, and in July 1965, I accepted a job as a civilian in the Office of the Secretary of Defense.

For my father, this was an inexplicable decision. It was one thing to get some experience in a firm like Boston Consulting, which was run by a smart business guy like Bruce Henderson. But working for the government? This could ruin me forever.

Shortly after I accepted the job in July 1965, my father wrote me a letter in which he explained his views:

> *You asked me if I had any experience in passing judgments on government activities and government employees and my answer is yes. When we decided to take over our California building I had to deal with the Maritime Commission in Washington. I found, to my utter amazement, the most appalling lack of business ability—not only in the top echelon of the Maritime Commission in Washington, but in the Departments of General Procurement and Storage. We must have found over $20 million*

worth of equipment in the California building when we started to take it over, which had been bought by the Navy Department. Some of the items could never possibly be used.

We had experience in hiring military men and former colonels right in our own organization. They just go along with the tide because they give up trying to change the way of life of the United States Government.

I simply hope it does not distort your outlook because you have such a wonderful future ahead by operating on good, sound business principles.

You might wish to keep this letter so that you can compare it with your experience after a year or two and perhaps even later when I may not be around.[1]

My father's views about the government were typical of the views of many small-business people around the country, not only in 1965 but also when I came back to the government as commissioner of internal revenue thirty-two years later. This was part of the chasm in attitudes that I had to bridge between the public and the IRS.

In October 1965, I walked into the Pentagon, knowing nothing about the military or defense programs but part of the cadre of analysts hired by Enthoven to provide quantitative analysis for the secretary of defense. On my first assignment, a messenger showed up pushing a grocery cart filled with paper volumes of a military staff plan responding to President Charles de Gaulle's order to move all NATO facilities out of France. This plan had an astronomical cost and would have required more construction in Belgium than the country's gross national product. It was not hard to write a memo showing that a more economical plan needed to be developed. So started my career as a defense systems analyst.

For three years, I worked harder than I ever have before or since, analyzing one problem after another sent down from McNamara and Enthoven. The work, dealing daily with equally hard-working people in the military services, was high pressure intellectually and personally, but also rewarding because of the obvious importance of what was at stake. It was also often immensely controversial, since our job was to challenge traditional assumptions and cherished programs of the military services.

In the 1968 presidential election, candidate Richard Nixon made a speech in which he promised to wipe out the Pentagon's so-called whiz kids, who were ruining the military by overriding seasoned military judgment with their pointy-headed thinking. When Nixon won, our leader Enthoven immediately resigned and many of the rest of us in the office made plans to leave.

Then another surprising turn of events changed my plans.

Nixon appointed Melvin Laird, a wily and experienced congressional leader, to be secretary of defense. David Packard, the legendary founder of Hewlett-Packard, was appointed deputy secretary. Packard asked some of us to sit in on several of his initial briefings and afterward to give any comments that might be helpful. I remember one briefing by the Army Corps of Engineers on the backlog of military construction. With no hint of irony, the briefer said that at the current rate of progress, the backlog would be worked off in 109 years. Afterward, Packard asked us to provide him with some options that would be more practical than waiting a century to fix this problem.

Packard soon decided that the systems analysis office could be valuable to him and decided not to abolish it after all. Ivan Selin, an intellectual phenomenon who got his engineering Ph.D. from Yale at nineteen, was appointed acting head of the office, with me as his deputy. During the next year, we managed to complete some major projects for Packard and Laird without stirring up too much controversy.

Back to Business, but Not to Promote Concerts or Make Mobile Homes

Selin and I were developing a close relationship with both Laird and Packard. Nevertheless, after about a year, Laird told Selin that it was not politically possible to get him confirmed by the Senate, because he was a holdover from the previous administration. Clearly it was time to leave.

With three other colleagues in the office, we began to discuss the idea of forming a company. We all had entrepreneurial instincts, and only Selin had hit age thirty. We figured that if we were going to start a business, now was as good a time as any to take the leap. The only small item we lacked was a plan for what kind of business to start.

Since none of us had any real business experience or an idea for a specific product to produce, we tried to think of a business that might allow us to build on our experience and reputation from working in defense, but without actually being required to sell anything to the Defense Department. (After we started our company, we did no business with the Defense Department for the first five years.)

Despite its name, the systems analysis office did not have anything directly to do with managing computers. But we did use them as much as we could for our analysis. We realized that the Defense Department and many large companies were spending millions to buy large IBM 360 computers, but that these computers were being used to do the same mundane work that had been done on card-punch machines. So we decided to start a company to help large companies and government agencies use the computers they were already buying to run their businesses better.

That was about the extent of our business plan as we began to go out to find some financing. Helped by a key reference from David Packard, who encouraged our entrepreneurial ambitions, we obtained a venture investment of $300,000 from Lehman Brothers. On February 2, 1970, we incorporated American Management Systems (AMS).

We worked for state governments putting in budget systems, a railroad developing a customer accounting system, and a manufacturer automating a distribution system. Pat Gross, one of the founders, got AMS started doing work for banks, and Frank Nicolai, another founder, set up a back office to support the growth. We made a breakthrough in 1976, when another of our founders, Jan Lodal, convinced New York City's newly established financial management agency to give AMS the contract to replace the city's ancient budgeting and accounting systems as part of solving the city's financial crisis.

By 1979, AMS had grown to almost $48 million per year in revenues, relatively large then for an independent service company. This growth allowed us to go public with an initial offering of shares.

We had grown fast simply by selling and then performing projects for clients one after another. We figured that if we did projects that were successful for our clients, we'd get more—not a bad basic business philosophy. But, by 1981, our "just do it" management style began to fall apart. For the first time, our growth slowed down and we reported a loss. Our outside directors, representing the investors, decided that we had to "get organized." I was asked to become chief executive officer and to develop a definite business plan. We organized the company into business units specializing in industries such as government and banking, cut out some losing ventures, and regained profitability.

For the next ten years, AMS continued to grow rapidly, expanding into the telecommunications industry, establishing a network of offices around the United States and Canada, and beginning to do business in Europe. By 1992, the company attained revenues of over $300 million, the stock price was more than 250 times what the original investors had paid, and we convened our whole executive group for a year-long strategic planning exercise to decide on what to do next.

As we reflected on AMS's business in the strategic planning exercise, we realized that over the years many things had changed about the AMS business, but the one constant was the continuity of relationships with clients and employees. Most of our twenty-two straight years of growth could be traced directly to people who worked with us once and who trusted us enough to work with us again. Although less personal than the kind of relationships my father and mother had built their businesses on, the principle of building on relationships of trust was very similar. Just as my father had done when he adjusted to prohibition's wiping out his wine label business, we could replace product lines. We could not, however, replace our essential relationships.

Our team agreed on an aggressive plan to grow for the rest of the decade. As part of this plan, I recommended to the board that one of our colleagues, Paul Brands, be appointed CEO while I remained chairman of the board. The plan worked well, and AMS continued to grow rapidly, reaching revenues of almost $1.2 billion in 2000.[2]

I had no plan to leave AMS and no thought of taking any new job, let alone a government job. On top of that, I was a Republican businessman with no connection to the Clinton administration and no experience in the tax field. No wonder the first question people often ask me is, How did you end up as IRS commissioner?

CHAPTER 3

You're Gonna Do What?

From Businessman to Taxman

RETURNING TO MY OFFICE at AMS after a meeting one day in February 1997, I found a pink phone slip with a message from an executive search firm about its assignment to find a business executive to be IRS commissioner. The message requested me to call back with any suggestions. Putting a businessperson in charge of the IRS seemed to me like a sensible idea, and several candidates came to mind, so I returned the call.

After listening to my suggestions, Norbert Gottenburg, the recruiter, asked if I would consider the job. I explained that this didn't make any sense for me. My plan was to gradually phase down my work schedule at AMS to allow me and Barbara more free time. Taking another high-pressure job of any kind would be completely inconsistent with this plan.

Over the next week, Gottenburg pressed hard for me to agree to meet with Treasury Deputy Secretary Larry Summers. I was reluctant to take up the time of a top official when I knew that I was not a real candidate, but Gottenburg convinced me that it would still be helpful for the Treasury Department to hear my insights on how to recruit a businessperson for the job.

On February 27, 1997, I walked into the Treasury Department for the first time.

Treasury is housed in a nineteenth-century building that looks very much like a fortress for guarding money. (In fact, inside there is a cash room, once used to dispense cash to vendors and employees.) High officials work amid original nineteenth-century furniture and fixtures. On the walls are framed artifacts, like early specimens of U.S. currency.

Yet this image of slightly faded gentility doesn't mask the raw power that resides in the cabinet department that occupies the building. Situated immediately east of the White House, it is a center of power not only in Washington but in the world. It is ground zero for managing rapid-fire daily events in the world financial markets, the U.S. economy, and Congress. It is as though a Wall Street bond house had its trading floor in a museum.

Despite the formality of the surroundings, the august nature of his duties, and his reputation for being a brilliant if sometimes acerbic intellectual, Deputy Secretary Summers struck me as informal and engaging. He immediately offered me a Diet Coke from an inexhaustible supply in his closet, and asked me to call him Larry. He launched into an explanation of why the administration needed a person with strong management experience to run the IRS. It was the largest civilian operation in the federal government and needed astute management, especially of its troubled computer program, he said.

I said that it sounded like a good idea to recruit a businessperson, and I suggested some names. But I explained that the job did not fit my plans to phase down my work activities. We ended the meeting. I figured that it would be the first and last time I would be in the Treasury Department.

That was on a Thursday. The following Sunday night, I was surprised to get a call from Treasury Secretary Robert Rubin. He got right to the point—he would like to talk to me seriously about taking the IRS job. The job was "the most important management job in the civilian government," he said, adding that my background in the information systems industry might make me the right person to fill it.

Thinking about this conversation over the next few days, I decided that it would not be right to keep the conversation going. I called

Rubin, agreed that the IRS needed a business-savvy commissioner, and urged him not to hold up the department's search trying to recruit me, as I would not take the job.

Over the next month, my curiosity aroused, I started paying closer attention to press articles about the IRS's situation. There was plenty being written about IRS problems, and I could see why Rubin and Summers wanted a commissioner with management and technology experience. It looked like a huge and risky turnaround situation, but with a lot of upside potential to make things better for the millions of people who dealt with the IRS. I began to think this might be one of those rare situations in which there were enough forces aligned to make real change possible, especially because Rubin and Summers seemed so committed.

A few weeks later, Summers called again and asked if I would be willing to reopen discussions. I returned to the Treasury Department, and Rubin's assistant walked me through underground tunnels filled with heating pipes. We were heading to the basement of the West Wing offices, where Rubin was meeting with the White House staff. Sounding very much like Enthoven thirty-two years earlier, Rubin stressed the importance of the job for the country as well as the contribution I could make.

By then Rubin was becoming a legend in Washington. He had given up one of the most prestigious and lucrative jobs in the business world, as CEO of Goldman Sachs, to take a staff job helping newly elected President Bill Clinton formulate economic policy. After being appointed treasury secretary, he continued to live in a hotel room during the week, spending every waking hour managing the endless and critical economic problems of the growing but shaky domestic and international economy. He was spending his Sunday nights back home in New York doing things like calling people to be IRS commissioner. Coming from Rubin, the statement "It's a way to give something back" meant something.

The IRS management and technology problems were clearly daunting, but at least they were the kind of problems that I had experience dealing with during my years at AMS. I could see myself assessing these problems and taking action to solve them. But it was also obvious that making fundamental, and inevitably controversial, changes in the agency would require backing from the top. My major question to Rubin was whether there was a real commitment by the leaders of the government to change the IRS. This was by far my biggest concern in considering whether to take the job. If I was going to change my whole life to take this job because of the chance to make a difference, I wanted to be sure it was a real opportunity to fix things and not just a public relations job. Rubin assured me of his commitment to real reform of the IRS, a commitment he kept even when the going was tough.

Over the next few weeks, I talked to Summers about the problems that needed to be confronted immediately, including the looming specter of the Year 2000 date change for IRS computers. When I asked about authority to recruit a senior management team, he quickly assured me that I would be permitted to do this. To my everlasting regret, I never mentioned the budget. I naively thought that if solving the problem was as vital to the country as the treasury secretary and deputy secretary obviously believed it was, then the IRS would surely get the relatively small budget increase it might need.

Summers also agreed with my request that I be allowed to discuss my possible appointment with Congressman Tom Davis, a well-connected Republican from Virginia whom I knew well and respected. When I told Davis why I was there, his first reaction was exactly the same as from other people when I told them I might be taking the job of IRS commissioner—a widening of the eyes in amazement as though to say, "You're gonna do what?" Recovering, he immediately walked me over to the nearby office of Representative Rob Portman, who with Senator Bob Kerrey was cochair of the commission that had already spent almost a year studying the IRS.

Portman knew the issues cold and did not sugarcoat anything. Although he personally was very serious about improving the management of the IRS, he was well aware that many in Congress saw bashing the agency as a cheap way to get headlines or raise money. He mentioned the anti-IRS fund-raising letters and warned that I would be stepping into this political cross fire. But he also said that, if I was willing to risk it, there was a real opportunity to improve the way the IRS worked. Portman promised to do anything he could to help me.

Within a week I was shaking hands with Rubin on the deal.

On the day Secretary Rubin officially offered me the job, May 14, 1997, the tax column on the front page of the *Wall Street Journal* ran one of its pithy humor items: "Great job for masochists? Former IRS

Commissioner Donald Alexander offers this thumbnail description of what it is like to run the embattled agency: 'The hours are impossible, the pay is lousy—but you get lots of abuse.' "[1]

When news of my nomination appeared in the press in early June, the reaction from my friends was summed up by one who said incredulously, "If that's what you want, congratulations."

Close and distant friends also began telling me their own stories about dealing with the IRS. One told me about how many hours he spent getting busy signals calling the IRS simply to get proper credit for a check. Others sent clippings about the IRS's threatening to shut down a girls' softball team and going after employment taxes from golf caddies.

Many of the comments were funny, or at least intended to be. One of my AMS colleagues sent me an article on supercomputers; another asked if I would be moving to West Virginia (the site of the IRS's biggest computer center). But my daughter, Allegra, made me laugh the most, saying, "But Dad, you don't even do your own tax return."

A Rude Awakening: Finding Little Support in the Administration

I knew that I would soon be in charge of an organization of a hundred thousand employees, with old creaky computer systems, lots of unhappy taxpayers, and a torrent of money to collect. Apart from that, I knew next to nothing about anyone or anything at the IRS. Unlike all previous commissioners, I was not a tax expert. Obviously, I had a lot to learn, and I badly wanted to get started.

I picked up whatever IRS documents happened to be available in the Treasury Department offices to start reading, while anxiously awaiting the go-ahead to begin serious preparation for the job. Meanwhile, I was given a mountain of paperwork required by the lawyers in four different agencies that needed to vet my appointment.

Instructions from the treasury political staff were plain: Don't talk to anybody, period. They said that when the time came, there would be plenty of experts at the Treasury Department to prepare me.

As weeks went by with no plan and no action for me to prepare for actually doing the job, it began to dawn on me that there was a fundamental difference between what I thought I was coming to do at the

IRS and the prevailing view within the administration I was joining. The White House and most of the Treasury Department, apart from Rubin and Summers themselves, had little interest in the substance of IRS management. They saw the raging IRS issues as a tactical political battle between the Clinton administration and an unholy alliance of congressional Republicans and one maverick Democratic senator who were using the IRS to get attention for their own agendas.

My first battle was not going to be inside the IRS or with Congress. It was going to be within the administration. Clearly, we had to deal with the continued attacks on the IRS and to communicate that the administration was committed to taking action. But I thought that we had to do this by thinking through and winning support for a plan for making real change. We could not succeed just by inventing something to announce in press releases, as seemed to be the prevailing method of the administration.

Even after I was given permission to go to the IRS to begin learning something about the organization I was slated to take over in just a few months, an assistant in the Treasury Department intervened to call a halt. The Department was worried that I would do or say something that might create a political problem. My role was to lend my résumé so as to buy some quiet time from the critics. The rest was incidental. When I suggested how we could explain my efforts to learn about the IRS before my confirmation, a treasury staffer curtly dismissed the idea: "You ran an IT company." What did an IT guy know about politics?

Eventually we reached an uneasy accommodation that allowed me to meet with a few people in the IRS headquarters building. As I began talking to the IRS executives, I found that they were only too glad to have someone listen to what they thought their real problems were. None of them thought that they were doing just fine. I also started reading thousands of pages of available studies and reports. Because of the work of the restructuring commission, a large and valuable library had been put together.

As I studied the situation, I saw one pending decision that I thought needed attention immediately, because it would have implications long after I took office.

As the criticism of the IRS from all sides had mounted, the treasury had pushed even harder to show that it was doing something about fixing the agency. The department's biggest step was announcing a new technology program. Over the previous year, Summers had canceled most of the previous program and hired a chief information officer (CIO) from outside the IRS to develop a new plan.

The new CIO, Arthur Gross, was a smart and experienced but very aggressive former state government official who had put together a seven-volume blueprint for what the IRS's technology should be. He then released a draft request for proposal, or RFP, to the government contracting industry to bid on a fifteen-year, multibillion-dollar contract to manage the new program. By coincidence, this huge set of documents was published the very day I shook hands with Secretary Rubin to accept the job as commissioner. I left the treasury building lugging a big box of documents to my car.

Years before, I had bought a farm in Maryland on the waters of the Chesapeake Bay's Eastern Shore, which I used as a relaxing weekend retreat from work at AMS. Now, one day after I accepted the IRS job, I was relaxing on Memorial Day weekend by studying volumes of the IRS technology blueprint spread out on the porch table overlooking the water.

At one level, this blueprint was a monumental achievement. For the first time, it provided a relatively complete, if ugly, picture of the systems that the IRS actually had. It also laid out a high-level design of what a coherent set of modernized systems might look like. All of this was good.

But as an immediate plan of action, it made me shudder. It presumed that the IRS's organization and operations would remain largely unchanged, with just new computer systems to support them. This was an assumption I certainly was not willing to make. It would just lock in old ways of doing business. The plan also called for selecting one contractor, called the *prime,* to manage the program. But the RFP set up the contract in such a way that the IRS would provide all the money to the prime, without requiring the contractor to accept any of the enormous risk in making the program work. These were big problems.

But the most compelling problem was that it made no sense to launch this big program at that time. Every bit of management capacity in the IRS information systems staff would be required for the next couple of years to fix the Year 2000 problem, and the IRS was under tremendous pressure to fix a wide range of management and service problems as well. I was being appointed IRS commissioner, I thought, precisely to make sure all this stuff worked. So what sense did it make to issue the biggest information systems contract proposal in IRS history before I would even take office?

I resolved that I would have to find some way to get this program delayed, even though I wasn't supposed to be saying anything about my views before my confirmation. My wife, Barbara, captured the situation perfectly: "You have to do something while appearing to do nothing; it's usually the opposite in government." But I didn't think that delaying this RFP would be all that hard. What could be easier than delaying something in the government?

I met with Summers in June, and my most urgent topic was the technology RFP. Noting the inherent riskiness of such a large program, I urged that the RFP be delayed for six months or so until we had time to review it thoroughly along with everything else going on at the IRS. We agreed that I could not get involved in such a sensitive topic before being confirmed in office, so the treasury staff would have to handle the issue with the IRS in the meantime.

Suddenly, in the middle of September, I was stunned to learn from a treasury staffer that the RFP had indeed been delayed—by all of two weeks! It would be out before I was even in office. No one in the Treasury Department had done anything about delaying it, and in fact, the legislative staff had continued a full-court press with Congress to push the RFP forward as fast as possible in order to show that the administration was doing something about the IRS's problems. During my time at the IRS, despite many provocations, I rarely lost self-control. But this time I did. I could feel myself becoming red-faced and shaking, almost shouting that this was the kind of disaster that I thought I was appointed to prevent.

I immediately went to see Summers, who frankly acknowledged that the failure to delay the RFP was a mistake. Eventually, the Treasury Department and the IRS decided to put out a preliminary version right away and to delay the final version by a few months, into early 1998. Under this time frame, if I wanted to change this complex and critically important program, I would have to change it after it had already been under way. I would also need to work on it in my first couple of months in office, when the pressure of other matters was at its most extreme.

I viewed the premature RFP as a serious setback before I even started the job. For the technology program itself, the RFP would have bad long-term consequences. The IRS would have a harder time getting accountability for performance from whichever vendor won the prime contract. Even more important for me, the situation confirmed my deepening fear that the preoccupation of most people in the Treasury Department and White House, which was winning the daily political and public relations battles swirling around the IRS, could seriously interfere with what Rubin and Summers had hired me to do. If I couldn't even get a delay of a few months in a technology RFP, what chance did I have in getting far more difficult changes accepted?

I had learned a hard lesson and decided to forge ahead, while vowing to confront any future issues more directly with Rubin and Summers before I was overtaken by events.

Confronting the Big Question: Did It Still Make Sense for Me to Take the Job?

The congressional schedule bears some resemblance to that of an elite college. Fall semester starts in September. The students take frequent breaks, have occasional rowdy incidents, stay up all night before exams, and then go home for Christmas. As the September semester in Congress geared up, the Senate hearings on abuse of taxpayers dominated the headlines.

As the negative headlines spilled out almost daily, and the IRS reform legislation began to gain momentum, the White House political and press staffs escalated their pressure on the treasury to manage the press coverage. The idea was to steal the thunder from the restructuring commission and the Republicans in Congress. The favored technique for doing this was to invent some catchy new thing for the IRS to announce.

By October, Vice President Gore's customer service task force came up with a long list of ideas, like rewriting the hundreds of different notices the IRS sends to taxpayers to make them more readable. While many of these ideas were good, most of them were complex and expensive to implement. Without proper planning, they could cause massive damage to an already terrible situation by raising the expectations of taxpayers far beyond what could be delivered. But the White House was demanding that more actions be ready for a planned announcement by President Clinton.

One morning I picked up the *Washington Post* and read a story that the White House was planning to appoint thirty-three citizens panels, one for each IRS district, to be watchdogs over the IRS. No one at the Treasury Department or the IRS had even been informed about this proposal before it was announced, and the White House had no idea what these panels were supposed to do. It was just a way to steal a headline, while leaving the IRS to figure out how to handle the years of complex and controversial issues that were sure to follow from it. Meanwhile, as the incoming head of the organization, I was on the sidelines together with the rest of IRS management.

I called Rubin and said that we had to meet, as it seemed that we might have very different ideas of what needed to be done about the IRS. In that meeting, I gave him a graph that portrayed two opinions of

FIGURE 3-1

I used this graph with Secretary Rubin in October 1997 to contrast my view of IRS performance with the administration's view. My line started at 40 percent. I started the administration's line at 75 percent.

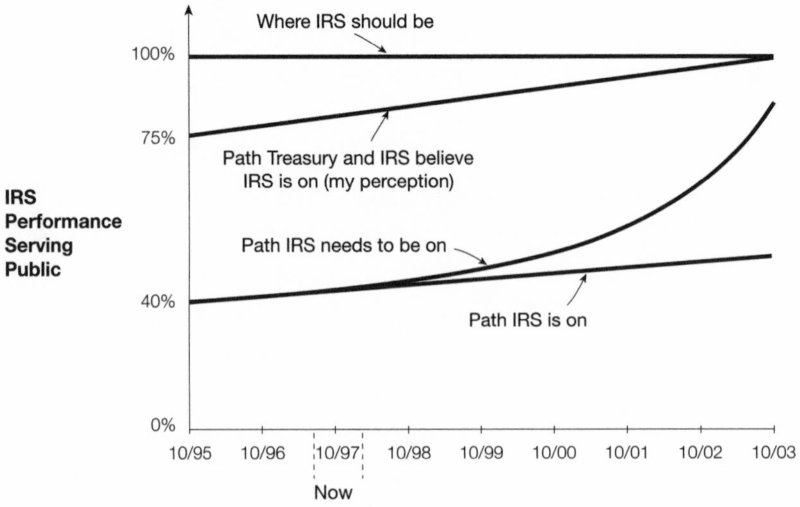

how effectively the IRS was actually serving the public. One line—representing the administration's point of view—started at 75 percent and sloped solidly upward. The line representing my opinion started at about 40 percent and stayed almost flat.

"You think the IRS is only performing at forty percent of what it should?" Rubin asked.

"In terms of how it serves the public, yes," I replied. "That's why the hearings had so much impact, because tens of millions of people have personal experiences that let them identify with the stories told by the taxpayers on TV."

I added that any attempt at announcing quick fixes—whether new IRS notices, a premature technology program, or thirty-three citizens panels—would backfire. We needed a sustained and fundamental change in the whole way the agency worked.

Rubin asked me the basis for my assessments. I cited surveys, the IRS's own statistics, and the anecdotal evidence I was collecting.

He said that, even if I was right, I could not be like a CEO who came in and wrote everything off to get a clean slate. I agreed, saying that there was plenty of good to build on and that it was possible to make clear progress step by step. As I was to do many times over the next five years, I stressed my belief that eventually the changes would improve the IRS's effectiveness in enforcing tax compliance as well as in service to the public. But it was essential to have realistic expectations about the depth of change and the time required. In the meantime, I pointed out, the strategy of responding to daily events by inventing things to say in press releases was failing even on narrow political terms, because the press and Congress saw through it. This approach just produced more criticism that the administration was not serious about fixing the IRS.

I handed Rubin a page titled "What Is Needed to Achieve Acceptable Performance," with big boxes showing that modernizing the organization and the soft items such as attitudes and training were on a par with technology.

After the meeting, I wasn't sure that Rubin and Summers shared my belief that fundamental change was needed. I was even less sure that they could control the strong pressure from their own political advisers and from the White House to treat the whole thing like an election campaign rather than a serious management problem. So I called Summers. In light of what we all now knew, I said, he and Rubin might want to rethink my appointment. If they thought I was not the right person for the job, I would leave quietly.

A few days later, at a follow-up lunch, they made it clear that they still wanted me to take the job. This meeting was a turning point for me. I believed I could count on support from the Treasury Department's top management, although I knew the trench warfare with the political and public relations types in the administration would continue. I reaffirmed my commitment and plunged into the confirmation process.

It is customary for those nominated to political office to offer courtesy visits with each member of the Senate committee responsible for the nomination. Because of the tremendous focus then on the IRS, many senators took up this offer. I began these visits in September.

As I had minimal experience dealing with members of Congress and none testifying, the Treasury Department assigned David Williams, an experienced professional from the legislative office, to prepare me for these meetings. Williams had worked on the Hill for fourteen years and had learned its sometimes devious ways and annoying quirks, but without adopting them himself. He had an uncanny ability to anticipate what each senator would say and to help me think through the best answers to questions without my falling into the trap of seeming to agree with everything and everybody. I later recruited him as my first senior executive from outside the IRS. He took charge of the whole IRS communications organization and remained an invaluable member of the senior management team for my whole term.

In most of these meetings with senators, two things happened: I listened to their views of the IRS, which often included personal stories and experiences in dealing with the agency, and they asked me why I was taking the job.

One senator told me about a personal encounter with the IRS over a single missed employment tax deposit. This incident happened twenty-two years earlier, but it had made such a searing impression that he still remembered such minute details as the exact quarterly payment that was missed. Another senator summed up a common theme: "A letter from the Labor Department is like a speeding ticket, but one from the IRS is like a capital case."

These meetings with the senators on the Finance Committee were the start of the relationships that I knew I would need to build with members of Congress and other key stakeholders after I became commissioner.

When I visited Senator Kerrey, he summed up his conclusions from working on the restructuring commission for a year. Reforming the IRS would take ten years, he said. This sounded right to me, and I cited it during my confirmation hearing. Senator Kerrey also asked me if I had a dog. When I said yes, he said, "That's good, because you'll need a friend."

In the Bull's-Eye

On October 23, 1997, I was the only witness at the table in the crowded Senate hearing room, with television lights and cameras staring at me while the senators looked down from their seats.

They all wanted to make their points about the IRS but were nevertheless friendly to me. The occasion was ready-made for some colorful comments

Senator William Roth began: "It is, indeed, a pleasure to welcome you, Mr. Rossotti. I want you to feel welcome here, and not like the officer sent to Little Big Horn as the replacement of General Custer." In a more serious tone, he added, "Mr. Rossotti, you have the opportunity to do great things in this agency. Never in my recollection has an agency been so ripe for change. Great leaders disdain the beaten path. Great leaders, as Lincoln taught, seek regions heretofore unexplored. This is the kind of leader we need at this time to take charge of the Internal Revenue Service."[2]

Senator John Breaux, an exceptionally influential Democrat from Louisiana, summed up what he thought would be my biggest problem: "There is an incredible amount of distrust, mistrust, and misunderstanding about the legitimate and proper role of the agency."[3]

Echoing the comments he made in our private meeting, Senator Kerrey warned, "You are the bull's eye." He cited a Billie Holiday tune

FIGURE 3-2

Senator Bob Kerrey drew this chart during my confirmation hearing to make his point that lots of people would be giving me orders. At the top he wrote, "Good luck in the bull's-eye."

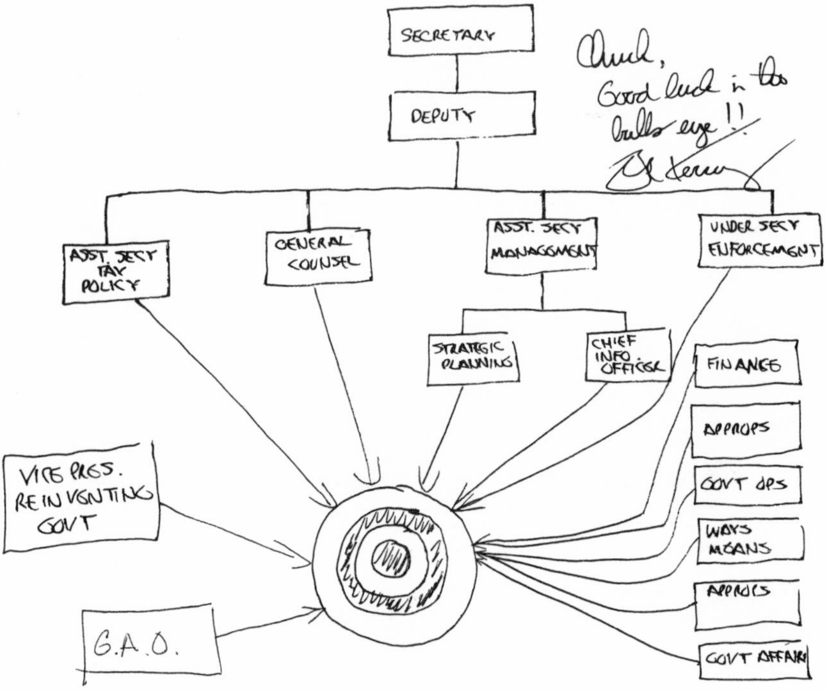

that was popular in his office, "Nobody Loves You When You're Down and Out." "Remember that, Mr. Rossotti," he concluded.[4]

After making his comments, Kerrey drew by hand a diagram of all the agencies and people who would be shooting at me in the bull's-eye and sent it to me with his signature. I framed it and hung it in my office.

After the white-hot hearings and political clashes between Congress and the administration, my confirmation by the Senate was almost an anticlimax. Republican Senator Phil Gramm of Texas summed up the point of view of many members: "This hearing and the debate on your nomination is not really about you, it is about a realization that this committee and the country have come to, that the IRS is out of control." Senator Gramm leaned back and added, "So anybody that wants this job under these circumstances probably ought to have it."[5]

About two weeks later, the Senate voted ninety-two to zero to confirm me as IRS commissioner. I thought that perhaps they feared if they didn't act quickly, nobody would take the job.

CHAPTER 4

Promising Everything to Everybody Will Not Get Us There

Regaining the Initiative

I THOUGHT I MIGHT be killed in the line of duty my first morning on the job.

On Thursday, November 13, 1997, after Treasury Secretary Robert Rubin swore me in as commissioner of internal revenue, we were scheduled to drive together to the IRS's television studio in suburban Maryland for a nationwide video conference with several thousand IRS employees. The secretary would introduce me as the new commissioner, and then we would both answer questions from the audience about the Senate hearings.

As we were walking out of the Treasury Department to drive to the noon video conference, the latest world financial crisis intervened, in the form of an urgent phone call for Rubin. At 11:48 A.M. we finally got into the secretary's armored limo, which was driven by two Secret Service agents who either were determined to get the secretary to the studio on time, or were testing their skills at getaway driving. Putting a flashing red light on top of the car, they roared down Fifteenth Street, crossed six lanes of traffic on Constitution Avenue, careened around the corners, and accelerated onto the Southeast Freeway, making the thirty-minute drive to the Maryland IRS building in eleven minutes flat. Going directly on camera from the car, I was sure the IRS employees would think their new commissioner looked scared to death, which I was. But not about the video conference.

On my first morning, I had already been taught one basic fact of life about the world I was entering: Uncontrollable daily events could easily dominate my day. I was determined that I would not let this happen. I would respond to the events as necessary, but I would keep my focus on what I came to do, which was to make the IRS work better. To do that I needed a plan.

Making My Point with a Doorstop

The next day was my first official day in my office at the IRS Washington headquarters, a massive stone structure built in the 1930s. It occupies two full blocks on Pennsylvania Avenue, smack in between the IRS's two political masters: Congress on Capitol Hill and the president in the White House. Inside the seven floors of the building are two-block-long corridors that look so much alike that even people who have worked there for decades sometimes get disoriented. You can, however, tell when you are approaching the commissioner's office, because the walls are lined with pictures of former commissioners—mostly unsmiling guys with glasses and black suits—including the first commissioner, George S. Boutwell, who was appointed by President Lincoln to collect taxes for the Civil War.

What struck me most when I first entered the building were the closed doors that lined the long corridors. My first act as commissioner was to put a rubber stop under the door to my office suite. I asked Belinda Smith, my trusted executive assistant whom I had convinced to come with me from AMS, to let everyone in the office know that I didn't want that doorstop removed.

I already knew that the grapevine in the IRS worked faster than any official communications channel. So I decided to use it to get across the first message I wanted to convey to our work force: that we had to have honest, open communications internally if we were to have any hope of effectively confronting the problems we faced. What better way to make this point than to prop open my own door?

Another way that I could open up communications was to spend as much time as I could talking to people in and out of the IRS, and especially outside Washington, before making important decisions. I was able to visit about a dozen IRS offices around the country in my first three months on the job.

Reversing a Downward Spiral of Unkept Promises

But in the world I had just entered, many things could not wait for me to get ready to make decisions. My situation reminded me of the guy whose famous tombstone inscription, in Boot Hill, Arizona, read, "I was expecting this, but not so soon."

I received the first blast on my second day in the form of a letter signed by Senators William Roth and Daniel Moynihan, the chairman and senior Democrat on the Finance Committee. They wanted to know what I was going to do about a particular IRS collection manager, whom a national magazine story accused of whipping up a frenzy among his employees, urging them to seize taxpayer property to make his statistics look good. In Senator Roth's opinion and that of much of his committee, I was appointed to fix such problems. They believed I could show my stuff by immediately solving their list of tangled taxpayer cases and disciplining the people responsible. I realized that failing to act on this issue, which was their top priority, would so undermine my credibility that they would pay little attention to anything else I said.

It was immediately clear how hard it was going to be to deal with even the few specific cases of interest to the committee. A magazine article exposé may point to a problem, but it doesn't provide the hard facts needed for an organization to take disciplinary action against an individual. The taxpayers testifying to the committee had heart-wrenching stories, but many of the cases stretched over many years and came with inches-thick files.

During my early visits to Capitol Hill, I was also asked by some senior senators to give immediate attention to another matter. Congress had passed a law mandating that almost all businesses, some with only one or two employees, use a new Treasury Department electronic payments system to deposit cash for payroll taxes. The purpose was to reduce float, thereby speeding up receipt of tax revenue by the government. The IRS regulation implementing this law caused a near riot in the small-business community. Confusion was rampant. Many small-business owners thought that the IRS would now simply take money out of their bank accounts, the mere thought of which was enough to arouse their worst fears about Big Brother. In my first few days, I had to try to calm things down and kick off the months of work needed to develop a plan that both met the mandates of the law and was acceptable for the small-business community.

But these were only two of the can't-wait problems that demanded attention in my first few days. Pressure was on the IRS from every direction to do something about the problem du jour. Here I saw the vicious circle in which an organization in crisis can find itself—promising everything and delivering nothing.

The way the vicious circle worked at the IRS was obvious: Someone powerful would insist that the agency do something about a particular issue—like the taxpayer and employee cases identified by the Senate Finance Committee or the complaints from small business about the electronic deposit system. These powerful advocates were often unaware of, or uninterested in, any of the other problems demanding attention. The treasury would press the IRS management to commit to a specific action plan with the shortest possible deadline, to show it was doing something about the problem. The IRS would write a letter agreeing to do things to solve the problem. More and more of these promises would accumulate, with little prospect of implementation, further undermining the credibility of the management.

Meanwhile, the IRS headquarters would try to implement some of these promises by sending directives to various subordinate units or field offices. On the receiving end of a never-ending stream of often confusing directives from headquarters, the people in these field offices did whatever they could to comply—which usually was relatively little—while wondering what planet the management in Washington was living on.

I put together a small team just to make a list of all the changes that the IRS had promised to implement. These promises were made in response to pressures from many sources—the six congressional committees that officially oversaw the IRS, the vice president's customer service task force, hundreds of audit reports, numerous task forces of IRS employees around the country, mandates in recently passed legislation, the IRS taxpayer advocate, and the several IRS advisory committees of tax accountants and other practitioners.

The changes proposed by these sources ranged from small to big items. One said the IRS should change the text of letters it sent to foreign addresses to stop referring to the "IRS local office," because there was no local office. Another said the IRS should change its mission statement. When the team came back with a preliminary list that added up to five thousand line-item recommendations, I said stop counting. The IRS was like a car stuck in the snow. The more the driver raced the wheels, the deeper the rut got.

There was no way that the IRS was going to solve anything by reacting one at a time to five thousand proposed changes in the way it did business. Promising everything to everybody would not work. The IRS had to make far fewer promises but then actually follow through on the ones it did make. But how could this be accomplished when all the powerful external pressures, especially from the treasury and the White House, were to react immediately to every demand?

I found one key ally who had the experience to understand the deadly spiral the IRS was in, and the clout to help us break out of it.

Nancy Killefer came to the Treasury Department as assistant secretary for management and chief financial officer shortly before I was nominated as IRS commissioner. As a top-ranking director at McKinsey, one of the world's leading management consulting firms, Killefer had worked for years with major companies that needed to change to survive. At the peak of her career, she responded to Rubin's call that she take a few years out of business to help the treasury deal with the profound management problems in the IRS and elsewhere. In a treasury staff filled with policy wonks, former Wall Street traders, and would-be political strategists, she was almost alone in understanding that fixing a big organization required more than issuing press releases.[1]

Killefer and I decided to set up one unified program to manage all the short-term service improvement projects in the IRS. To make it work we had to take some strong steps immediately. We directed that no projects, even those already under way, would proceed without going through this new management program. She and I agreed to cochair the steering committee, a break with past practice in which the IRS and the Treasury Department all too often worked independently and failed to share information. And most important, we worked hard to recruit the best possible executives to run the program, our first foray into finding change leaders inside the IRS.

Bob Wenzel, an IRS veteran who started as a collection officer on the streets of Chicago, helped run the vice president's customer service task force and knew Killefer, who first introduced him to me. Tall and athletic looking, he was always immaculately dressed in a way perfectly appropriate to the occasion, whether his attire was a starched white shirt at an official ceremony or pressed khakis at a barbecue. His attention to dress was one of his ways of showing respect for the people he met with, much as a military officer might wear the precisely correct uniform as a sign of leadership. He was living in California on what he thought was his final assignment before retirement. During my first trip to the West Coast, we spent a day together, and I realized that he had a deep commitment to changing the IRS so that it could better serve the public. He recounted how he had decided on a career in public service as a boy, recalling with pride how it was his job to raise the American flag every morning for his father, an immigrant who had started a small flower nursery business. Over the years, he had held almost every job in the IRS and was immensely respected by people at every level.

I reached Wenzel at home in Fresno the Sunday before Christmas. While waiting to pay for my Christmas tree, I talked to him on my cell phone. We discussed the impact he could have if he extended his time a few more years to help turn around the IRS. He agreed to come back to run the new program Killefer and I were setting up. (Despite our best antibureacratic efforts, the program acquired the long moniker Taxpayer Treatment and Service Improvement Program.)

That Christmas tree phone call turned out to be one of the most important I ever made at the IRS. Less than a year later, Wenzel became deputy commissioner and was instrumental in making the massive changes we carried out throughout the IRS. When I left office in 2002, the Bush administration appointed him acting commissioner pending confirmation of the new commissioner.

Killefer and I agreed we needed a few more leaders to make the program work. She agreed to assign her deputy, Lisa Ross—a talented young executive recently recruited from Marriott—to help Wenzel manage our short-term improvement program. We rounded out the team with a Washington-based IRS career executive, Judy Tomaso, who knew so much about IRS headquarters that nothing would escape her net.

Within a few months, Wenzel's team winnowed 5,000 proposed changes to about 1,000 that deserved serious study. After a marathon session of several days, we agreed on 157 near-term initiatives that we would commit to carry out in the next twelve to eighteen months. These projects had a common purpose: making tangible improvement in service to taxpayers. We knew that without visible evidence that the IRS was changing, the rest of our plans would have little credibility. The projects included such actions as longer hours of telephone service, more consistent desk guides for employees talking to taxpayers, and better updating of addresses to reduce the volume of undelivered mail.

For two years, we used this priority-setting process to manage a large number of short-term changes, which began to turn around the public's view of IRS service. Later this approach became a part of a new strategic planning process to set priorities in the IRS budget. Our drastic pruning of the overloaded list of promises was a tangible example of the basic principle that, in the face of overwhelming pressure, it is important to do a limited number of things that one can deliver on, not simply to promise everything to everybody.

"Drop Dead Date" Redefined: Y2K

Still another critical short-term problem loomed. Because nearly all computer systems had been written with dates abbreviated to two digits (such as 99 for 1999), when the first date in the new century arrived the computers would be confused, thinking that January 1, 2000, was January 1, 1900. If not corrected, this computer confusion would cause massive errors and the IRS could probably never fully recover.

Allowing minimal time for testing and correcting unexpected last-minute problems, we had only eighteen months left to do all the work needed to fix the systems. Three days before I was sworn in, I spent most of the Veterans Day holiday with several IRS executives from the information systems office to scrutinize the Year 2000 problem.

The size of the problem was even more staggering than I had imagined. Not only was the IRS one of the largest computer users in the world, but it depended on some of the oldest systems still in use—some dating back to the 1960s and 1970s. And the IRS had purchased products from almost every vendor in the computer industry.

Fixing all this in the time available would be a fearsome challenge for any organization. But I was stunned to learn that the Office of Management and Budget (OMB) within the White House had provided no funds whatsoever for the Year 2000 conversion in the budget for the 1997 fiscal year. This refusal to provide funding had delayed the start of critical work, thereby increasing the cost of fixing the problem and increasing the risk that we would fail.

The situation was not all bleak. A few months before I arrived, a small group within the IRS information systems department, led by veteran Bob Albicker and new CIO Arthur Gross, had insisted that a serious commitment was needed to fix the Year 2000 problem. In the summer of 1997, Gross actually told a congressional committee that the IRS Year 2000 program was a "death march," successfully alarming the relevant parties. (Deputy Secretary Summers later jokingly warned him not to be "inadvertently memorable.")

Despite being initially ridiculed by the OMB, Gross and Albicker had forged ahead and set up teams to begin work. Had this not been done, my task would have been near hopeless. In that Veterans Day meeting, we expanded the management program and insisted on commitment from top leaders throughout the agency. While this commitment was a necessary step, we knew it would put even more pressure on IRS resources and management for the next two years.

As I learned more about the Year 2000 problem and the other pressures on the IRS, it became even more evident to me that it was too soon to launch the big new technology program that had been planned before my arrival. But I had failed to get the Treasury Department to delay the release of the technology request for proposal, which had already been sent in draft to the contracting industry in October 1997.

I knew that the two teams of vendors must be burning hundreds of thousands of dollars per month to fund their proposal teams and that they would soon be using every lever they had to get the IRS to move ahead as fast as possible. Using polite but pointed language, the vendors made it clear in meetings that the IRS would be blasted by everyone in the computer industry, and by their supporters in Congress, if it failed to proceed on schedule with this procurement. This was a practical example of the special problems of operating in a political fishbowl, but it was the world I was working in. What little time I could make available for this issue in my first few months, I spent trying to fix the substantive problems I had already identified in the draft RFP, such as the lack of adequate accountability by the prime contractor. Making these changes in the document also had the advantage of pushing back the start of the program to a time when we would be better prepared to manage it.

The process for preparing the president's annual budget request to Congress is like the irresistible force of the universe. It moves on, regardless of what else is happening. In a pattern that was to become all too familiar over the next five years, the OMB had largely ignored everything that was swirling around the IRS, including the Year 2000 problem, the six new tax bills Congress had passed, and the massive reforms Congress and the public were demanding. Setting aside almost everything else for a few days, I put together information for Secretary Rubin and Deputy Secretary Summers. I asked their help in including in the budget at least some modest recognition that the IRS was in crisis and that fixing it wouldn't be free.

Getting to the Source of the Problems

As pressing as all these immediate problems were, they were not my biggest worry during those first few weeks in office. My biggest worry was that I would never get beyond managing short-term issues, and therefore that I would fail to make the fundamental changes needed to make the IRS deliver acceptable performance.

If we just reacted to events better than the IRS had in the past, nothing fundamental would change. The skepticism of most longtime observers of the IRS would be confirmed. Even the one big long-term initiative that was planned, the technology modernization program, would fail if it continued to be designed as a technology program isolated from change throughout the IRS. I could end up patching the obvious damage without ever moving the IRS onto a new and better path. And if nothing really changed in the IRS after the enormous crises of the past few years, the results for the taxpayers, the IRS, and the U.S. economy could be disastrous.

Worst of all, I worried about how to overcome the relentless pressure to react. Meeting with several key treasury officials shortly after I took office on what to say to the press about the Senate hearings, I realized that this worry was all too real. I started with my by-now familiar point that we had to be careful to promise only what we could actually do. One official replied that he understood the need for the IRS to vet administration press releases announcing actions the IRS was supposed to take. But we had to be realistic, he said: Without the pressure of political and press events, the IRS would not have reacted at all.

I stifled a reflex to respond sarcastically by pointing out that this formulation at least had the virtue of making the IRS commissioner's role clear: to edit press releases dreamed up by treasury and White House staffers. Instead, I laid out why I thought his reasoning was backward. The IRS was in so much trouble in large part because it had grown entirely reactive. If we continued this approach, we'd never actually change anything. We'd just continue reacting by making announcements that nobody took seriously, undermining our already disastrous relationships with many stakeholders.

I added that to make real changes that would permanently and substantially improve the performance of the IRS and that would garner the support of the IRS's many diverse constituent groups, we had to have a serious plan. And it had to be a plan that we worked closely with our many stakeholders to execute. Reacting to the day's events was not a serious plan.

Pitching a Plan

I had started discussing with Rubin and Summers in September the elements of the plan I was developing. My key point then had been that modernizing the IRS would require changes in both hard items like organizational structure, technology, and measurements and soft items like attitudes, training, and relationships. I also put together a one-page list of priorities for my first ninety days. On the top of the list was the preparation of an overall plan for these far-reaching changes, which I put there to show that this was every bit as important as reacting to daily events.

Developing a broad plan for the IRS required very little imagination.

As I had reviewed thousands of pages of studies and reports, I found that almost every idea that anyone could reasonably suggest to improve the IRS had already been proposed. In the early 1990s, an internal IRS task force proposed major improvements such as eliminating unnecessary filing requirements, consolidating the management of telephone operations, and using more market research data to guide compliance operations. More recently, the vice president's customer service task force and the restructuring commission produced reports with many useful recommendations. Many of the proposals had been tried on a small scale in the IRS, although few had been fully implemented.

Clearly the problem was not a dearth of good ideas but a failure to select the important ones, to forge them into a coherent plan that people could understand, and, most important, to follow through by implementing the massive changes that would be required. I thought it would take six months after I started at the IRS to develop a broad but realistic plan.

By December, I realized that we didn't have six months. We didn't even have two months. The Senate Finance Committee scheduled a public hearing on IRS reform in late January 1998. I realized this might be a critical date for presenting our own plan for the IRS. If we missed this chance to present our own plan, we might be overtaken by events as Congress and the administration negotiated the IRS reform law that was moving through Congress. Although the time was punishingly short, I resolved to make an all-out push to consult with the necessary people and get approval to present a top-level plan at the Senate hearing.

To provide an uninterrupted block of time, Summers and Killefer agreed to meet after regular hours on January 5, 1998. At 7 P.M., we assembled in a drafty basement conference room with boxes of Kung Pao chicken and Moo Shi pork. For three hours, we discussed what was strong and weak in the IRS and how it could be changed to become a modern organization that did a better job in both service and compliance.

We listed sixteen pages of specific comparisons between how the IRS worked now and how it should work in the future. We covered changes needed in the agency's goals and guiding principles, in business practices for customer service and compliance, in organizational structure, in roles of management, in ways of measuring performance, and in the effective use of technology. Altogether we were proposing major changes in nearly every major aspect of the IRS, in order to put more focus on understanding and serving taxpayers, to streamline and increase accountability in the IRS's internal organization, and to bring the IRS's ways of doing business more in line with modern business practices. Far from dealing mainly with technology, as the last modernization blueprint had done, this plan provided for the comprehensive changes that were needed to increase the IRS's performance for taxpayers. To convey its broad scope, we dubbed our new plan "Modernizing America's Tax Agency."

Summers and Killefer liked the direction, but were concerned that the massiveness of the changes, especially the reorganization, could distract people so much that the IRS would essentially fall apart before it was put back together again. I acknowledged the risk, but pointed out that the IRS was already demoralized and under attack, with no end in sight. If we had a plan of our own, it would provide a positive goal that people might rally around.

This meeting began an intense week-long debate over how much of this plan we should outline at a public hearing. Once the plan was out in public, we would be making a tangible commitment to it.

In five years at the IRS, I got very few pleasant surprises. By far the most important of the few I did get was the reaction of the top IRS career executives to my proposal for a broad modernization plan, which involved changing the most long-established aspects of the IRS.

Abolishing hallowed IRS districts and regions was akin to abolishing divisions in the army, but the top IRS executives didn't flinch. The afternoon before my Chinese dinner meeting with Summers and Killefer, I had gone through the whole thing with Mike Dolan, the deputy commissioner and most senior leader of the career executives. Dolan told me I would be surprised at how much support I would get from the executives for big changes. After all, the career people were the ones who had done the dozens of studies that were never implemented. The two other most senior executives at headquarters, Dave Mader and John Dalrymple, were similarly supportive.

Killefer and I were in almost continuous conversations with other treasury officials over how much risk was involved in imposing so much change and how to lay out the plan publicly. As so often happens in such debates, people got cold feet and looked for ways of watering down groundbreaking proposals. Dolan and his senior colleagues argued strongly for laying it all out, saying that the organization could handle the change and still operate. This gave me strong ammunition to argue with the Treasury Department against the watering-down approach.

On January 13, Killefer and I met with Rubin and Summers to seek approval to go forward with the plan. Rubin had two big questions: How destabilizing would the transition be? What would happen to the enforcement functions?

I said that the right way to look at it was to compare the proposal to the path we were already on, which was reactive and destabilizing without any clear end point. No matter what we did, there would be some destabilization and some fall-off in enforcement results over the next couple of years. But by having a positive plan, we would reverse the decline and, over the long term, raise the effectiveness of enforcement. I pointed out that the IRS's enforcement approach was out-of-date and slow to respond to the most serious compliance problems. An IRS that was in closer touch with its taxpayers and more able to adapt would in time be much more effective in achieving compliance with the tax law.

In the end Rubin ended the debate with six words: "It sounds good. Let's do it."

Walking out of the meeting with Rubin, we were all in a high mood. In eight days we had gotten treasury support for a plan that called for the biggest changes in the IRS in fifty years. Someone said we ought to break out the champagne. I said that this would be like Eisenhower drinking champagne after giving the order for the Normandy landing. Maybe we should wait till we got ashore.

We took stock of the huge job ahead. In the two weeks before the Senate hearing, we were determined to consult with every key person who had a stake in the proposal. We wanted people to hear directly from me what we were proposing and why. We wanted to emphasize that while the proposal laid out at a high level where we wanted the IRS to go, the real work was in developing and implementing a plan to get there. We intended to ask everyone we consulted to participate in doing this.

One of my first visits was with Bob Tobias, the president of the employees union, called the National Treasury Employees Union. Starting in the 1970s as a junior lawyer on the staff of the union, Tobias had taken on the IRS management many times in legal and political battles. A thoughtful and articulate speaker, he had the personal air more of an intellectual than of a tough union official. In the 1990s he had tried, with mixed success, to move to a more cooperative relationship with IRS management. Well connected in Congress, he had served as a full voting member of the IRS restructuring commission led by Kerrey and Portman.

I pointed out that he could see as well as anyone the negative consequences of the IRS's instability. Public anger at the IRS had led to cuts of fifteen thousand employees in the last few years, despite more and more tax laws and more tax returns. The purpose of the modernization plan was not to make further staff cuts but to get the best out of the people we had. Some people would be displaced and would have to retool for new jobs, but we would ask people at all levels to participate in developing the plan. Tobias understood my logic, but he had seen dozens of IRS plans come and go. He remained skeptical.[2] But he agreed to participate in a video conference with union chapter presidents around the country to explain the plan and to defer other contentious issues that would have interfered with explaining our proposal.

As the January 28 date for the Senate hearing approached, I was in almost continuous conversations about the plan, fielding phone calls on the way to meetings and back. I felt like the senator who told me of being in a meeting and looking down at a printed schedule. His aide leaned over and whispered, "Are you trying to see where you go next?" The senator replied, "No, I'm trying to figure out where I am now."

I met with groups of managers and employees in headquarters. I conducted back-to-back ninety-minute video conferences with thousands of IRS managers and union officials around the country. I visited or telephoned key members of Congress, former commissioners, and representatives of tax accountants and lawyers.

With strong support from Killefer, I managed to bull through OMB, which had to give approval of all testimony by agency heads, and which made a last-ditch effort to water the plan down to just some vague principles. (OMB and the White House staff were preoccupied at that moment with preparing for President Clinton's annual state of the union address and wanted us to find a "happy taxpayer" to sit in the audience to show that they had already improved the IRS.)

I also briefed key members of Congress. Senators Roth and Moynihan liked the whole idea immediately, because they thought that it held the prospect of permanent change in the way the IRS worked. The members of Congress who had served on the restructuring commission were supportive, because they saw our plan as following through on many of their recommendations.

The IRS audiences were pleased that they heard the proposal directly from me before I presented it to Congress and the public. But, like the baseball fans who are used to being told "wait till next year," they weren't betting on anything big actually ever happening.

The hearing itself was like pushing on an open door. This time I was in front of the bright lights at the witness table not only to respond to charges and problems but to propose a positive plan.

I summarized the whole plan in one chart, which was entitled "Modernizing America's Tax Agency." It set out three goals—for service, compliance, and productivity—and five *levers of change*—management, organization, business practices, performance measurements, and technology—in order to reach the goals. For the next two years, this chart became the touchstone of where the IRS was going.

Just as we hoped, the thrust of press coverage reported that the IRS was taking the initiative to fix its problems. The Associated Press called it an "ambitious restructuring plan," noting that "as lawmakers argue

FIGURE 4-1

Modernizing America's Tax Agency

I used this chart at the Senate hearing in January 1998 to summarize my plan for modernizing the whole IRS, not just the technology. It listed new goals (and guiding principles) and five levers of change.

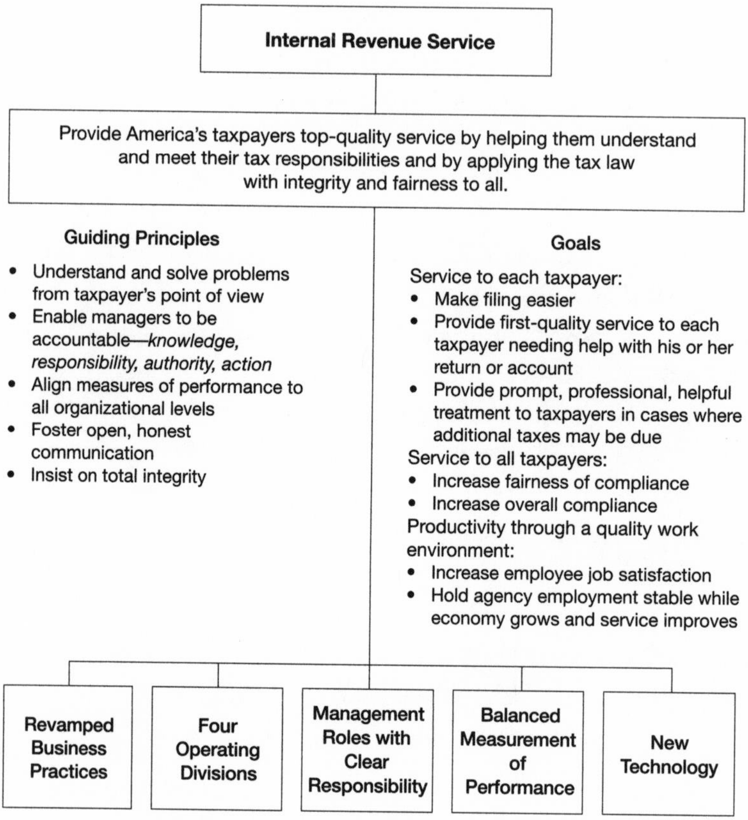

about the scope of legislation to overhaul the agency, [Rossotti is] moving quickly to have it clean up its own act."[3]

Of course, informed observers of the IRS maintained their doubts about how real all these changes were going to be. "He's obviously shown that he's got significant public relations skills," said Lawrence M. Hill, a tax attorney for Brown & Wood LLP in New York. "The question remains whether the Commissioner, as well as Congress, are enacting changes that are more than improving the public perception of the service, but also will substantively improve the process for taxpayers."[4]

We had succeeded in laying out a plan. The question now was whether we could use the plan to move the IRS to a new and better place without crashing along the way.

CHAPTER 5

If You Already Have an 83,000-Page Rules Manual, Will More Rules Solve Your Problems?

Legislating Change

SENATOR WILLIAM ROTH, chairman of the Senate Finance Committee, was clear. He wanted to write the rules into the tax code itself.

In the spring of 1998, the law that was designed to make the biggest changes in the IRS in forty-six years was in the final stages of drafting and negotiation. As far as the IRS was concerned, this was like rewriting its constitution. But the U.S. Constitution fit on ten pages, while the IRS already had an 83,000-page manual to prescribe every detail of its operations. Would writing more rules solve the problems of the IRS?

In March, Senator Roth invited me for a private meeting to discuss the provisions he was proposing. In the four months since I had taken office, I had met regularly with Senator Roth, usually visiting his office in the Hart Office Building late in the afternoon. Consistent with his manner when dealing with people directly, he always greeted me warmly, inviting me to sit in a chair to his right, with his two key staff members facing us. We would usually chat a little about his Saint Bernards and my Labrador retriever before getting down to business. Now we were down to the language of the bill—a very serious matter, since these provisions would become the law of the land and would be very hard to change.

Senator Roth's draft legislation provided all the authority needed to implement the plan I had proposed in January, including the biggest reorganization since 1952. But he was also determined to add specific mandates and rules he believed would fix problems described by taxpayers in his dramatic hearings the previous September.

I argued that, with the general authority he was providing in the bill, we could permanently fix the IRS's problems without adding detailed rules on such things as what exactly to print on the millions of different letters the IRS sent to taxpayers. Such prescriptions were bound to be costly in time and money and were bound to lead to the kind of unintended consequences that detailed laws often produced. I showed him how one proposed rule would increase, rather than decrease, the number of busy signals taxpayers would receive when calling the IRS. A far better approach would be to set forth what he wanted the IRS to achieve and then follow up carefully to make sure we were doing it.

But Senator Roth feared, as did so many other long observers of the IRS, that the agency would probably never permanently change. One commissioner might temporarily make some changes, but in the end, the bureaucracy would return to the old ways of doing things.

"No matter how much we trust you to do the right thing, we know that you won't be commissioner forever," he told me.

The specific rules stayed in the bill.

A Floating Constitutional Convention

By the time of this meeting with Roth, Congress had been debating what to do about the IRS for almost a year. I thought of this process as a kind of floating constitutional convention for the IRS. It was kicked off by the restructuring commission's June 1997 report, which had proposed sweeping changes in the way the IRS was governed externally and managed internally. But even before the commission made its final report, the Clinton administration was arguing about its proposals.

The debate began to take on the trappings of a modern political campaign, complete with dueling press releases, the recruitment of political allies on both sides, and, occasionally, snide comments about the motives and competence of the other side. Members of the restructuring commission were quoted as saying that no one from the Treasury Department even knew the address of the IRS building. Administration political operatives implied that one of the commission's proposals would let private individuals decide who should be audited.

As I stepped onto this political battlefield in the fall of 1997, I wondered why there was a big argument going on at all. Usually, when people in Washington argue about taxes, it is easy to understand why there is an argument: It's about who's going to pay more and who's going to pay less. But now the argument seemed to be about how to manage the IRS. Why would that be such a hot political topic?

I soon learned one of the peculiarities of managing change in a government agency: The political players seldom think management proposals are really about management. They instinctively assume that some deeper political motive must be in there somewhere. In this case, many members of the administration, Congress, and the press believed that there must be bigger and more sinister motives behind these IRS reform proposals, such as an undermining of the whole tax system or a push for public support of big tax cuts. Believing that the management proposals must be a cover for a political agenda, this political community felt obliged to oppose the proposals reflexively.

During the year-long debate over the IRS reform law, the greatest controversy of all was not about the IRS itself but over who would *watch* the IRS. The restructuring commission had whipped up a storm when it proposed in the spring of 1997 to create a board of directors with members from the private sector to govern the IRS.

Comparing the proposed IRS board to the board of directors of a private firm, the cochairmen, Kerrey and Portman, said it would "provide the IRS with the continuity, accountability and expertise it needs to modernize its operations and to recover the confidence of the public and Congress."[1] Portman added that "the Commission decided an independent board was needed because Treasury did not have enough management expertise or time to manage the agency."[2]

The Clinton administration reacted strongly against this proposal because it saw the plan not as a route to better governance of the IRS but as a power play to take away control of a key agency from the administration and to insert opponents of Clinton's policies on the newly created board. These political suspicions about the board were completely dominating any substantive discussion about how to fix the IRS.

In my discussions with Rubin and Summers in the summer of 1997, I suggested that the administration would gain more by supporting the reform bill and negotiating its details than by appearing to oppose the whole idea. I had no success with this argument. But when a few key congressional Democrats signaled that they were no longer going to oppose the reform bill, the White House decided in October that the big argument was lost and it was better off joining the winning side. The *Washington Post* reported that "the White House reversal came after administration officials sensed they were losing the debate and Clinton personally consulted with Senator Bob Kerrey, a co-chairman of the commission, to try to find a way out of the political box."[3]

The administration's political view, however, had not changed. The White House simply shifted its tactics from outright opposition to negotiating limits on the powers of the board. Would the board have powers over IRS enforcement functions? Over the budget? Over personnel? Over reorganizations? Would the treasury secretary be on the board? Could the board hire and fire the IRS commissioner?

The essence of this negotiation was over how much power and influence the new board would have as compared to other institutions, such as the Treasury Department or the Office of Management and Budget, that also had some jurisdiction over the IRS. Senator Kerrey's hope had been that the new board would unify direction provided to the IRS by those who oversee it, getting the commissioner out of the bull's-eye, at which multiple, conflicting players were throwing darts.

In the end, the political compromises that produced the reform law gave significant powers to the new board without taking any powers away from anyone else. The IRS was like a subsidiary company that had its own external board of directors, but also still reported to the corporate headquarters of a large conglomerate with its separate staffs and board of directors.

Another player had been added to the many already overseeing the IRS, and the commissioner was still managing in the bull's-eye.[4]

Seeking Authority Without Micromandates

Suspicions about political motives didn't explain all the arguments for and against the reform proposals that started with the Kerrey-Portman commission and moved slowly through Congress during 1997 and 1998.

Some people opposed the reform proposals because they didn't think that the IRS *could* be changed in any significant way. All the talk of reform of the IRS was just a waste of time, they thought, and just diverted attention from reforming the tax code. "Restructuring the IRS without rewriting the tax law it administers is like trying to turn a Winnebago around without taking it out of the garage," said Michael Graetz, a Yale tax law professor and former treasury official.[5]

Still other groups supported the idea of a law to reform the IRS—but not because they thought there was much serious chance of changing the IRS. They saw the bill as an opportunity to pass some long-stalled pet ideas such as increasing the interest rate on certain corporate tax refunds and giving accountants privileges previously reserved for lawyers.

As sometimes happens when people choose sides in a fight, the debate took on a life of its own. The practical purpose of the reform proposals—to make the IRS do a better job of what it was assigned to do—was at risk of being lost in the fog of a mini–political war.

After the administration changed its stance in October 1997 to support passage of a reform law for the IRS, the confused argument with political overtones continued, but the process did provide me a chance to work quietly on shaping the bill.

It felt to me like I was trying to turn around a bankrupt company that had fallen into the hands of a warring creditors committee. Would the angry bondholders give the new management enough leeway to run the company to pay off the debts for everybody, or would they sink the company by imposing conflicting and unwieldy restrictions? This comparison was not just in my imagination. Waiting for a meeting with a senator one day, I was chatting with his staff aide, who had generally been very positive about working with us. I mentioned that it would be good if Congress would let us run the IRS like a business, without too many detailed instructions. She replied that this wouldn't work, because "if the IRS was a business, it would be a bankrupt business."

As the law moved from the initial proposals of the restructuring commission through the House and Senate, the political war over specific provisions continued at each stage.

A proposal in the House to change the burden of proof in favor of some taxpayers in tax court cases caused a short but intense firefight. One lawyer told me that passing this provision would destroy the foundation of the American tax system. But who could resist the argument made by the chairman of the Ways and Means Committee? "In our system of justice, criminals have more rights than taxpayers," Representative Bill Archer of Texas said.[6] "It's high time we changed that." The burden-of-proof provision stayed in.[7]

Even before my confirmation hearing, I began to discuss the problems of the IRS with Roth and offered some of my ideas for how the agency could be changed. At the end of my confirmation testimony in October, he said he had concluded that I was "dedicated and committed to real reform of the agency."[8] Once Roth reached this conclusion, we could share views and work together on the reform bill.

But sharing views and working together did not always mean agreeing. And there were a lot more people pushing and pulling on this bill than just Roth and me. So the floating constitutional convention continued. I realized that we had to work hard on both fronts: getting *into* the law the provisions that we needed to change the IRS, and keeping *out* of the law as many damaging micromandates as possible. In the end, I got both—the authority I wanted and the micromandates I didn't want.

I put the top priority on people.

From my earliest discussions with Summers, I had said that no commissioner could successfully change the IRS, since almost everyone else in a leadership position had spent his or her entire career at the IRS. A larger number of senior executives with experience and successful track records on the outside were needed. To do this, we required the authority to bring in a limited number of top executives without the cumbersome and lengthy process generally required in the federal government. What was even more controversial, we needed the flexibility to pay somewhat higher compensation than was generally available for government executives.

We also needed authority for other changes in how we managed people, such as how we evaluated and paid managers and how we recruited entry-level accountants and other professionals.

Summers committed his support to these proposals, and Roth was receptive to giving me the authority that I needed to make changes in the IRS. But even that support was not enough. We were worried that we would be stalled to death as everybody waited for everybody else to approve. In March 1998, the Senate Governmental Affairs Committee scheduled a hearing on the issue, giving me a chance to testify publicly and, with Killefer's help, to get support from the rest of the executive branch. The hearing cleared the way for this key authority to go in the bill.

The plan I testified about in January 1998, for modernizing the entire IRS, included a major reorganization. It was surprising that this huge undertaking gained support in Congress faster than anything else in the plan, because reorganizations are usually threatened by interest groups that think they will lose influence. Roth saw the reorganization as a way to show that real change was happening to a bureaucracy that, he feared, would never change. Senator Moynihan of New York, the ranking Democrat on the Finance Committee, a remarkable wit and towering intellectual, only occasionally weighed in about the IRS, but he threw his support behind the proposed reorganization. He saw it as a rare move to pare back what he believed were inevitable tendencies for government organizations to grow so inwardly focused that they became detached from the outside world. Even the Small Business Committee, which had no official jurisdiction over the matter, issued a statement in favor of granting me authority for the reorganization.

Could there be such a thing as too much support from Congress? Apparently so. When the Senate Finance Committee proposed to extend the authority of the commissioner to include the IRS lawyers, the backlash was immediate. The restructuring commission and most other people who studied the IRS found it peculiar that everybody in the IRS reported to the commissioner except the IRS lawyers. Although they were called IRS lawyers and were located in the IRS building, the lawyers bypassed the commissioner and reported to the lawyers in the Treasury Department. The only people who did not find this arrangement peculiar were the lawyers themselves, who reacted vociferously to any hint that the IRS's lawyers should be part of the IRS.

The protests of the lawyers always seemed off-key. They sounded like a philosophy department that protested reporting to the same dean as the other academic departments of the university by asserting that they were being made subordinate to the building and grounds department. But in this case, purity of management principles had to be tempered by political reality. I knew that this issue about the lawyers was so explosive in the Treasury Department that it could poison the whole effort to get a helpful law passed. I agreed to ask Roth to scale back this authority for the commissioner. On one occasion, I was walking from one meeting to another on Capitol Hill when a car was sent to intercept me so that I could immediately issue a statement, drafted by treasury staff, opposing the proposal to give the IRS commissioner authority over the IRS lawyers. Never before had I received so much help from the treasury staff.

The law was supposed to help us change the IRS to run more like a well-managed business. Every business I had ever worked with made daily business decisions about how much effort to spend collecting money owed by a customer and when to acknowledge reality and write off a receivable. I wanted increased authority for the IRS to be able to make these kinds of businesslike decisions on collections, and I knew that Roth and his committee were receptive. But here we again collided with the tax lawyers in the Treasury Department. They seemed to believe that writing rules about collecting money was the same thing as collecting money. It was like thinking that the bank with the most fine print on the back of its bank statements would be the most profitable bank. But we persisted and won some of the authority we wanted for deferring or compromising amounts owed.

There was a pattern here. We were getting the authority we asked for to implement our plans. This was the good news. The bad news was that more and more detailed instructions for the IRS were being added to the bill. The House bill had about twenty-eight provisions setting out detailed rules, and the Senate bill increased that to about seventy.

One congressman made the point colloquially that only very specific rules would tame the huge IRS bureaucracy: "The IRS is too big and too mean," said Congressman Dick Armey of Texas, the House majority leader. "Once this bill becomes law, the IRS will just be too big."[9]

Sentiment that the IRS would never really change its basic ways spilled over into one particularly troublesome provision that required the IRS to fire employees for a list of offenses that soon became known as "the ten deadly sins." One of the firing offenses included violation of the tax code, Treasury Department regulations, or the IRS's internal manual—a body of text of over eighty-three thousand pages. Here Congress seemed not only to be adding more and more rules but to be saying that any employee who violated just one would automatically be fired. We argued that this provision would appear to employees as if they would receive capital punishment for a simple error. Why not give us the authority to manage our work force to meet the goals that Congress had set?

By the time of my March meeting with Roth, it was clear that the die was cast. Congress would give us authority to change the IRS but would not bet on its ever actually happening, except to the degree that legislation included highly specific rules. All the specific rules stayed in the bill, although we did get some helpful wording changes.

In June 1998, the House passed the final bill and the Senate followed a few weeks later. The *Washington Post* reported that Congress passed the bill because it was "fed up with complaints of lousy service and mismanagement at the IRS." The newspaper reported that the 402 to 8 vote set in motion "the biggest changes since 1952 at the agency that has more direct contact with citizens than any other in government."[10]

The day the bill passed, I was called over to Capitol Hill to join a press conference on the lawn in front of the Capitol—in a place that the media called the swamp. Here were gathered all the bill's movers and shakers from both parties and both houses: Senators Roth, Kerrey, Moynihan, Bob Graham, Orrin Hatch, John Breaux, and Charles Grassley; and Representatives Archer, Portman, Nancy Johnson (Republican, of Connecticut), and Charles Rangel (Democrat, of New York). We posed for a group picture and then went back to work. Reforming the IRS had become popular enough to produce a brief moment of bipartisan unity.

On July 22, 1998, I went to the White House for a bill-signing ceremony with President Clinton in the East Room. A White House legislative aide commented to me while we were waiting that "this ceremony is an example of the power of the presidency to manage what the public thinks. People will think that the president proposed this bill even though he opposed it until it was inevitable that it was going to pass in Congress." Despite the twisted way it happened, political calculation and good government had finally come together.

Regardless of who proposed the IRS reform bill and who opposed it, we were now going to have to implement it.

CHAPTER 6

So Many People, So Much Distrust

Rebuilding Relationships

THE TAXPAYER WAS SHAKING slightly as he opened the shoe box holding his tax records.

It was Saturday morning, November 15, 1997, two months after the dramatic Senate hearings in which taxpayers complained about horrible tangles with the IRS, and two days after I was sworn in as commissioner of internal revenue. The IRS was holding its first Problem-Solving Day, which was scheduled in thirty-three cities around the country. In each city, the local IRS office would set up an open house where taxpayers could come in at a convenient time to meet face-to-face with IRS experts, who would try to solve any lingering problem on the spot. I had gone to Baltimore to see for myself how this new idea would work and to hear about problems directly from taxpayers. I arrived just as the office was opening, and a small line of taxpayers had already formed in the makeshift reception area set up in the lobby of the downtown federal building. Local television stations and even CNN sent reporters to interview taxpayers as they filed in and out. Treasury Secretary Robert Rubin visited to lend his support.

The IRS district director and all his chief managers were there to make sure this unprecedented event went off as well as possible. IRS employees were set up with desks scattered throughout the first floor area. Specialists, such as lawyers and bankruptcy experts, were on call in case they were needed.

After chatting with the IRS managers, I asked to join an IRS employee who was working cases with taxpayers. The man with the shoe box, who looked as though he was in his early thirties, sat down. Seeing that the taxpayer was nervous, the IRS employee—a collection officer—did his best to put the man at ease by smiling, leaning back in his chair, and greeting him with a cheery "How are you this morning?" I sat in a chair nearby and explained that I was just observing how this new open-house idea was working.

As he opened the shoe box, the man said he had not filed a tax return for several years. He said he knew he should have been filing, but he had gotten behind one year and then was not sure what to do, so he had done nothing. As the years went by, he just put his records, such as W-2 forms

FIGURE 6-1

Listening to people on the front line was part of rebuilding trust. On November 8, 1997, I sat with a taxpayer working with an employee at the IRS's first Problem-Solving Day.

Source: Sarah L. Voisin / *Washington Post*

from his employers, in the shoe box. Now he wanted to get things right if he could. The IRS collection officer patiently reviewed the man's records and over a couple of hours helped him prepare his back tax returns. As it turned out, the man had a very simple return, and when all the calculations were in, he was due a refund of several thousand dollars.

As the man left, he looked like someone who had just been told that he didn't have cancer after all. I asked him why he had decided to come in now. He said he had thought of it before, but he had been too afraid of approaching the IRS by himself. He had read in the paper that a lot of people would attend this open house, so he hadn't been as afraid.

I talked to a number of taxpayers that day, and of course, most of them weren't due refunds. But none of them was a criminal, either. Like the man with the shoe box, many had let their problems linger because they didn't know what to do and were too afraid or too confused to go to the IRS. Most were pleased with the help they had received that day in sorting out long-stalled tax problems.

I also talked to some of the IRS employees, many of whom had volunteered for the extra time on Saturday. Almost all of them were proud that they had straightened out so many problems for taxpayers.

Driving home, I couldn't stop thinking of how heavy a price both taxpayers and IRS employees were paying for the distrust that had built up over the years.

As the weeks went by, I was learning fast that the distrust went beyond taxpayers' fear of the IRS. Distrust characterized relationships inside and outside the agency. IRS employees didn't trust management. Field managers didn't trust the national office. The IRS and the Treasury Department staffs didn't trust each other. Members of key congressional committees, as well as their staffs, distrusted almost anything they got from the IRS. Many groups representing taxpayers, especially those from small businesses, were actively hostile. Even vendors essential for the Year 2000 fixes didn't trust their huge and important client.

The IRS situation was completely at odds with what I had learned in my parents' businesses long ago and had applied in my twenty-eight years with AMS: that relationships of trust were the cornerstones of success. Here at the IRS we had relationships of distrust. And they were the root cause of many failures.

A few weeks after going to Baltimore, I visited the IRS office in Dallas, where about one thousand frontline IRS employees dealt with taxpayers every day on the phone or in person. After meeting with the managers in charge of the office, I met separately with groups of ten to twelve employees without any managers being present. I arranged for the management and union each to solicit volunteers for these small meetings from a cross section of employees.

Most of the employees in these small groups had worked at the IRS for ten, twenty, or even thirty years and had never met a commissioner except in a large ceremony. The employees in the first group were assembled in a small conference room, set up in typical government fashion with bare walls, nondescript chairs, and a slightly battered conference table. They didn't know what to expect, and there was dead silence when I walked in. I said I was there just to hear whatever they thought I ought to know about the IRS. I asked each person to say a couple of sentences about himself or herself, and then we opened up the discussion.

The traumatic Senate hearings and the ensuing bad publicity were on the minds of all the employees. Why were they being unfairly attacked, when they were only doing the job they were required to do? One employee told about being insulted by an acquaintance who asked how he could work for an organization that abused people for a living. Quickly the discussion moved to who was at fault for all this trouble. Some blamed the senators and the press, but soon the conversation shifted to management.

For the rest of the meeting, I heard complaint after complaint, story after story, about what management was doing, or not doing, to put the IRS in such a sorry state. Managers were just paper pushers who wouldn't know a good case from a bad one. Managers were not interested in anything but statistics to make themselves look good. Managers got away with stuff that employees were punished for. Managers wouldn't lift a finger to help the employees get what they needed to do their jobs. Managers reduced a quality-improvement initiative to a sham checkoff exercise by putting tick marks on every single item on a quality-improvement report. There was no doubt from the members of this group—they didn't trust management one bit.

Just before visiting Dallas, I had visited Oakland, California, where thirty executives in charge of the IRS activities in the Western Region were meeting. During dinner, I had talked informally with several of the executives. They too were distressed and unhappy about the criticism of the IRS and the problems that were being uncovered. Opinions diverged on many things, but one theme came through clearly—the IRS national office was strangling them with directives. If they could just be left to operate more independently, they could solve a lot of these problems on their own. There was not much confidence in management from this group, even though they were managers themselves.

Of course, back in Washington I had already seen the problem from the other end of the telescope. IRS management in Washington felt intense pressure from the Treasury Department, the White House, and Congress to react to whatever events were reported that day. In response, the IRS national office would often produce hastily written directives for the field offices. But as these endless and often confusing directives were transmitted to the front lines through management layer after management layer, the people on the receiving end concluded that management was the source of their troubles. The explosion of protest from the small-business community about the mandate to use the electronic deposit system—which taxpayers transmitted into hostility to employees in the field—was just one example of the IRS management's creating ill will and distrust, although the agency was just trying to respond to a congressional mandate.

Nearing a Point of No Return

Lack of trust magnified every problem. There was no clearer example than its impact on the critical job of fixing the IRS's computers to work after January 1, 2000.

After a few months of working on this problem, I realized that one of our highest risks was posed by the dearth of people who understood the details of the IRS's old systems well enough to fix them without breaking other things as they went along. Some of the computer code was written in languages that had not been widely used for at least twenty years. Over the years, programmers had modified this old computer code thousands of times to make it work with new tax laws, sometimes using clever programming tricks to get around the limitations of the equipment or software. To fix code like this, one had to know it from experience, and we had no time for new people to get the experience.

A very limited number of IRS employees had the necessary experience, and many of them were eligible for retirement immediately. Meanwhile, the market for programmers in Washington was white hot. Every month more of these critical employees were leaving—not surprisingly, since no one had told them in any meaningful way that they were needed or valued.

As each experienced employee left, the already excruciating pressure was ratcheted up on the remaining employees. Having very little trust in IRS management to turn this situation around, employees were prone to listen to those who said that anyone who stayed at the IRS information systems department would be forever tagged with the blame when the whole tax system came crashing down.

The IRS management was trying to fill in the gaps by using contractors. While this approach made complete sense, it only added to the suspicion among the employees that the contractors were being positioned to take over their jobs and that the IRS employees should get out while the getting was good. The contractors in turn picked up the hostile signals and began to suspect that they would become scapegoats if the systems failed.

The IRS was rapidly approaching a point at which the systems could not be fixed in time, regardless of how much money it spent. The agency was like an airplane that was flying over the ocean and burning too much fuel to get to its destination but was too far from home to go back. The only possible salvation was to reduce the amount of fuel we were burning—in this case, the number of experienced employees who were leaving.

The only way we could turn around the prevailing pessimism was by talking plainly with the employees, not painting a rosy picture, but instead laying out the problem and asking them to be part of the solution. Bob Tobias, the president of the union, together with Bob Albicker and Toni Zimmerman, two of the most respected IRS information systems executives, agreed that the only approach that might work was for the four of us to meet directly with the employees. For an entire morning, nine hundred employees crammed into a cafeteria to talk with us about this problem, with most of the time spent on answering employee questions. We pointed out that the IRS obviously needed every experienced information systems person we could get, and that the country's welfare depended on them. We explained that we had a practical plan that would succeed if everyone committed to it. To back it up, we provided a temporary 10 percent salary bonus and promised retraining in new technologies for every employee, once the Year 2000 crunch was over. As we followed through on the statements made in this meeting, attitudes and retention began to improve.

This was plugging one hole in one dike. How were we going to turn the tide of distrust that impeded progress across the whole IRS?

Rebuilding Relationships, One at a Time

People often refer disdainfully to a large organization like the IRS as a bureaucracy. In business, critics often charge underperforming old-line companies with being too bureaucratic. Often, the implication of this term is that the organization is faceless. Customers, employees, and other stakeholders don't see themselves as dealing with real people. But, in reality, every organization, no matter how large, is made up of individual people—people who have relationships with other people inside and outside the organization. Building on the good relationships, and rebuilding the ones that are broken, is the key to regaining trust throughout the organization.

Among the many items of reading material given to me while I was preparing for confirmation were the results of an employee survey. One section asked the employees to rate their agreement with the statement "There is trust between employees and management." This statement got one of the lowest scores in the survey. Very few employees indicated that they trusted management—a statistical verification of the distrust that was expressed in my meetings with employees.[1]

But another statement in the survey got a much higher score: "There is trust between *me* and *my* manager."[2] Most employees indicated that they did trust their own manager. At the end of several of my small group meetings, I had asked the employees how they felt about the person who directly supervised them. The majority said their own manager was a good person who did his or her best but was thwarted by other higher-ups.

Even taxpayer surveys, most of which rated the IRS poorly, gave predominantly good marks to the professionalism of IRS employees with whom taxpayers had personally dealt.

This seemingly contradictory result was not surprising. People have a far more reliable basis for judging people they work with directly than those they don't know. And most of the IRS managers and employees were competent people who were doing their best, often fighting serious obstacles, to do what they were asked to do. So when a person finds things going seriously wrong with an organization he or she is dealing with, who is likely to be blamed? Obviously, the people he or she doesn't know. *Management.*

We couldn't immediately solve all problems; management would inevitably be blamed when things went wrong. But to accomplish anything, we had to reverse the IRS's death spiral of distrust. Relationships of trust mattered in the IRS as much as they did in my father's business or at AMS. When relationships are strong, people will believe that the people they trust will do their best to fix the specific problems.

As a critical first step, I could personally work on building relationships with a circle of people who were most important to the functioning of the IRS. Over time, we could expand this circle by setting up the IRS so that more and more of IRS management built more and more direct, trusting relationships with people inside and outside the agency. Over time, we could replace the abstraction of management with meaningful relationships of one person to another.

To build relationships, I had to travel. I had to find opportunities to meet with people in settings that encouraged them to get below the surface—to tell me what was truly on their minds and to solicit their support on fixing the real problems we were facing in trying to change the IRS. It was hard to do this in Washington, where time was chopped into tiny pieces, especially for members of Congress. So I sought opportunities to visit key members in their home districts. It was also important to meet with tax practitioners, business groups, and IRS employees on their own turf and in small groups, where they would feel freer to talk. On trips, I sought out local newspapers and television stations; their coverage helped me put a face on the IRS.

The week of April 15 is the moment of the year when people are thinking about taxes and reading stories about the IRS. Senator Ben Nighthorse Campbell of Colorado, then chairman of the subcommittee that appropriates funds for the IRS, had scheduled a field hearing in Denver for April 14 and invited me to attend.

He had planned an official congressional hearing at which local taxpayers could testify. Afterward I could explain what we were doing to fix the kind of problems they reported. We knew that this might become another occasion for emotional attacks on the IRS. Several of the taxpayers likely to testify were innocent spouses, people who were stuck with unpaid taxes on joint tax returns when their husband or wife left them.

A room at Denver University was set up like a congressional hearing, with Senator Campbell presiding, faced by a witness table and rows of chairs for the public. Television cameras from local stations were lined up next to local newspaper reporters to cover the hearing.

Two panels of witnesses testified, telling their lengthy stories of unfair treatment in the hands of the IRS. One woman told of having her house seized for taxes she didn't know her husband had run up, claiming that the IRS forged documents to get the house before the required notice period. A tax accountant claimed that her partner died because of frustration with the IRS.

When it was my turn to speak, Senator Campbell helpfully noted that I could not comment on the specific cases right there. He gave me every chance to say how we were working to improve the way the agency worked. IRS employees from the local office were present, and they promised to follow up on each case and to keep Senator Campbell informed.

After the hearing, on the way to lunch, Senator Campbell told me of his Native American background and of his early experience as a migrant farm worker. His first break came when he was able to join the Teamsters Union, and he has remained a dues-paying member ever since. He was a member of the U.S. Olympic Judo team, drove a Harley, wore a pony tail, and made jewelry in addition to being a Republican senator and chairman of an appropriations subcommittee.

Some of his constituents, including people in the information technology business, joined us for lunch. The senator listened intently to our discussion about how the IRS's old systems caused problems for taxpayers. In fact, some of the problems reported that morning were in part caused by the inability of the IRS's old systems to properly keep track of taxpayers who filed joint returns and then divorced while taxes were still due.

On the way home, I reflected on what I had accomplished on the trip, which took more than a full day during a period of intense time demands. As my press experts had warned, I probably drew more television coverage to the taxpayers' complaints than might otherwise have happened. Yet, deep down, I was sure it was the right thing to do, to listen to the taxpayers and to get to know Senator Campbell a little better. Maybe Woody Allen was onto something when he said that "eighty percent of life is just showing up."

The next day was tax day, April 15, and I had plenty of chances to face the public and try to make the case that the IRS was changing. I attended a morning congressional hearing and then moved on to a National Press Club luncheon meeting, where I gave a speech broadcast live by National Public Radio. The press club's method for managing the clamor of reporters is to require them to write their questions on three-by-five cards, which are handed up to the moderator.

For the last question, the moderator said, "This question is from your wife, Barbara: What time will you be home tonight?" I replied, "Same as always, I don't know." This answer got a good chuckle from the audience, who knew that being IRS commissioner was not the best job for a person who wanted to get home for dinner every night.

Connecting with the Front Line

One of the great values of building a wide circle of relationships within an organization is that the process of building them decreases the chances of making poorly informed decisions and increases people's confidence that the changes a leader proposes are based on reality. Coming in cold from the outside, there was no way I could feel confident making decisions about changing the IRS, or even explaining the IRS to other people, without a better sense of what employees actually did every day when they were working with taxpayers. I also knew that employees and first-line managers believed that upper-level managers had long since lost touch with the reality that frontline workers faced every day.

One way I could gain a better feel for the work, and encourage upper managers to do the same, was occasionally to go to work with some employees who were dealing with taxpayers. Early on, I did this by going to Problem-Solving Days and listening in on phone calls with taxpayers. But I also wanted to go out with the employees who visited taxpayers' homes and businesses to collect money and audit tax returns.

"The commissioner wants to do what?" people at headquarters asked incredulously when they heard of my interest. Had the pressure gotten so bad I was losing my grip? No one could remember a commissioner going out on collection or audit calls. What about security? Would the taxpayers object? Would the employees object? Would the union object? Was it ethical? Was it legal?

I persisted. On a trip to New Orleans, I went on my first call with a revenue officer (the IRS term for employees doing collecting in person). Our first stop was at a strip mall to meet with a dry cleaning shop owner who had been in business for more than ten years and had fallen behind on employment tax deposits. We sat in his little office behind the front counter where he took in the clothes. The revenue officer introduced me and simply said I was visiting from Washington and was accompanying employees. The taxpayer explained that he did not have the cash to pay the overdue taxes, but was negotiating a loan to cover them as well as other bills. On the way out, the revenue officer explained to me that the account was already more than eighteen months overdue before it had been sent to him for collection and that 30 percent of the balance was interest and penalties built up in that time. Why would management wait this long to send the account out for collection, making it harder for both the taxpayer and the employee? It was a very important question for which I had to find the answer.

In Detroit, I went out on an audit with a revenue agent, the IRS's term for the accountants who audit complicated tax returns. The taxpayer was a medium-sized manufacturing business, and we went into the office of the company's comptroller for the opening meeting. The agent identified certain items on the tax returns for which he wanted documentation. The comptroller replied that he would be glad to provide the requested documentation, but asked if the agent was aware that a previous audit had been completed less than two years ago. The earlier IRS agent had concluded that these very items had been reported correctly. Talking with the agent on the way home, I learned that there was no routine way for the agent to have known about the details of the prior audit—or even that an audit had been completed. The IRS systems did not provide this information to the agent, who simply was given a stack of paper returns to review. Here was another example of a critical problem that would have to be solved: The IRS was wasting its own time and that of taxpayers by auditing people who did not need to be audited, as IRS records should have shown.

Over the years, I continued the practice of visiting with frontline employees as they worked with taxpayers. I have no doubt that I learned more than I could have learned any other way about how the IRS really worked. Equally important, I believe this practice was critical to establishing credibility with employees and taxpayers that the massive changes we were proposing were soundly based. And, as my own travels became known, managers at all levels were encouraged to get out of their offices and spend time with employees doing the everyday work of the IRS with taxpayers—showing that management consisted of real people who were not disconnected from reality.

Into the Lion's Den

Obviously, visiting one small-business taxpayer at a time would not change minds on a national scale. Yet, nowhere was the distrust of the IRS greater than among groups that represented small-business taxpayers. Almost 45 percent of the cash that comes into the treasury for taxes is sent by small businesses. And most of the small businesses are *really* small, with just a few employees and very little time to spend coping with a blizzard of tax forms. Over thirty million are self-employed sole proprietors. I needed to reach out to the powerful small-business associations with chapters around the country and representatives in Washington.

Shortly after taking office, I invited the leaders of several of these organizations in for one-on-one meetings with me just to chat and hear what was on their minds. One of the most vocal advocates for small-business owners was Jack Faris, who ran the National Federation of Independent Business. A politically savvy Tennesseean who had deep connections throughout Congress and a big constituency of small-business owners throughout the country, Faris was a great conversationalist who loved to tell stories about the sometimes quirky way small-business owners thought about the world.

Benny Thayer, who ran the National Association of Self-Employed, was a tall African American entrepreneur who had had numerous business ventures of his own. Thayer had started his association to represent the growing number of individuals who made a living as sole proprietors, and he represented them loyally and effectively.

Faris and Thayer were used to hearing complaints from their members about the IRS, over such items as the mandates to use the electronic deposit systems and overly complex tax accounting rules. On their first visits with me, we each spent most of the time telling stories. I was able to connect pretty well by talking about the problems I had myself when AMS was a start-up business. Their one specific request was that I come to one of their meetings and meet face-to-face with their members.

Faris's federation was then involved in a widely publicized campaign to sunset the tax code. The campaign called on Congress simply to abolish the code by December 31, 2000. Although this campaign was directed against the tax code, much of the anger spilled over to the IRS. Some of the federation's literature called the tax code the "IRS code." As a symbol of its campaign, the federation used a poster consisting of a stop sign superimposed over the letters "IRS."

At the peak of this campaign, in May 1998, over a thousand small-business owners came to Washington to lobby Congress. I was scheduled to speak to the whole assembly in a packed hotel ballroom. The room was so big that bright spotlights and television cameras were focused on the speakers on stage to transmit pictures to screens around the room. When Faris told the crowd that the next speaker was the IRS commissioner, a dull murmur of "whooooo" went around the room, as though to say, "Who does he think he is, Daniel bearding the lion in its den?"

Faris introduced me in the most positive way possible, stressing that I was the first business guy to run the IRS. I made a short speech and then opened it up to questions. A few were openly hostile, such as, "Is it true that anybody who criticizes Clinton gets audited?" But most just recounted problems the person had with his or her taxes or the IRS or both. One person asked me to look into a certain regulation, which I agreed to do. In the end they thanked me for coming and wished me well. Of course, they still wanted to sunset the tax code.

Thayer invited me to attend one of the many smaller meetings he held routinely around the country. For one of them, he rented a small auditorium in the upper reaches of the Texas Rangers baseball stadium. Walking through an area displaying memorabilia from the team, I joined his meeting of about one hundred self-employed businesspeople from Texas. I spent the morning alternating between telling small-business stories, hearing their anecdotes, and listening to suggestions about how we could improve the IRS.

For the rest of my time in office, I continued to meet regularly with Faris and Thayer and to attend some of their meetings. The IRS was able to solve some of the problems they brought up and not others. Faris and Thayer strongly supported our modernization proposals and later began to bond with the team that ran the IRS's new small-business and self-employed division. When Benny Thayer died unexpectedly, I felt I had lost a true friend. After I left office, Jack Faris sent me a handwritten thank-you note. The appreciation was mutual.

People Are Good, Bureaucracy Is Bad

The big sports story of the summer in 1998 was the torrid pace of home run hitting by Mark McGwire and Sammy Sosa. As McGwire closed in on Roger Maris's record of sixty-one homers, a clever *New York Times* reporter created a hypothetical question about gift tax due from a fan who might catch the record-breaking ball and give it back to McGwire. An IRS spokesman, trying to answer the reporter's question during Labor Day weekend, fell into his trap.

The next day, I read this headline in the *Boston Herald:* "Mac Fans Brushed Back by an IRS Pitch." "Leave it to the IRS to sound a sour note in a moment of triumph," the article began. "As Mark McGwire bore down on Roger Maris' home run record last week, an Internal Revenue Service official knocked a foul that threatened to bean any fan foolish enough to do the right thing." The IRS spokesperson had said that any fan "who shagged the Cardinal slugger's sixty-second home run ball, then gave it back to McGwire, would be liable for a huge tax."[3]

More than innocent-spouse cases, more than small-business owners losing their businesses, more than IRS modernization failures, the prospect of the IRS taxing this hypothetical good-hearted fan unleashed the fury of the American people, not to mention their representatives in Congress. This was what people thought of when they talked about a faceless bureaucracy.

I got two calls from Senator Roth, a call from the Senate floor from Senator "Kit" Bond, a letter from Senator Moynihan, and a letter signed by eight senators saying they were confident that the "baseball fans at the IRS" could certainly devise a solution to this senseless problem. Without checking with anyone at the IRS, White House spokesman Mike McCurry said that the IRS assessment was "about the dumbest thing I've ever heard in my life."[4]

Stuart Brown, the IRS chief counsel, personally took charge of finding a legal way to solve the problem. We got out a statement that same day, saying that if a fan caught the ball and gave it to McGwire, the person would not be taxed. In the release, I said, "Sometimes pieces of the tax code can be as hard to understand as the infield fly rule. All I know is that the fan who gives back the home run ball deserves a round of applause, not a big tax bill."[5]

The press grudgingly gave us credit for not being so pinheaded after all. I was told one of the television commentators read my quote to the national audience at the beginning of the game in which McGwire hit his sixty-second homer. By the skin of our teeth, we had turned a potential public relations disaster into something that made it seem as if real people worked at the IRS, even people who knew what the infield fly rule was.

This seemingly small incident gave me a real lesson in how people form their opinion about whether they can trust an organization to do the right thing. Real people are good, even if they occasionally make mistakes. Bureaucracies are bad, even if they mostly do what they are supposed to do.[6]

Staying on the Road and out of the Ditch

One of the ways we were trying to overcome the accumulated distrust of the IRS was by building relationships directly with people who were important to the agency. My premise was that people have a reasonably reliable basis for judging other people whom they have direct experience working with. But what if that direct experience turned negative? What if someone important to the IRS worked directly with us on one specific issue, even a little issue, and had a bad experience? This could undermine our whole effort.

Congressional offices sent thousands of letters to the IRS every year, many directed to the commissioner, about specific tax cases, employee complaints, and IRS rules and regulations. Part of the job of building trust was to improve the handling of this routine correspondence. If we handled these requests badly, we risked making a bad situation worse by reinforcing the preexisting distrust. But some of these requests raised even bigger stakes, because members of Congress felt so strongly about a matter, they would ask me to look into it personally.

I asked several former commissioners how they handled such situations. One told me a long story that he remembered decades later. The then chairman of an appropriations subcommittee had called to complain that the IRS had "wrongly" denied one of his constituents a deduction for a business expense, which turned out to be expenses the man had incurred when his daughter had come to Washington to be a Mardi Gras princess. The commissioner had told the congressman that his constituent should appeal through normal channels, and if the deduction was still denied, he, the commissioner, would ask the chief counsel to review the decision. The deduction was still denied, the congressman persisted, and the commissioner had invited the congressman to come in with his technical expert to discuss the matter with the IRS technical expert.

When the meeting convened, the congressman had brought not a technical expert but none other than the majority leader of the House of Representatives, hoping to win through pressure what he couldn't win through persuasion. Fortunately, as soon as the majority leader heard about the frivolous issue, he had stopped the meeting, declaring it not worth his time or the IRS commissioner's.

This far-out story made a couple of practical points for me. Ultimately, the cases had to be decided on the merits, no matter who was exerting pressure. But it was also vital in such situations for the commissioner to show that he had carefully considered all points of view before reaching a decision. Often, with a little work, the agency could propose a solution that was both within the rules and acceptable to those making the request.

In one instance, a member of Congress described to me how he had worked for years to get passage of a tax provision that encouraged investments on certain Native American reservations. But the provision would not take effect until the IRS issued regulations defining where and how the incentive could be taken. At the same time, the provision had a fixed expiration date. The congressman called me to explain that the delay in issuing the regulations was effectively nullifying this provision, which would help raise people out of poverty in his state. I found that the regulations were stalled because they required not only the usual complex coordination within the Treasury Department but also input from the Interior Department to define certain boundaries of reservations. I asked my ace assistant, Kirsten Wielobob, to work on this issue, and she cut through this maze and got the regulations out. In this case, my personal intervention at the behest of the congressman made a big difference for his constituents and was the right thing to do.

In another case, a senator called me about a tiny school district that was facing enforcement action by the IRS for failure to pay required payroll taxes. The problem had started when a former bookkeeper embezzled the money. In such situations, the law makes the responsible officers, such as the school board members, personally liable for the taxes. This tax code provision was a potential disaster for this poor school district and the volunteers who served on the school board. As usual, there turned out to be complications, such as how an insurance bond would be applied. Negotiations between the IRS and the school district were stalled in part over confusion on both sides over these complications. I asked Val Oveson, our national taxpayer advocate, to look into the case himself. He convened meetings of the local people and worked out an acceptable solution.

Choosing to personally handle certain matters as commissioner was similar to the choice I sometimes made as CEO when clients complained about decisions made by individuals in our company. In such situations, a leader can fall into the ditch on either side of the road. If he or she just brushes off the client and blindly supports the decision of the team, the leader both misses an opportunity to find out whether there is substance to the client's complaint and surely makes the client feel that the organization is unresponsive. If a leader just orders up something to please the client, the integrity of the organization is undermined. The right approach is to take the complaint seriously while ultimately making the decision on its merits.

Although hazardous, handling sensitive situations carefully is critical to building the right relationships with stakeholders. I viewed it as an essential part of the job, as well as a valuable reality check for me on what was really going on in the organization.

In December 1998, the schedule was even more packed than usual, as we tried to juggle all the balls in the air and to free up some time for a Christmas break. Floyd Williams, the IRS legislative director, advised me to attend a reception being held on Capitol Hill sponsored by the Tax Coalition, a network of women staffers on the tax committees. This informal network had expanded to include a lot of people we regularly worked with in and out of government. The program consisted of little skits and parodies of the funny (at least to insiders) things that happened in the tax business in Washington that year. To my astonishment, they sang a song about me, to the tune of, of all things, "That's *Amore.*"

When the Code is so thick
That it just makes you sick
Ring Rossotti.

When the public is mad
'Cause the service is bad
Call Rossotti.

When morale is so low
There's no lower to go
Please call Chuckie

Tax reform, we don't need
It's a new IRS
With Rossotti!!!

I hadn't laughed so much in weeks. It was a delightful Christmas present, and I took it as a nice sign of progress in trust building.

PART II

Fixing the Plane While Flying to a New Destination

CHAPTER 7

Will People Always Hate the Tax Collector?

Changing the Culture

"How does it feel to be the most hated man in America?" a reporter asked me a few months into my term as commissioner.

That reporter was just one of dozens of people who offered their opinions about my position as chief tax collector. A few months after his comment, I was crammed in an economy airplane seat. I asked a man next to me if I could put my cup of Coke on his tray, since my computer took up all my tray space. He asked me where I worked. When I told him, he smiled and said, "Have you ruined anybody's day today?"

The attitude that tax collectors are bad people is an ancient one. Bible stories lumped tax collectors with such unsavory characters as drunks, gluttons, heathens, prostitutes, and other societal outcasts. According to one of the readings, while Jesus was having dinner at Matthew's house, many tax collectors and sinners came and ate with him and his disciples. When the Pharisees saw this, they asked his disciples, "Why does your teacher eat with tax collectors and 'sinners'?" On hearing this, Jesus said, "It is not the healthy who need a doctor, but the sick."[1]

I heard of many incidents that showed how personally such entrenched attitudes affected IRS employees.

Bob Wenzel, the deputy commissioner, told me a story about moving to a new neighborhood near Detroit as a young IRS manager. He and his wife went next door for a party, where all the new neighbors introduced themselves and told where they worked. When Bob bent down to pick up a napkin, all the men took the opportunity to move to the other side of the room, as though he bore a contagious disease.

A respected senior manager in the IRS Chicago office shared a similar story. She had grown up in a poor neighborhood and had worked her way through college. Later she had joined a group that worked in the neighborhoods to encourage kids to stay in school. At a meeting in 1997, when her name was announced at a luncheon to recognize the volunteers, the audience booed at the mention that she worked for the IRS.

Jokes at the expense of IRS employees abounded on Web sites and around water coolers: The IRS agent goes to a psychiatrist and says he's depressed because he's the most hated person in the world. The psychiatrist says, "You're not the most hated person in the whole world. In the United States, maybe, but not the whole world."

Experiences and stories like these, repeated over and over, led many employees to conclude that taxpayers were natural adversaries. Having heard me speak about the need to turn around the public's declining view of the IRS by improving service, many thought I was naive. The prevailing opinion was that the public's negative attitude toward the IRS would never change.

On a hot August day in 1998, I traveled to Brooklyn, New York, for a town hall meeting in a community college auditorium. A standing-room-only crowd of 350 IRS employees overflowed the room. It was the most raucous group I'd seen so far, and they weren't in the mood to listen to a speech.

One revenue officer reenacted what a taxpayer did the previous week when the officer visited his business and announced that she was from the IRS. Imitating the taxpayer, she stood and put her hands up, as in a holdup, prancing around to give the whole audience a view. The crowd roared and applauded, relishing this depiction of what taxpayers really thought about IRS employees. "Maybe we should change the name of the IRS," she said, implying that nobody would ever react positively to anyone associated with the IRS.

A smart aleck in the back picked up the theme that trying to please taxpayers was a fool's errand: "All we're doing is making it easy for the deadbeats to get away with not paying." I replied with my little riff about how we could provide good service, treat people right, *and* be effective in collecting the taxes, using enforcement action when we needed to. Seeing from the body language the obvious skepticism of the crowd, I ended by saying, "Of course, you don't believe any of this, so you'll just have to wait and see." The same guy shot back in his most sarcastic voice, "How did you guess?" "You're from Brooklyn," I replied, unleashing a little applause, but realizing how tough it was going to be to bring this group around to thinking of taxpayers as anybody but adversaries.

Six months later, I attended a town hall meeting with about two hundred employees in Richmond, Virginia. The crowd was much more subdued than the one in Brooklyn, but some of the attitudes were still the same. One veteran revenue agent stood up and made an impassioned little speech. "Why are we giving up on the bottom line? We need to recognize that the taxpayers are adversaries who are out to pay as little as possible."

The attitudes of many tax experts were even more hardened than those of employees. They thought that people *should* hate the IRS. At a cocktail party in Washington in the fall of 1998, the conversation moved to the recently passed IRS reform law. Two former congressional staffers ridiculed the whole idea of the new law. Reform the IRS to make it more friendly to taxpayers? The IRS is supposed to collect taxes, not make friends. The agency is not doing its job if it's not making people unhappy.

It reminded me of a joke about a company that had particularly bad service. We joked that the company's customer service slogan must be "We're not happy until you're not happy."

Using the term *kinder, gentler IRS,* some tax experts commonly trivialized the idea of an agency that provided good service and treated people properly. They believed that you could either have a kinder, gentler IRS or an effective IRS that collected the taxes—but not both. When the IRS announced one particular enforcement action, an expert, betraying a typical view, commented, "Now the IRS pendulum has begun to swing back from being 'kinder and gentler' with taxpayers to putting greater emphasis on making sure they pay taxes that are due."[2]

Getting Out of Pendulum Prison

Eight months after I took office, I had a new law governing the IRS and a radical plan for transforming it. But a big part of the success or failure of transforming the IRS would depend not on reorganizing or replacing technology but on changing basic attitudes about how the IRS *could* do its job. I and my top team would have to convince honest taxpayers that the IRS was on their side, and employees that most taxpayers were not necessarily adversaries. We would have to disabuse outside tax experts and IRS employees of the notion that the agency could not deliver good customer service while collecting taxes effectively. This meant we had to get beyond the swinging-pendulum model of doing business.

In the swinging pendulum model, the IRS would, at best, shift its emphasis from enforcement to service when the complaints got too great and then back to enforcement when the political pressure eased. As long as this swinging-pendulum model prevailed, it not only reinforced negative attitudes the public and the IRS held about each other, but also served as a built-in excuse for shoddy performance in the IRS. If IRS employees believed that taxpayers would always complain about the agency, it was too easy to dismiss complaints about poor service. If satisfying taxpayers was not a realistic objective, IRS management and its OMB overseers would fall back on the crutch they historically used to justify the agency's budget. That crutch was a narrow set of statistics that the IRS thought could be most easily measured, namely enforcement revenues collected by the seizure of taxpayer property or the assessment of deficiencies in audits.

Poor performance in dealing with taxpayers not only drove the public's opinion of the agency lower, but also impeded the ability of the IRS to perform any aspect of its mission. It was impossible to convince such hostile taxpayers, and the politicians who represented them, that their interests were served by effective enforcement of the tax law. The demoralizing, yet widely popular, attacks on the IRS in the years before I took office made it devastatingly clear that the organization which dealt with the most people in America could not perform its essential mission for the country if it continued also to be the lowest rated in the country.

I did not believe that anything inherent in the IRS mission made this result necessary. The swinging pendulum was a theory of organizational performance long out-of-date in business. Few modern businesses would argue that they couldn't provide good customer service because they had to make money for shareholders; most companies would say the opposite—that satisfied customers were necessary for the business's financial success. The best-performing businesses focus on improving performance across the board.

On my side of this argument, I had some compelling information about the way the tax system works in America. The vast majority of Americans try to pay their taxes honestly. In fact, 98 percent of revenue comes in without any enforcement intervention by the IRS, and over 80 percent of taxpayers say they would not cheat even a little bit.[3] My view was that there was no good reason why the IRS could not be—and could not be *perceived* to be—on the side of this vast majority who are trying to comply. This view was completely consistent with the idea that the IRS would use its enforcement authority vigorously whenever necessary to collect the taxes from the minority who would not pay what they owed.

Reforging Familiar Tools

I needed to make into reality my very different view of how the IRS was supposed to work in an organization of a hundred thousand people spread across the country. And through their work every day, these IRS people had to convince millions of taxpayers the IRS was changing. To begin, I decided to reforge tools already familiar in the IRS organization: the mission statement, the goals, and the system of performance measures.

I had begun to grapple with the IRS's mission statement and goals as soon as I became commissioner, reviewing many prior studies. People in the IRS took these expressions seriously and were accustomed to referring to them as guidance for many decisions. In my first testimony, I had summarized my view of the IRS's mission, testifying that the IRS serves taxpayers in two distinct ways: First, "we serve *each* taxpayer with whom we deal directly, one at a time. In each and every one of these interactions we should provide first quality service and treatment. Second, we serve *all* taxpayers by ensuring that compliance is fair. Our tax system depends on each person having confidence that his or her neighbor or competitor is also complying."[4] Senator Roth responded helpfully by including a section in the IRS reform bill passed in July 1998 explicitly directing the IRS to write a new mission statement that placed greater emphasis on serving the public.

In my years at AMS, I had observed many organizations, big and small, embark on developing a new mission statement. Books and articles have been written about the subject. The only common conclusion is that hazards abound. The process can become endless with committees and consultants. Or, the CEO can so dominate the process that nobody believes that his or her own views counted. The product can become so long and vague that it says nothing and inspires nobody. The content can be so divorced from reality that it produces cynicism or black humor.

To tackle the job of writing the new mission statement, I turned to one executive, Judy Tomaso, asking her to solicit views widely, but quickly. I asked her to propose a list of proposed mission statements that focused in a balanced way on how we served taxpayers. I then convened our senior management team for one meeting to consider the options. Then I made the final decision.

In September 1998, we published the new twenty-seven-word mission statement for the IRS: "Provide America's taxpayers top quality service by helping them understand and meet their tax responsibilities and by applying the tax law with integrity and fairness for all."[5]

The outside reaction was mostly favorable, though one former commissioner, reflecting the old-line view that the IRS was an enforcement agency that wasn't there to help people, couldn't resist sarcasm: "I thought H&R Block already had a mission statement."[6] Privately, I was actually glad to read this, because it underscored the pervasive view we were trying to change.

Inside the IRS, employees and offices posted this mission statement on walls, desks, and computer screens within days. Discussion about the mission statement tended to grow out of one common question: Why did it not use the words *collection* or *enforcement?* I answered this question many times, finding that the ensuing discussion prodded people to think about what was changing. The words *applying the law* are synonymous with *enforcing the law,* I would point out, but without the historically narrow association with statistics. The IRS applies the law in many more ways than seizing property or investigating crime.

But the biggest question among many employees was not about the words. It was about whether the IRS management meant them. Was this just the latest flavor of the month? Performance measures had always been an important tool of IRS management. Promotions and awards were often driven by them. How would these quantitative measures of success change with the new mission statement? If the enforcement revenue king was dead, what would replace it?

You Get What You Measure

The employees were certainly asking the right questions. The IRS had been trying and failing to develop appropriate measures of performance for forty-four years.

In 1954, the IRS implemented a project to "establish production standards so that both supervisors and employees know what is considered normal." The intent was to let everyone know, in quantitative terms, what was expected of them. But the agency soon concluded that the standards appeared to cause a "worsening of the enforcement picture."[7]

IRS attempts to fix the system by redefining the standards created new problems, and in 1959, congressional criticism caused the IRS to issue a new directive, which stated flatly: "Dollar production [meaning tax revenue collected] shall not be used as the measurement of any individual's performance."[8]

Such cycles of tinkering with the measurement systems were often followed by strong criticism, and then new rules, decade after decade after decade. When congressional hearings in the 1970s focused on allegations that taxpayers were mistreated as a result of production quotas, Commissioner Don Alexander issued a new directive stating that "individual case or dollar goals—formal, informal, or implied—are not permitted and will not be tolerated."[9] He was essentially repeating, only more strongly, the 1959 directive that nobody in the IRS would be given a quota for how much tax revenue he or she should bring in. And yet, some system was needed to measure performance, so the IRS periodically tinkered and Congress periodically criticized. Finally, in 1988, Congress passed the first law prohibiting production goals or quotas.

How to use numbers to judge success is one of the most fundamental problems leaders of any organization face. The wrong measures can create highly perverse results. When authors in Soviet Russia were paid by the number of words they wrote, they produced very long, but highly repetitive, books. And when car factories in the United States were rated mainly on the number of cars produced, manufacturers sent out a lot of lemons.

The right measures can be a powerful tool to improve performance. When Paul O'Neill, as CEO of Alcoa, began rating people based on how few workdays were lost to injuries, safety increased to unprecedented levels. When General Electric began an intense focus on measuring quality, the number of defects in products—from turbines to washing machines—dropped to extraordinarily low levels.

Even sensible numbers, however, such as quarterly reports of corporate earnings, can drive people to bad behavior if they become obsessed with them as a sole and mindless badge of success or failure. Enron and WorldCom were only two of a stunning string of corporate accounting scandals that showed how a blind focus on a few numbers can destroy an organization.

Unfortunately, the IRS had a history of putting too much emphasis on too narrow a set of numbers, mostly those that counted enforcement revenues, while ignoring other important measures. In Oakland, California, I met with employees whose job it was to review the quality of collection cases handled by telephone. The reviewers were unhappy that their quality ratings were not being used by IRS managers to fix persistent quality problems. The managers largely ignored the quality ratings because no one used them to evaluate the managers' own performance. One quality reviewer said, "We tend to judge ourselves by our best intentions while judging the taxpayers by their last worst act." If all attention was on quantity, then quality would take a back seat.

If an organization's use of the wrong numbers, or its erroneous use of the right numbers, can do enormous damage, it is equally true that no organization can succeed without using numbers to judge its success. Numbers may not tell the whole story, but they tell part of the story in a way that words alone cannot, even in organizations for which profit is not a performance goal. Attendance at church services is certainly not a complete measure of the spiritual health of a congregation, but it is an essential number for the parish leaders to know.

Recognizing that any successful organization must use numbers to manage performance, Congress passed the Government Performance and Results Act in 1993. The act required federal agencies to establish "performance measures . . . expressed in objective, quantifiable . . . forms."[10]

By the time of the Senate hearings in September 1997, just before I took office, misuse of statistics had again become a central focus of the criticism, showing again the power and persistence of a badly constructed measurement system. Senator Roth said in his opening statement, "While the use of quotas is specifically prohibited, it appears to be commonplace. . . . I believe this is outrageous, a major problem that has become part of the agency's culture."[11] "What we need to do is to drive a silver stake through the heart of this quota process . . . and kill it, kill it, kill it for good," Senator Richard Bryan of Nevada told me at my confirmation hearing a few weeks later.[12]

This time, even Vice President Gore said the IRS would swear off dollar quotas completely, as he explained in his report on IRS customer service: "One of the points the IRS front-line employees made to us over and over again is: 'You get what you measure.' If you have a performance measurement and rewards system based on dollar goals, it can drive employees toward actions that can lead to problems in their relationship with taxpayers."[13]

Immediately after the September 1997 Senate hearings, Acting Commissioner Mike Dolan had suspended the use of nearly all performance numbers throughout the IRS. The reform law, passed in July 1998, contained a prohibition, even more sweeping than previous laws, on using "enforcement results" to suggest goals or to evaluate "any IRS employee."[14] What's more, other parts of the law mandated quarterly certifications by every manager and severe penalties for violating this prohibition.

But we still had to get the work done in the agency. And the Government Performance and Results Act still mandated that the IRS have quantitative performance measures.

Years earlier, Commissioner Larry Gibbs had stated the heart of the problem I was inheriting: "The problem with our policy statement is that it tells our people what not to do. It says, 'don't use enforcement statistics.' I don't think that this helps someone on the front line very much, to tell them what not to do."[15] The IRS was like a sailboat without sails in the middle of the ocean. Numbers were the essential power source in the IRS for so many years that when they were taken away the boat was nearly adrift. Our urgent task was to create a new set of measures that could again power the boat, but that would not unintentionally send it off in the wrong direction.

Our management team had to find a way to tell the IRS employees at all levels what they *were* expected to do and how their success *would* be measured. And we had to do this in a way that measured what we really wanted to happen in the new IRS, not just what had always been measured or what was easy to measure.

Getting It Roughly Right Rather Than Precisely Wrong

When I took office in 1997, the IRS already had a project under way to develop a set of measures built around the idea of the balanced scorecard. First laid out in a 1992 *Harvard Business Review* article by Robert Kaplan and David Norton, the idea was that no single measure of performance could effectively capture the reality of any significant business operation, because true success over time demanded attention to more than one purpose. To retain customer patronage and goodwill, a business had to satisfy its customers; to produce valuable products or services, a business had to train and motivate employees; and to attract stockholders and lenders, a business had to produce excellent financial returns. I believed that this idea was fundamentally sound, had worked elsewhere, and could in principle be applied to the IRS, which also had to be successful in more than one dimension to achieve its mission. The application of a balanced scorecard was one area where the IRS could very profitably learn from others' experience—where it could, in the jargon of business journals, import best practices.

But dozens of questions had to be answered to convert a useful concept to a new way of managing much of what one hundred thousand people did every day:

- What does *customer satisfaction* mean in the IRS? How do you measure it? How do you use it?
- What are *business results* for the IRS, now that all measures of dollars collected are banned? How do we get quality to be part of the equation?
- Why do we care if employees are satisfied? How does it relate to productivity and the business measures?

I asked Bob Johnson, a thoughtful IRS field executive, to take on the job of converting the idea of balanced measures to something real that could be implemented. Recruiting more than seventy-five managers and employees from every part of the IRS, Johnson began to work out thousands of details. Bob Tobias, president of the employees union, was an active participant in this process. Recognizing that the IRS could not operate without using numbers as part of its management process, he focused on helping Johnson come up with the right set of measures and the right ways to use the measures.

Working out a new way of measuring performance for a big, complicated organization is a hard job anywhere. In the IRS, it was like walking through a minefield in which the mines had been laid over forty years of battles. The misuse of enforcement statistics and the poor treatment of taxpayers reported in the wrenching Senate hearings triggered investigations of IRS managers. These investigations had continued throughout all of 1998.

Enforcement statistics were at the core of the distrust between management and employees. Almost all the statistics used to rate managers were not supposed to be used to rate employees, but employees readily got the message about how important it was to deliver those statistics to their managers. As one employee testified: "Now, if I am a manager and

I have a goal to obtain ten of a certain item and I have ten agents working for me, I think you know what I am going to do, I am going to tell each of my subordinates that I want them to do one of these actions. If one of them does three, then I am going to praise that person. So what is happening is that the goals are being used indirectly because it is forbidden to use them directly."[16]

Instead of an open, well-understood, and positive way of motivating people toward a common goal, the previous measurement process became a shadowy system that sowed conflict.

The practical effect of the complexities surrounding this issue was to create objections from lawyers, executives, or union representatives to any specific proposals for the new measures. Critics could easily say what was wrong with any particular proposal—it might be illegal, it might not be accurate, it might be misused, it might not be understood. To get to a practical solution, I kept falling back on the advice I got from my first boss in the Pentagon, Alain Enthoven: "It is far better to be roughly right than precisely wrong."

Mission Possible

By January 1999, our top team was ready to launch the new system of balanced measures. About six hundred IRS field managers and union officials came to Atlanta for the first training sessions, the first time in recent IRS history that they were assembled to hear the same message at the same time. All veterans, they had been through the endless cycles of tinkering and breakdowns in how numbers were used in the IRS, and they were skeptical that anything was going to change as a result of this meeting. Seated at round tables so they could work in small groups on the exercises that were part of the training, they packed the ballroom of the downtown Westin Hotel. Showing the reserved attitude of the attendees, an unusual quiet came over the room as the meeting was about to start at 7:30 A.M. sharp.

Suddenly, the lights were turned down and the ballroom was nearly dark.

Bob Wenzel and I knew we had to acknowledge to this well-informed audience that the IRS had failed many times to solve this intractable numbers problem. But we also had to get across our belief that, this time, nothing would stop us from getting it right.

A person ran up the aisle to deliver a package to Wenzel on stage as music sounded and video clips of daring deeds flashed on the screen. Our theme was "Mission Possible." I slunk up the aisle in a long trench coat, Sherlock Holmes hat, dark glasses, and black gloves, joining Wenzel to open the package and start on the mission. It was not exactly award-winning drama, but it did beat the dull introductions to most IRS conferences.

As the meeting proceeded, Nancy Killefer drew on her years of management consulting, citing examples from leading companies like IBM and Federal Express to explain how performance measures had evolved in the private sector—from a focus solely on accounting numbers to one that included the perspective of customers and employees. Bob Tobias and several respected IRS executives endorsed the changes. Slowly the substance began to come through to the managers.

We knew that these meetings were just a kickoff. Once we started getting new sets of numbers, people throughout the organization had to learn how to use them to help change the way they worked with taxpayers and with each other. For the next three years, in countless meetings, training sessions, formal and informal talks, and, most importantly, everyday interactions of frontline employees with taxpayers, the IRS struggled with making this change a day-to-day reality.

One of the perennial debates was whether the very idea of customer service and customer satisfaction made any sense in the tax business. Sometimes even taxpayers complained about being called customers. The ever-quotable Michael Graetz said that "he would rather be a werewolf than a customer of the IRS."[17]

One night I was having dinner with the heads of the tax administration agencies from several other countries, and the topic came around to the idea of using the word *customer* in our business. Sir Nick Montagu, the head of the United Kingdom's Inland Revenue and a well-read and witty Englishman in the best tradition of top British civil servants, told how he responded to the complaint that taxpayers weren't customers, because they didn't have a choice about paying taxes. He replied that it was like the answer to determinism as a philosophy of life. It didn't matter if determinism was true or false, as long as everyone behaved as though it was false. It doesn't matter whether taxpayers are really customers as long as everyone in the agency behaves as though they are. We all agreed to designate Sir Nick as the official philosopher of tax administration.

Most people in the IRS, however, were not philosophers. They confronted practical questions every day, such as how to satisfy people while telling them they had to pay money they didn't want to pay. A key mental breakthrough depended on getting people to realize they were not struggling alone with these nasty either-or questions. Every profit-making business faces the problem of satisfying both customers and company financial objectives. No business can be successful by choosing between satisfying its customers and satisfying its stockholders.

By May 1999, I had honed my arguments. I made this false dichotomy the main topic of my speech to a meeting of all IRS executives. "It might seem to many people that because we are in the tax administration business we are unique and cannot be compared to private companies that strive for customer satisfaction," I began. "This is not true, and we are not unique."

Every business, I pointed out, has to balance customer satisfaction with business results. I used pricing to make my point. "To make a profit and stay in business, every business has to charge a certain price. While most customers would like to pay a lower price, no business can afford to say to its customers: 'We want to keep you satisfied, so if you don't like our price just tell us what you would like to pay.' "

I argued that it was our job as leaders to help our employees develop the skills to meet the needs of taxpayers while also achieving the agency's business goals. I added that this challenge included knocking down myths, and I took the opportunity then and there to knock down three of the most common:

- No, customer satisfaction does not require letting taxpayers pay whatever they want to pay.
- No, customer satisfaction does not mean failing to raise legitimate issues in an exam.
- No, customer satisfaction does not mean failing to collect money that is due.[18]

I had many discussions with employees about how these changes in our mission and goals affected them. In one conversation, a manager said he found that his whole way of thinking had changed. Previously, if a taxpayer complained or pointed out a mistake by the IRS, this manager's first reaction was to insist that it wasn't a mistake, and even if it was, it didn't matter because the taxpayer owed the money. Now he realized that there were often more ways to solve the taxpayer's problem. He said that the twin goals of serving each taxpayer *and* achieving compliance really made sense to him now.

Putting the Pendulum to Rest

Over the years that this change was gradually taking hold in the IRS, we expected an onslaught of criticism from many external sources who could not believe the IRS could ever walk and chew gum at the same time. As the IRS reported declines in traditional enforcement statistics, IRS watchers of many stripes proved to us that they were indeed clinging to the tired pendulum theory.

In 2001, a *USA Today* story headlined "Please, IRS: Stop Playing Nice Guy" said: "The good news for taxpayers this year is that the IRS seems to be living up to its mandate to reinvent itself as a kinder, friendlier place that emphasizes satisfying customers rather than terrorizing taxpayers with audit threats." Showing its penchant for the mindless cliché, the paper continued: "the bad news, unfortunately, is that fear seems to be what motivates some taxpayers to be honest. Once dreaded for its aggressiveness, the IRS has gone soft."[19]

As was so often the case, even this well-intentioned but oversimplified article confused the idea of the IRS going soft with the hard reality of what was actually causing declines in enforcement statistics, namely, the time-consuming micromandates in the reform law and the declining size of the work force. In another paragraph, the very same article noted: "While the boom economy and bull market have increased the number of individual and corporate taxpayers to more than two hundred million—and dramatically upped the complexity of their returns—the IRS has simply been unable to keep up. Hampered by Third World technology, a shriveled work force and a mandate to hold taxpayers' hands, the IRS has fallen further and further behind in its efforts to stop tax cheats."[20]

Some confusion was natural in the midst of such massive change, and of course, the confusion was reinforced by the enormous and often conflicting press coverage of the IRS. A big part of my job was to keep the focus on the ultimate purpose of improving performance in all aspects of the IRS mission. Over and over I repeated this message: Our purpose was not to move an imaginary pendulum one way or the other a few degrees, as we had done for the better part of a half-century. That's relatively easy but not particularly useful or long lasting. Our purpose was to improve the *entire way* the IRS works and to get out of this pendulum prison once and for all.

Confronting the Force Behind the Bureaucracy

A big part of my effort to change attitudes inside and outside the IRS was aimed at breaking down the perception that the agency was a mindless bureaucracy. One reason people most dislike dealing with large organizations is that the organizations seem like bureaucracies in which people march according to rules, even when the rules seem patently at variance with common sense.

As an organization grows larger, its leaders must work hard to fight the tendency for rules to override common sense. As AMS grew, I experienced this dilemma many times. In one incident, some employees went to a business meeting dressed inappropriately, creating a backlash from an important client. An executive in our human resources department said we should prescribe a dress code to avoid such problems in the future. I replied that, despite this incident, we could continue to rely on the common sense of employees, as we had done successfully for years—and for matters more important than deciding what to wear. The executive countered that "we are now too big for common sense," to which I answered that if we ever got too big for people to use common sense we would be too big to be successful.

No organization is too big for common sense, but organizations of any significant size do require some rules, so that large numbers of people can make decisions within appropriate limits. In the IRS, which had substantial authority over taxpayers and their money, it was necessary to have even more extensive rules, to let taxpayers and employees know what standards would be applied in the millions of cases that the IRS handled every year. But if we wanted to change the attitudes of taxpayers and employees toward each other—and avoid being overly bureaucratic and being perceived as such—we had to make sure that these rules took into account the real world that taxpayers lived in. We had to provide our employees rules that comported with common sense.

This meant that IRS headquarters, and especially the lawyers at headquarters, had to change their attitudes, too, because they were the ones who wrote the rules. Our frontline revenue agents audited taxpayers, but it was the rules written by lawyers in Washington that told the agents what to do.

Changing the attitudes of expert groups such as lawyers is often difficult in any organization, because the experts have the apparent weight of deep technical knowledge to back up their opinions. In the IRS, changing the lawyers' working relationship with the rest of the IRS was an even more intractable problem, because the lawyers were organizationally independent. In these tough situations, the top leader of the organization must personally intervene in specific matters to show the experts unmistakably what change is expected.

I had such a matter thrust upon me before I even took office. In September 1997, Senator Bryan of Nevada told me of a tax court decision that could suddenly change the way three hundred thousand casino workers, such as cocktail waitresses, blackjack dealers, and bartenders, were fed.

Almost all casinos in Nevada required their employees to stay on the premises during working hours. In return, the casinos provided free meals in an employee cafeteria. Until lawyers representing the IRS won a tax court case against one casino, none of these meals was ever treated as taxable income to the employees. Had this ruling been upheld, it would have required the employees and employers to pay millions in back taxes and would have drastically increased the cost of continuing to provide meals to these middle-income workers.

The casinos, the unions, the politicians, the press, and anyone else who counted in Nevada were in an uproar over this decision. All were determined that the status quo should be restored. While the case was still under appeal, the Nevada congressional delegation was able to get a provision included in the IRS reform law in July 1998. This provision fixed the problem by amending the legal standard for meals to be tax free.

The lawyers in the IRS building who drafted interpretations of tax laws often worked on the same sections of the tax code for years. As a result, the lawyers often acted as though they alone knew what "their" section meant. Although they seldom if ever met field employees who implemented the rules they wrote, their legal interpretations extended to minute details. In this case, one month after the law intended to fix the casino meals problem was passed, the lawyers drafted a detailed training manual for agents in Nevada to ensure that their view of this new law would be followed to the letter.

Immediately, the casino industry got a copy of this manual, and another storm broke. The details in the manual drafted by the IRS lawyers made it impossible for most casinos to meet even the relaxed requirement of the new law. Both Nevada senators called me over to an emergency meeting in a room off the Senate floor in September 1998 to protest strenuously that the IRS was moving the goalposts. I received a follow-up letter signed by thirty members of Congress saying that the IRS was failing to implement congressional intent.

The more I learned, the less sense this dispute made. Although clothed in technical tax jargon, the issue boiled down to whether the casinos' policy of requiring the blackjack dealers, bartenders, and cocktail waitresses to stay on the premises during the shift was really necessary. The casinos said it was necessary for security and efficiency. The government tax lawyers in Washington disagreed.

"What was the cocktail waitress supposed to do," I asked, "go out to McDonald's in her costume? And how did government lawyers in Washington know what security procedures a casino in Las Vegas needed? Were we supposed to think that they spent all this money on facilities and meals just to save some taxes on the value of these meals?"

In a tone that a professor might use with a particularly dull student, one of the Treasury Department staff lawyers snapped back at me, "Everyone knows there is no serious legal issue here; the taxpayers just don't want to pay the tax."

We were at a standoff. Although the rules these lawyers wrote were published and implemented by the IRS, and the IRS commissioner was responsible for defending them to Congress and the public, none of the lawyers was under the authority of the commissioner. This paradoxical situation was a peculiar but unfortunate consequence of the political compromises needed to get the IRS reform bill through.

I saw this situation as an almost perfect example of why people thought the IRS would always be hated. Here you had an impenetrable bureaucratic machine for writing rules with no practical input either from those affected by them or those implementing them. This process deflected all accountability from the lawyers who actually wrote the rules. The whole setup made the casino case too important for me to just go along.

Although I couldn't rewrite the rules, I could stall their release. To see firsthand how the casinos operated I traveled to Las Vegas. There I saw the security procedures, the employees' eating rooms, and their special entrances and dressing rooms—all of which made the IRS tax case seem as unreal as the faux New York skyscrapers in the desert.

Then, in May 1999, I learned that the three judges who had heard the taxpayers' appeal had come to a different conclusion from that of the treasury lawyer who had vehemently insisted to me that the case was so black-and-white that it did not even present a serious legal issue. Instead, the judges unanimously overruled the tax court decision that created the problem in the first place. The appeals court ruled that the casinos had practical reasons for keeping their employees on the premises for meals: "While reasonable minds might differ regarding whether a 'stay-on-premises' policy is necessary for security and logistics, the fact remains that the casinos here operate under this policy. Given the credible and uncontradicted evidence regarding the reasons . . . underlying the 'stay-on-premises' policy, we find it inappropriate to second guess these reasons."[21] It took a court of appeals decision to impose common sense on the IRS lawyers.

Years of wasted effort and unnecessary animosity had been generated by this one case. And this was by no means the only senseless issue that the lawyers insisted on pursuing. In another case in Minnesota, the IRS lost a court decision concerning minor amounts of taxes on income received by three hundred retired farmers from a cooperative. The IRS lawyers wanted to use a technical maneuver to keep up the legal war on these retired farmers.

If we wanted to change the IRS and its relationship with the public, we had to change the relationship of the IRS with its own lawyers. By personally intervening in a few matters, I showed what I was expecting. I gained an ally in the chief counsel, Stuart Brown, who understood the change that was needed. He asked me to work with him on a new mission statement for the counsel organization. We also started bringing in field agents to work directly with lawyers drafting new rules. Later, I made a key move by persuading the counsel's office to appoint Kevin Brown, an extremely talented lawyer and leader who shared my view of how the IRS and its lawyers should work together, to supervise many of the lawyers in the field. But still, changing the way the lawyers worked with the IRS was one of the hardest of all the changes to implement.

Taxpayers Respond

We started to get positive feedback from taxpayers about the changes in the IRS faster than I expected. Much of this positive reaction was caused by the frontline employees' taking the new guidance to heart and working hard to improve their interactions with taxpayers.

In November 1998, the Chicago IRS manager, who a year earlier was booed in a meeting of neighborhood volunteers when her IRS affiliation was announced, instead got resounding applause this time.

In December, Pat Schroeder, an old friend who became president of the Association of American Publishers after retiring from Congress, brought in about twenty-five financial managers from large publishing companies for me to hear their views. Two managers volunteered that they already saw a positive difference in dealing with and getting information from the IRS.

In February 1999, I testified at the annual filing season hearing with the House Ways and Means Committee. The hearing was surprisingly positive. Congressman John Lewis of Atlanta told a story about a woman in his district who broke down in tears because she was so happy with the help the IRS gave her in getting a refund faster.

In early April, I got a cold call from a U.S. attorney in a Southern state. As soon as I heard who was calling, and not knowing what to expect, I figured this call must mean trouble. I picked up the phone and heard the voice of a courtly Southern lawyer. He literally started off the call by saying, "You've pulled off a miracle." He went on to say that he had spent thirty years as a tax lawyer before becoming a U.S. attorney and knew a lot about dealing with the IRS. In the last thirty to sixty days, he had had several occasions to deal with a variety of IRS people, some for his personal business and some for his official business. In every case, the IRS people were extremely helpful and had gone out of their way to solve his problem. He viewed this as such an extraordinary change that he wanted to call me personally. This call left me nearly speechless. I didn't get many cold calls from people making compliments.

The press coverage beginning in the April 1999 filing season also began to change dramatically, with headlines like these:

> "IRS Offering More Taxpayer Help As Filing Season Begins" (Associated Press, 5 January 1999)
>
> "Senate Panel Applauds Changes at IRS" (*New York Times,* 15 April 1999)
>
> "IRS to Consider Severe Economic Hardship in Settling Unpaid Debts" (Associated Press, 20 July 1999)
>
> "IRS Tax Filing Change Eases Burden for One Million Small Businesses" (Associated Press, 27 November 2000)

In the summer of 1999, the latest Roper survey showed that public rating of the IRS had turned sharply up, after trending down for years to its all-time low in 1998.[22]

What I found remarkable about this positive feedback from taxpayers was that it started *before* we implemented any of our plans for major changes in the way the IRS worked.

By any objective measure, the IRS still had poor customer service; slow and inaccurate data due to ancient computer systems; inadequate training; out-of-date manuals; burdensome regulations; senseless rules and court cases; and a creaky, slow-moving organization. Most of the taxpayer rights procedures mandated in the reform law had not yet been implemented. We had not yet implemented our new measurement system.

Almost the entire change was initially accomplished by IRS frontline employees' getting the message and taking their own steps to do whatever they could to do a better job for taxpayers. And many taxpayers and employees saw the difference almost immediately. This turnaround was, for me, the most impressive demonstration I had ever seen of people's natural desire to do what is expected of them in an organization. This desire is what creates the power of simply laying out a clear direction for change.

Many employees told me directly how they sensed the change. In one of my small meetings with frontline employees, I met a man who had worked his way up from the mail room to be a customer service representative answering taxpayer phone calls. He told me he had watched all the television coverage of the IRS. He said that when a taxpayer tells a story on television about how he or she was not treated right, he just tells his friends, "That's the old way. Things are changing now."

Then there was the case of Michael Gallagher, an IRS employee who designed tax forms in IRS headquarters. For fourteen straight years, Gallagher had done everything he could to get permission to print pictures of missing children on the blank pages in the IRS's tax form booklets. Statistics showed that one out of six kids whose pictures were widely publicized was found. A law on the books specifically permitted federal agencies to print these photos, and the White House had sent out memos encouraging the agencies to do so. Other agencies, including the U.S. Postal Service, had done it. The dollar cost to the IRS for the printing was zero, since the pictures were only to be put on pages that would otherwise be blank. Gallagher's proposal was turned down year after year because managers at various levels thought that using this blank space to help find missing children was incompatible with the IRS mission. But in 1999, after we focused the mission on people as well as money, everyone up the line quickly approved the proposal and the IRS started printing the pictures.

Later, I attended a ceremony in which the National Center for Missing & Exploited Children gave Gallagher an award. By then, the IRS had printed 750 million images of missing kids and several kids who were pictured had been recovered. Some of the kids came to the ceremony to thank those who had helped.

It wasn't all happy news. For every good day there were bad days. We still heard taxpayer horror stories, and many employees were still confused over where all this was leading. Objective measures of service were still far too low. Traditional enforcement statistics were declining. Would the pendulum swing back? Some old-timers with connections to Capitol Hill staffers tried to start a movement to have me fired for ruining collections.

But clearly the change was starting. Perceptions were changing. Now we had to make it real and permanent. We had to deliver on the commitments in our new mission. We had to do a better job of serving taxpayers and collecting the taxes. Most of the change still lay ahead.

CHAPTER 8

When Everybody Is Your Customer and the Tax Code Is Your Bible

Providing Quality Service

ALMOST EVERY ADULT American is a customer of the IRS. Many need help to comply with the complex tax code or to do routine business with the IRS, as I saw many times during my tenure.

One taxpayer was a self-employed landscaper in California earning $33,000 a year. He had an installment agreement with the IRS for monthly payments to pay off some back taxes. He called the IRS toll-free phone line because he had missed two payments when he had separated from his wife and had had to move out of the house. An IRS employee in a call center in Salt Lake City talked him through his tax accounts and found that he still owed a few hundred dollars that was accumulating interest from old tax years. She found out how much he could afford to pay, and worked out a new installment agreement to cover all his payments. She reminded him to be sure to file his new return on time to avoid penalties and interest.

Another taxpayer was a busy businessman who traveled constantly. He sent in his mother's simple tax return with a check for the tax due. He then received a notice saying the tax due on the return was not paid and would accumulate interest and penalties until it was paid. Repeatedly getting busy signals on the phone number printed on the notice, he finally reached an IRS employee and found out that the notice was a routine mistake. The check had been missed because it was stuck to the form.

A husband and wife had started a construction business eighteen months earlier. They had used a payroll service that was supposed to file their payroll tax returns, but it had failed to do so. Working out of the office all day, the couple could only do paperwork on nights and weekends. They called the IRS's toll-free number at night, but the problem was too complicated to solve on the phone, because several forms for several time periods covering several employees were involved. The amount they owed was increasing every month because of interest and penalties. The family came into the IRS office on a Saturday morning to go over all the paperwork needed to fix the problem, and they worked out a payment arrangement.

These stories are a mere drop in an ocean of contacts that people across America have with the IRS every day and every year in the course of trying to pay their taxes.

If people are trying to pay their taxes, should the organization that takes their money at least try to take it as painlessly as possible?

The answer, historically, has been "Not necessarily."

For years, the IRS was not sure how much effort to devote to responding to calls, visits, or other requests for help from taxpayers. Why? Because the OMB overseers, who set the ceiling on IRS funding, were only interested in how much enforcement revenue the IRS brought in from audits and overdue collections. At one point in the 1980s, the OMB actually directed the agency to shut down much of its taxpayer assistance operation because the OMB thought it didn't bring in any revenue.

The lack of service from the IRS put millions of taxpayers in a Catch-22. In one year, the IRS sent 109 million notices to taxpayers about their accounts. Most of the notices told them they owed more money than they thought they owed. The taxpayers were required to respond and usually needed help from someone at the IRS to do so, but they often could not get through to anyone.

By the mid-1990s, the telephone had become the main way to deal with the IRS on routine business, since service in local offices had been cut back and mail was slow and ineffective for many subjects. But all too often, the taxpayers just got busy signals or long waits. Even when the taxpayer did get connected, the IRS employee often could not solve the problem. Either the IRS's archaic computer systems didn't provide the right information, or the complexity of the questions exceeded the employee's ability to answer. And some topics were just too hard to deal with by phone, especially when the taxpayer had mountains of paperwork or spoke limited English.

The IRS was like a bank whose owners had directed it not to spend money on providing service to customers, except to those whose loans were long overdue. Eventually, the good, paying customers, who paid almost all the money the IRS received, started banging on the door to get information about their accounts and help in paying their taxes.

The frustration and rage of honest taxpayers trapped in this box produced complaints to Congress, press stories, and demands that something be done. "Our constituents can call up their bank or credit card company and get the status of their accounts over the phone," wrote Representatives Rob Portman and Ben Cardin in the *Washington Post* in 1997. Only 26 percent of calls to IRS taxpayer assistance lines were answered in 1996, they noted, adding that "if they are lucky enough to get through, they reach an IRS representative who too often lacks the information technology and training needed to answer questions and provide solutions efficiently."[1] The Senate hearings in September 1997 highlighted the hardship experienced by taxpayers, who had no way to untangle their problems with the IRS.

In Washington, as elsewhere, the squeaky wheel gets the grease. But what kind of grease did the White House and Congress want to apply to the shrieking IRS wheel?

Good Quality Service Is Not Produced by Decree

Since the 1980s, Congress had responded to taxpayer complaints by periodically passing tax code provisions known as taxpayer rights, such as requiring fixed notice periods before seizures. As criticism in Congress and the press built up in the fall of 1997, the White House was the first to start adding new mandates. It simply announced that the IRS would start providing telephone service twenty-four hours a day, seven days a week. Hearing of this proposal the month before I was confirmed, at first I could not believe it was advanced seriously. I even joked that "now we can give people busy signals twenty-four hours a day." Despite my strenuous argument that this 24/7 proposal would only make the already unacceptable service worse, the White House insisted on announcing it.

As the IRS reform bill went through Congress in 1997 and 1998, more and more mandates were added in an attempt to legislate improved service. One provision directed that hundreds of local phone numbers be published, despite there being no one in these locations to answer the calls. Another provision mandated that the IRS offer its phone services in Spanish—a good objective because of the increasing number of Hispanic taxpayers who spoke limited English. But now the IRS, which was having major problems answering tax questions in English, was directed to provide these complex services in another language.

Within the IRS, there were also attempts to make quick fixes. Most of these attempts backfired. To increase the number of calls answered, some IRS call-site managers imposed a limit on the time employees could spend on a call. On one of my first trips to a call center, one employee asked, "Would you rather have me help the taxpayer solve a problem now and avoid trouble later, or cut him off to take another call?"

There is no quick fix anywhere to providing first-class customer service. And providing quality service is even harder in the IRS than in most other large organizations. The agency answers more than one hundred million calls per year on the main customer service lines, answers twenty million letters, and serves over six million people who come into offices for help. And the tax law is complicated, so even a seemingly simple question, like "Why was my son not allowed as a dependent exemption?" can trigger five or ten other questions. Questions about taxpayer accounts can be even more complicated than tax law inquiries. People file and pay taxes every year for every taxpayer in their household or business, while their families, business situations, and finances change. And if the taxpayer gets the wrong answer, the problems for the IRS and the taxpayer can sometimes multiply to seemingly endless lengths.

One day I was calling a professor to check on a reference for someone I was considering hiring. After I got the reference, I listened to his complaint. He had four children and, for the first time, had to make estimated tax payments for them. He sent in four payments of $2,000 each. The IRS credited two of his children with $4,000 each and the other two with zero. The error required him to spend time on the phone until the problem was fixed. This was the simplest of accounting mistakes, but even tiny errors produce millions of frustrated taxpayers when multiplied by an astronomical number of transactions.

Trying to order the IRS to provide first-class service was like the czar of Russia issuing a ukase ordering that the next harvest must be a fine one.

Often, the biggest obstacle to solving a serious problem is getting beyond wishful thinking and accepting reality. That is why I fought so hard in my early days at the IRS, within the administration and in meetings with Congress on the IRS reform bill, against the notion that directives and quick fixes could ever address the IRS's serious service problems. I believed that the most important step was to make a deep and lasting commitment to providing quality service. The IRS would have to undertake the same long-term, painstaking process followed by other companies that have achieved quality customer service: understanding customer needs; setting out clear goals; organizing, motivating, and training employees; revamping plans and procedures; upgrading technology; measuring results; and learning from successes and failures.

By establishing a new mission and service goal, we made the commitment clear. The goal was to "provide top-quality service to each taxpayer with whom the IRS deals, one at a time." To achieve this goal, the IRS had to change the way work was done throughout the agency.

Getting Through, Getting the Right Answer

I made the improvement of phone service a high priority because it was the way most people did business with the IRS. To taxpayers, quality service meant that they could get their calls answered without too much delay, and then could get their problem solved correctly. To meet this need, the IRS would have to change the way telephone work was scheduled and managed across the country, and would need new systems to manage call traffic. Many of these changes could not be taken immediately, because they depended on reorganizing major parts of the agency and installing new technology. But once we made clear what the long-term goal was, we could make some changes incrementally to get there.

As usual in the IRS, some leaders understood the direction and took the initiative to move without waiting for final plans. In November 1998, I visited Ron Watson, who had moved from being the national customer service coordinator in Washington to take a customer service field job in Atlanta. A quiet, thoughtful man who had started his IRS career as a collection officer, Watson had moved into jobs managing customer service activities even when that was not considered a choice assignment. On his own initiative, he learned the specialized techniques that had been developed in the private sector for managing large telephone operations, but he was often stymied in implementing them within the IRS.

In Atlanta, I found that Watson and his local boss, Bob Johnson, had already begun to manage all the customer service sites in their region under a single team and to standardize operations. This was exciting news because it gave us a model for how to move the whole agency toward the long-term plan. It was also an example of how finding and supporting the "inside" change leaders is a key to making change really happen.

Only a month after my trip to Atlanta, I arranged for Watson and Johnson to come to Washington to meet with the key executives who managed telephone operations throughout the country. I limited the attendance so that we could meet in a small conference room next to my office, knowing that in the IRS, as in many organizations, people considered proximity to the boss's office a sign of how serious a meeting was. Talking to several executives before the meeting, I made it clear that its purpose was to discuss how, not whether, we would use Watson's approach as a model for the whole country. Using this model, within a year we started to manage the IRS's entire customer service telephone operation with the single goal of improving service to taxpayers, rather than as a collection of twenty-five individual sites, each doing things differently.

One of the first steps was rescheduling the work hours of employees. To provide good phone service, an operation needs to have enough employees at work when the customers call. But, because of the April 15 filing deadline and customer preferences, people don't call evenly. To meet customer demand, the IRS might need ten times as many employees on duty on a Monday afternoon in March as on a Thursday morning in August. We established a nationwide operations center in Atlanta. The center was equipped with new call-routing equipment, to do detailed advance planning and to monitor service continuously. With the support of this center, Watson and his telephone service staff rescheduled work hour by hour, day by day, for more than fifteen thousand permanent and seasonal employees and then adjusted schedules as conditions changed.

If lots of taxpayers started calling at 3 P.M., it didn't make sense to allow employees to work a 6 A.M. to 2 P.M. shift so that they could beat the rush hour traffic. Thousands of employees had to adjust the days and hours they were accustomed to working. This new way of managing was a big change for the IRS, where limited information had been available for planning, and work schedules were often based on traditional shifts. Although there was some grumbling from employees about having to change their long-established commuting and child-care patterns, most readily understood that they had to work when taxpayers were calling.

Improving scheduling helped to answer more calls, but it did nothing to help the far too many taxpayers who were getting wrong answers or were failing to get their problems solved correctly after they got through. Wrong answers would cascade into more notices, more letters, more calls, and more unhappy taxpayers.

No one felt this problem more than the employees, who were embarrassed when they could not answer the taxpayers' questions with confidence. In my small group meetings with call center employees, they invariably complained that they were being asked to answer calls on subjects for which they had not been trained. The reference manuals were huge paper books that were often out-of-date, and the employees' computers used nearly incomprehensible, 1970s-style codes.

An IRS employee in Nashville summed up the way many employees felt: "This job is frustrating enough without having to feel like an idiot because it takes so long to do things. The computer goes down half the time, sometimes in the middle of a conversation. It's difficult to access some things because of the way the command codes are."[2]

Improving quality and accuracy was critical. But how? The tax law is complicated and constantly changing, and the finances and family situations of 180 million individual and 6 million business taxpayers include every imaginable (and sometimes almost unimaginable) variation. Over the long term, modernized computer systems could take some of the burden off the employees, but new systems would not eliminate the need for employees to interact with taxpayers on the complex subject matter.

The traditional thinking was that more training would solve this problem. Indeed, we did increase training, but with limited results. Reviewing a survey in which two-thirds of the employees complained that their training was inadequate, I wrote to our senior management team. I explained that we were ensuring failure by expecting our employees and managers to be trained in subject areas far too broad and by relying on manuals and training courses that were unmanageable in scope and complexity. We had to fundamentally rethink how we organized our agents across the whole network.

No one could master all the subject matter, regardless of how much training was provided. But all employees could master some of the subject matter very well. If an employee was trained in answering questions about retirement accounts and then spent his or her days answering real taxpayer questions on retirement accounts, he or she could become extraordinarily proficient over time in this difficult subject. Training, practice, feedback, and pride in achieving quality work could raise the quality continuously. We began to retrain and certify employees in specific areas of subject matter, to distribute updates and training information to them electronically, and to use our new equipment to route to them the calls that they were qualified to answer. By taking this approach, we were giving employees the training and tools they needed to provide good service to taxpayers—one of our key principles throughout the modernization program.

Employees can't improve unless they know where they need to improve and recognize when they are performing better. As part of the program to improve service, we developed more useful ways to measure taxpayers' access to help, the quality of answers they received, and their overall satisfaction. We also measured employee satisfaction and productivity. Over time, the data helped every manager and employee know how he or she could improve.

Taxpayers calling the IRS began to see some improvement in service as early as 1998, mainly because the frontline employees were doing their best to make good on the new mission and goals. In 1998, the *Wall Street Journal* carried this item in its tax column: "IRS Commissioner Rossotti says it's easier to reach the IRS by phone but much work needs to be done. He quips: 'Two years ago it was impossible to get through on the phone to the IRS. Now it's just hard to get through. That's progress.' "[3] The objective measures of service were still poor, but independent surveys of taxpayers who called the IRS showed that taxpayers gave a rating of 3.7 out of 4 for the attitude and professionalism of our employees but only 2.1 out of 4 for the ease of getting through.[4]

As we implemented more and more of our changes in scheduling, call routing, training, and technology, service continued to improve year by year, although not evenly in all measures or in each period. Progress is rarely smooth when an organization is making major changes, and in fact, there are often temporary dips in performance. We regularly fought flaps caused by reports of poor service. In 2001, a single audit report, based on a tiny, unrepresentative sample of ten made-up questions, produced a story in a New York tabloid. Headlined "IRS Assistance Gets a Fat 'F,' " the story reported that IRS employees gave taxpayers wrong answers 47 percent of the time. It was a part of my job to deal with incidents like this, noting progress while keeping the focus of the organization on the work that still needed to be done.

Notwithstanding the occasional setbacks, the uptrend was clear. Normally critical of agency performance, the GAO reported to Congress in December 2002 that "IRS's telephone service improved compared with last year," explaining that "(1) telephone service was more accessible and accurate during the 2002 filing season than it was in 2001 and (2) IRS met most of its 2002 performance goals." The report noted that "in the area of accuracy improvement was greatest."[5]

The GAO wasn't the only party to notice the changes. In 2003, the *Wall Street Journal* wrote a story that would have been viewed as an April Fool's Day joke a few years earlier. Comparing the IRS toll-free hot line with three paid tax-advice services, the newspaper rated the IRS first, with comments such as "this service, run by the federal government, mind you, was polite, efficient and had the best answers."[6]

Meeting in Person

Although most taxpayers could do their business with the IRS over the telephone, some needed to meet in person. As in other areas, accepting this reality was an essential step to improving service.

Almost any banking or financial service a person could want is readily available by phone or over the Internet. Highly competitive companies have put huge resources and the most sophisticated technology into marketing these efficient and convenient electronically based services. Why then are there still branch banks on every main street and in every mall in America? Because some customers, in some situations, cannot meet their needs without them. One size does not fit all, for banking customers or taxpayers.

One day, I sat with a taxpayer who had come into a local IRS office with a professional accountant. He had divorced, moved twice, and fallen ill with a brain tumor. He hadn't filed a return one year and, a couple of years later, got a notice from the IRS demanding $5,000. He paid it. He got another notice, paid it too, but didn't file a return with the payment. Together with the withholding for the year, he had overpaid by about $4,000, but he still owed money for later years. Meanwhile, he was about to lose his job and he was going to be subject to failure-to-file and failure-to-pay penalties for the later years. After three hours of reviewing papers with the help of the accountant and a very skilled IRS employee, the problem was sorted out. Cases like this were impossible to resolve by phone, no matter how good the service was.

In 1997, the IRS local offices still had some walk-in sites to serve taxpayers who wanted service in person. Believing them to be expensive and obsolete, IRS management had given these sites even lower priority in funding and management than it had given other forms of service at the IRS, and OMB had done its best to have walk-in offices shut down completely. As a result, the walk-in sites were inaccessible, staffed by employees who received minimal training, managed as a sideline by the collection department, and lacked useful performance measures.

The sites were usually located in a room somewhere in a federal office building and were often intentionally hard to find. I found this out on my first visit to Baltimore for a Problem-Solving Day, an open house that the IRS had set up as an emergency response to the Senate hearings. My son, Edward, who then lived in the city, said he would come over to see what the event was like. He never did find the walk-in site, despite checking phone books and calling IRS phone numbers. Even the IRS employees answering the toll-free telephone number did not know the locations of the local IRS offices. Taxpayers learned about these sites through word of mouth.

Ironically, the cost of providing inadequate service in these sites was high, although the cost was buried in other accounts. When the lines of waiting taxpayers grew too long, local managers would pull accountants and field collectors, both of whom were paid more than the employees in the walk-in offices, off their compliance cases to staff the offices.

Providing quality service to taxpayers from local IRS offices required developing a whole new idea of what services taxpayers needed in this channel—in the same way that Starbucks or McDonald's lays out standards for the products and services its stores provide. Part of the idea was to provide a Problem-Solving Day every day, including, for the first time ever, the ability of any taxpayer to call the IRS for an appointment. To implement this plan, we needed a completely new organization, a new job category for employees, and a new set of performance measures. This entailed even more significant change than occurred for the phone services. Eventually, four hundred locations around the country became part of a professional field assistance organization.

Taxpayer Safety Valves

In the IRS, some taxpayer problems are just too tough for normal channels, even with improved service on the telephones and in local offices. And sometimes, IRS service just fails the taxpayer. The IRS had established ombudsmen in the 1970s to handle such hardship cases. As the volume of taxpayer complaints increased, the IRS and Congress periodically beefed up the size and powers of the IRS ombudsmen, who were called "taxpayer advocates."[7]

Even organizations with the best service can benefit from a safety valve for customers. For the IRS, the taxpayer advocates were a way of making sure that the IRS would meet the goal of providing quality service to every taxpayer, even if the agency didn't get it right the first time. And, by studying the problems that came to the taxpayer advocate, the IRS would have an invaluable way of pinpointing where improvements in its operations would do the most good for taxpayers.

But the IRS had made use of taxpayer advocates for twenty years, and still the tangled cases piled up, leading to Senate hearings and emergency reactions like Problem-Solving Days. The 1998 IRS reform law mandated the establishment of a national taxpayer advocate with a separate network of local advocates around the country to intervene when taxpayers needed help. Senator John Breaux of Louisiana, one of the strongest proponents of the taxpayer advocate provisions of the reform law, said he wanted to be sure that the taxpayers would always have "one person in the IRS who was on their side."[8] But would 180 million taxpayers get good service if one person was on their side? And, if a parallel organization of taxpayer advocates did everything that the rest of the IRS did, such as taking over audits from the auditors, would we need a second taxpayer advocate to handle complaints about the first taxpayer advocate?

The practical solution was to make taxpayer advocates effective safety valves for the small percentage of taxpayers who truly needed special help, while raising the quality of service throughout the whole IRS. No formula could achieve this desired but elusive result any more than directives would produce good service. We needed strong leadership and clear thinking about what it really meant to be a taxpayer advocate.

Fortunately, shortly after the reform law was passed, Val Oveson joined the IRS senior management team as national taxpayer advocate. A businessman and former state tax administrator, Oveson teamed up with a committed career executive, Henry Lamar, to set up a whole new organization inside the IRS, called the Taxpayer Advocate Service. They created new job categories, recruited and trained almost two thousand employees to fill the jobs, tackled the hardest taxpayer cases, and regularly called the attention of other senior executives to persistent problems experienced by taxpayers. Two years later, Oveson was succeeded by Nina Olson, a lawyer who had spent most of her professional life working with low-income taxpayers and others who needed help with the IRS. Oveson and Olson made sure that there was not just one person on the taxpayer's side, but rather that the whole IRS looked at everything from the taxpayer's point of view.

The IRS taxpayer advocates were indeed serving as a safety valve, as this letter, which I received shortly after leaving office in November 2002, indicated:

> *Please accept [our] gratitude for the extraordinary responsiveness and professionalism of the new office of the Taxpayer Advocate. We had been wrestling with growing penalties since 1997 that we believed erroneous; our* CPA *worked more than two years to have our claims addressed at all, but to no avail. I was assigned to a Senior Associate Advocate, who found our long-lost files and interviewed me at great length. This was followed by a letter in plain English reiterating the findings and timetable. At the end of the process, she made sure we were aware of all the determinations made and the reasons for them. I have asked myself whether I would be writing you had the decisions been adverse; I believe I would indeed. It would be impossible to work with such an advocate and come away feeling victimized or ignored.*[9]

Doing Business Electronically

We were making progress on service over the telephones and in local offices. But I also knew that unquestionably the *best* way to provide customer service, in any business, is to make it unnecessary. No one wants to spend time talking about his or her phone bill or tax return.

Allowing citizens to file returns and pay taxes electronically offered big opportunities to reduce the errors inevitably associated with processing huge volumes of paper forms. Making tax-law and taxpayer-account information accessible through the Web and automated telephones promised to save taxpayers and the IRS time. Tens of millions of calls, letters, and visits could become unnecessary. Here was a powerful way to use technology to improve efficiency and service.

The benefits were clear, but the obstacles were formidable.

The most obvious characteristic of electronic services is that they are electronic—entirely dependent on computers and networks—exactly the business in which the IRS had suffered such conspicuous failures.

One painful lesson from the failure of an early IRS project to offer tax filing over the Internet (the Cyberfile incident mentioned in chapter 1) was about security. Protecting the security and privacy of data about individual citizens in an electronic world was paramount, but very hard to do at the level demanded of the IRS, which was higher than that required for most private-sector services. Also, ancient IRS computer systems held access to all essential taxpayer data. Reliably and securely transmitting data from customer computers back and forth to these "legacy" systems was like hauling a cargo of gold on an unmapped road through a deep jungle at night with bands of thieves lurking in the darkness.

Challenging as they were, the security and technology problems were not the biggest obstacle to achieving the benefits of electronic services for taxpayers. The greatest hurdle was that millions of taxpayers and tax professionals would have to change their habits to start using these new services, and to do so voluntarily. In other words, the IRS would have to become an effective marketer—offering services that met the needs of customers and persuading people to use them. What a change! The IRS was used to writing and enforcing rules, not developing and marketing products.

Just as in many companies, the people who first set up the new electronic products in the IRS were a skunk works. At the time I arrived in 1997, the Web site was entirely managed by a few people in the forms-publication department. They fiercely protected the site's funky, un-IRS-like appearance and equally fiercely resisted proposals for improving it. But the very success of the site threatened its usefulness. It was growing so fast, and so haphazardly, that taxpayers were struggling to find what they needed.

Similarly, the electronic filing systems were first sketched out by a couple of programmers writing on a napkin. In 1998, Congress had set an 80 percent electronic filing goal, but at that time only about 15 percent of returns were filed electronically (and they were mostly simple returns filed by people who paid an extra fee to the preparer to get faster refunds).

I quickly learned why electronic filing as a product had a long way to go. Even in the 1040 family of forms for individuals, only the relatively simple returns could be filed electronically. Reporters often asked me if I filed my own return electronically. I had to admit that I didn't, because the IRS could not accept all the forms in my return. Almost all payments and all the complex individual and business returns were on paper. What's more, electronic filing was not entirely paperless. After filing the return electronically, preparers had to send in envelopes with separate signature documents and a voucher if payment was required.

I always loved people who were creative enough to push skunkworks ideas, and I wanted to build on the work that the innovative IRS people had done. But the new goal in 1998 was to make electronic services the main event, not a funky sideshow.

When I arrived on the scene, John Dalrymple, then chief operations officer, had already taken a big step by setting up an electronic tax administration office to lead the change—a situation in which a whole office became an internal change leader. In 1999, Terry Lutes, a particularly dynamic and voluble IRS executive, took charge of the program. Like most IRS executives, Lutes started his career in enforcement. After being assigned as a staff person in the new electronic tax administration office, Lutes plunged into learning the rapidly evolving world of the Internet and electronic consumer services. One of the first to understand the idea of marketing, rather than mandating, the use of IRS products, he became an acknowledged expert and leader throughout the agency and the tax software industry. With strong leadership from Lutes, the barriers to the use of the IRS's electronic services began to fall year after year.

When an organization is marketing any new product, a big part of the job is getting customers in the main part of the market to buy the product, moving beyond the early adopters. This means finding out what people really want and improving the product to meet their needs. Lutes's band of determined electronic-services (e-services) missionaries were constantly talking to preparers, software developers, taxpayer groups, and everyone in the agency who had anything to contribute. Even the IRS criminal investigators, previously viewed as naysayers on anything to do with electronic services, came up with creative ideas on how to substitute so-called shared secrets for a paper signature document.

Each year, the IRS offered improved services, including the option to pay taxes by debit or credit card or through an electronic payments system using the Internet. Taxpayers who couldn't complete their return by April 15 could even get an automatic extension with an automated phone call.

None of these improved services would be of much use unless people knew about them and changed their habits to make use of them. But marketing and advertising were as foreign to the IRS as an exotic language. Not only did no one speak the language, but no one knew anyone who spoke the language.

David Williams, our communications chief, and Frank Keith, a veteran media expert, helped our e-services missionaries learn the new language. Since the reform bill specifically encouraged electronic filing, we were able to secure a modest appropriation for paid advertising. We hired an advertising agency and design experts to improve the Web site and to produce promotional material. Television commercials featuring people explaining the concrete benefits that electronic filing provided them—faster refunds, less chance of getting one of those dreaded IRS error notices—started to appear when taxpayers were ready to file returns. A small cadre of e-file specialists in offices around the country helped tax preparers switch to e-filing. The efforts of this group of specialists were the forerunner of a more substantial sales effort that followed the overall IRS reorganization. Later, this foundation became an invaluable asset for broadening the use of marketing skills to educate the public about other tax issues.

By 2001, the electronic services were penetrating the mainstream of the market, with forty million returns filed electronically. "When it comes to taxes, more and more Americans are replacing their pencils and calculators with a mouse," an Associated Press story reported. "A record 30 percent of income tax returns are expected to be filed this year via computer." Experts cited many reasons for the increasing popularity of computers, the AP added, pointing out the advantages of "software that makes almost no errors, confirmation that a return was filed, simultaneous filing of state and federal returns and quicker refunds."[10]

Equally exciting was this headline on April 17, 2002: "IRS Surges Past Britney Spears in the Zeitgeist."

For the first time, the IRS had soared past both Britney Spears and the Japanese anime feature, *Dragonball,* into the number one spot on the "Lycos Fifty" top search terms.[11]

Our marketing program for IRS electronic services encountered external as well as internal obstacles. The most vexing was what businesses would call channel conflict. Equipment manufacturers like Hewlett-Packard often sell through dealers as well as directly to some customers. Conflicts develop over who is going to control sales to the end customers.

The IRS had its own unique version of this problem, because sophisticated software was needed both to prepare and to file returns electronically. A tax software industry had developed, with major companies like Intuit and H&R Block, as well as several smaller companies, selling software to individuals and tax professionals. After a return was prepared with their software, these companies transmitted the return to the IRS, handling any customer service calls and sometimes charging a separate fee to the customer for the transmission.

Proposals for the IRS to deal directly with taxpayers on electronically filed returns raised practical and political problems in the agency's relationship with the software industry. Just staying with the status quo, in which a few companies in the software industry essentially controlled the electronic filing gate to the IRS, might not satisfy taxpayers or allow the IRS to reach the goal of 80 percent electronic filing by 2007. But the IRS had no capacity to become a consumer software company. And the software industry was adamantly opposed to the IRS's "competing" with it, not hesitating to use its formidable lobbying clout in Congress to preempt any proposal for the IRS to deal directly with taxpayers filing electronically.

In the most remarkable turnaround of my term, Lutes worked with Chris Smith, a political adviser in the Treasury Department, and several very forward-thinking industry players, led by lawyer Steve Ryan, to negotiate an agreement that solved the seemingly intractable dilemma. In return for the IRS's agreeing not to offer its own software or Web site for electronic filing, the industry set up a consortium that had the effect of offering a free preparation and filing Web site for more than 60 percent of the taxpaying population.

By 2003, the IRS had added even more electronic services, allowing taxpayers for the first time to check on their refunds through the Internet. More than fifty million individual taxpayers, over 40 percent of the total, were filing electronically, a penetration rate far higher than the 10–15 percent penetration rate for online banking. Most of the cash coming into the treasury was coming in electronically; the IRS Web site during peak season was one of the most visited sites in the United States; and more electronic services were being rolled out for businesses and tax professionals.

Easing the Load on Small Businesses

Another way the IRS could reduce the time and money taxpayers spent doing their taxes was to get rid of rules that imposed unnecessary record keeping. Eliminating unnecessarily complex rules could also reduce the amount of scarce resources the IRS used in auditing taxpayers for minor technical violations.

IRS rules disproportionately affect small businesses, including self-employed people, who, in terms of share of time and money, incur the largest cost of complying with the tax code. Much of this cost occurs because businesses have both revenues and expenses and pay tax on the difference, an inherently more complex task than recording an annual wage from an employer's W-2 statement or interest from a bank's 1099 form. But the way IRS rules are written can also make a difference in how hard it is for small businesses to cope with taxes.

Some of the thousands of recommendations we sorted through during my first few months as commissioner held some good ideas for simplifying the paperwork for small-business taxpayers. We twice changed a rule to free millions of very small taxpayers with employees from the need to make monthly or weekly deposits.

But while we were searching for ways to ease the load on small-business taxpayers, lawyers at the Treasury Department were foiling our efforts by doggedly insisting on imposing a rule so confusing that, when taxpayers contested this rule in tax court, the judges couldn't agree among themselves on what it meant. Meanwhile, this rule was requiring the IRS to waste resources on such silly matters as how much gold dentists were using to fill teeth.

I first found out about this problem when I learned that the headquarters lawyers were ready to issue a ruling that would suddenly require thousands of small companies with oil and gas wells to start keeping books and paying taxes on an accrual basis, meaning that revenue would have to be estimated and taxes paid before the cash was received. The lawyers insisted that their rule was required by an earlier 1950s rule that said that companies who sold "merchandise" must account for "inventories." But the gas producers sold their gas straight out of their wells to the pipeline and had no inventories. Now, the lawyers suddenly decided these businesses needed to account for inventories, even if they had none.

I found that the implications of this bizarre rule were widespread. Dozens of cases arguing the intricacies of this accounting issue were actually in court. IRS lawyers were pitted against paving contractors, medical clinics, flooring installers, and even veterinarians. Ironically, this issue involved *only* small businesses. Since most businesses with over $5 million in revenue were required by law to use the accrual method, relatively little tax money was at stake.

Besides the very substantial and unnecessary cost to taxpayers and the IRS, the rules insisted on by the Treasury Department lawyers were ready-made ammunition for those who wanted to ridicule the IRS. As I wrote in one memo, it was impossible to explain why a plumber would be required to use accrual accounting if he installed enough new toilets but would not be if he fixed mostly old ones.[12]

Throughout 1999 and 2000, we had desultory and decision-less debates with the treasury lawyers while they tried to find ways to keep their fundamentally flawed rule intact. To accomplish this, they created more and more exceptions, making the rule more and more confusing. While the internal debate was going nowhere, the courts were making decisions that rejected parts of the existing rule. One ruling by the tax court required twenty-four pages to be explained, with eleven judges ruling one way and five the other; all this energy was expended over a onetime tax payment of about $50,000 by a generally compliant taxpayer.[13]

Still the debate went on. Finally, in December 2001, with much help from Mark Weinberger and Pam Olson, the new leaders of the tax policy office at the Treasury Department, we solved the problem by making accrual accounting optional for businesses with under $10 million in receipts, unless they were in certain clearly defined industries.

In the long blocks of look-alike corridors of the IRS building, there are remarkably few conference rooms suitable for even a medium-sized meeting. One room around the corner from the commissioner's office that is typically used for large meetings is long, narrow, and poor in lighting and acoustics. The old wooden table tends to separate people rather than draw them together. Even the dour atmosphere of this room could not contain the surprise and amazement of the small-business-community representatives when they heard the news about the new rule. They broke into applause after they read the press release—the first time this ever happened in the hundreds of meetings I attended in that room.

The torturous, three-year debate was over, and the IRS and small businesses could begin using their resources more efficiently than arguing over esoteric accounting details.

From this and other experiences, we drew the lesson that a strong, permanent group had to be created in our reorganized IRS. The job of this group every day would be to find ways of reducing the burden from IRS rules and regulations, especially on small businesses.

By December 2001, our broad program to improve service to taxpayers was showing results as seen by the ultimate arbiter: the taxpayers. Ratings of the IRS in public surveys showed a marked upturn from the lows of 1997 and 1998. This provided me a rare opportunity to send a memo to the treasury secretary, reporting good news and a bit of humor about the IRS.

Memorandum for Secretary O'Neill
December 18, 2001
From: *Charles O. Rossotti, Commissioner of Internal Revenue*
Subject: *Customer Satisfaction with the IRS*

In the last few months we have gotten results from two independent surveys that measure the attitude of the public towards private and public

FIGURE 8-1

IRS Approval Rating

The public's rating of the IRS declined during the 1980s and mid-1990s, reaching an all-time low, for any institution, in 1998. By 2003, it had rebounded substantially.

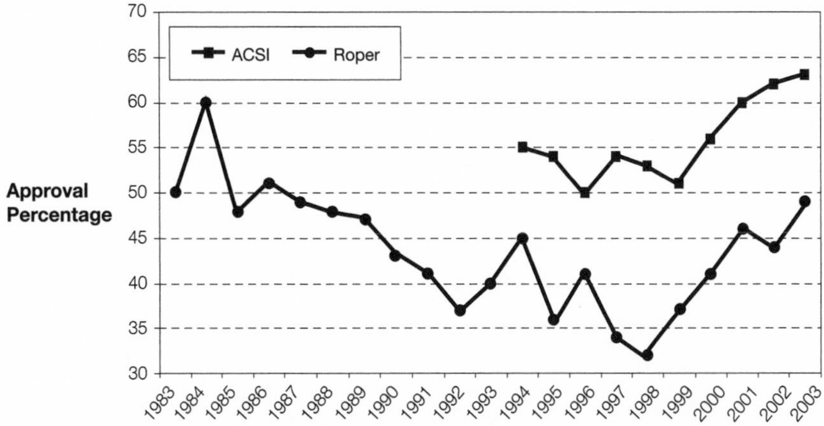

ACSI (American Customer Satisfaction Index) scores are based on a survey of five hundred individual tax filers. Roper favorability results are based on a survey of two thousand individuals.

institutions. One is the Roper survey, which has been measuring the "favorability" rating of the IRS and other government agencies since the early 1980s.

The other one, which came in this week, is the American Customer Satisfaction Index (ACSI), prepared by the University of Michigan. It is a well tested survey that is built around a model that measures "customer satisfaction" with a wide range of products and services in the public and private sectors.

Both surveys show the same thing about the IRS. Until a few years ago, the public rated the IRS very low, usually the lowest of any institution they measured. In the last three years, both surveys show strong uptrends.

The release of the ACSI survey produced some amusing press reports, including a front-page story in USA Today *reporting that customer satisfaction with the IRS was now higher than with McDonald's. This does*

> *not mean that people like paying taxes more than eating hamburgers. It just means that we are doing a better job of meeting their expectations when they deal with us.*

The IRS was improving its service to taxpayers, not by decree, but by a deep commitment to this part of its mission.

CHAPTER 9

When Are You Going to Fire the Management and Punish the Wrongdoers?

Reconciling the Past While Focusing on the Future

IN 1999, AT THE PEAK of the frenzy about making the government's computers continue to work after the century date change, I was testifying about the money the IRS would need for this Year 2000 work. One congressman asked me angrily who was responsible for programming these computers so badly that we had to spend the taxpayers' money to fix them. All you have to do is look at the calendar and you know January 1, 2000, is coming, he said, so, obviously, somebody made a big mistake. When are we going to find out who is at fault and fire them?

I was able to answer the Year 2000 question pretty easily, since the whole world had the same problem. But dealing with this line of thinking—looking back, seeking to fix blame, giving instant credence and publicity to allegations, judging the effectiveness of management by how many people have been fired—became a bigger part of my job at the IRS than I had ever imagined. I would be heavily occupied resolving allegations of wrongdoing from the past, even while I was trying to focus the IRS on how it could improve for the future.

A few months after the September 1997 Senate hearings, I received a call from a congressman who had long been one of the IRS's strongest supporters. He was hopping mad because no employees had yet been punished for mishandling the taxpayer cases reported in the hearings. He made it clear that they should be identified and fired immediately. He considered it my job to make this happen, and he was furious that I had not yet done so.

A few months after this call, in April 1998, the Senate Finance Committee held another set of hearings featuring more sensational charges about the IRS. I showed up on a Friday morning. Klieg lights glared down on the witness table in the committee room. I felt as if I were surrounded by guillotine-happy mobs in the French revolution. They wanted heads to roll, and I was the designated executioner.

After I laid out a long list of changes already under way at the IRS, one senator responded, "My question, though, is, has anyone lost their job as a result of both the hearings from last September and your initial review?"

Another senator commented that firing people could be a great morale builder for those still working at the agency. "In terms of morale of the IRS, I think firing about fifty of these people who are clearly abusing the system would be a good thing," he began. "Fifty people who were clearly bad actors and who had brought disgrace on a profession that I cared enough to dedicate my life to. I would feel good about it."

Another senator asked, "How many of the top executives are still in place?" He then continued beyond the normal boundaries in such hearings by naming one executive and repeating a list of unsubstantiated charges made against him three days before by a single witness.[1]

Members of congress get attention in newspapers and television by uncovering mistakes and insisting that the wrongdoers be punished. A large apparatus of inspectors general in each agency employs thousands of people to investigate and assign fault. Reporters covering these stories get front-page placement.

This combination of politicians, reporters, and inspectors general can generate tremendous pressure throughout an agency, and in April 1998, the pressure on the IRS was at its highest. After a solid week of sensational public accusations and demands for firings at televised Senate hearings, IRS employees at all levels felt embattled and confused. Many were embarrassed to admit where they worked.

Then, on May 1, I learned that Present Clinton was to devote his Saturday, May 2, radio address to the subject of abuses at the IRS. Despite frantic efforts and help from the Treasury Department to tone down the rhetoric, the president's speech lent his credibility to the charges. "Like

FIGURE 9-1

I appeared on Face the Nation *the day after President Clinton said in his radio speech that he was "outraged" at "citizens harassed and humiliated" by the IRS. Gloria Borger wanted to know when I was going to "clean house."*

most Americans, I was outraged by the testimony of last week's Congressional hearings on the IRS," Clinton said. He identified with "our citizens harassed and humiliated by what seemed to be an unaccountable, downright tone-deaf agency."[2] I felt as though my commander in chief had just stepped onto the battlefield to shoot my wounded troops.

The next day, I appeared on the Sunday morning television show *Face the Nation*. Waiting for the show to begin, one of the correspondents mentioned a comment she heard from a Republican on Capitol Hill: "I knew the IRS was a good issue when the president tried to steal it."

Of course one of the main lines of questioning to me on television that morning was "When are you going to clean house?"

Playing Solomon

For months I had been struggling with how to deal with this onslaught of allegations and the demands for punishing or firing those responsible. Demanding that heads roll in the IRS had been a surefire attention getter. But who should be punished, when the problems developed over many years, under many leaders and policy makers? And how much effort should we spend deciding whom to blame, when we faced urgent tasks ahead to fix the problems that caused the trouble?

I had no doubt about the right principles. Punishing people who commit serious violations of company or legal standards is vital to any organization. Failure to do so sets a terrible example and implicitly condones bad behavior. If management at any level is complicit in the offenses, or is seriously negligent, the managers responsible must be punished as well. And if the failure rises to the level of a potential crime, the facts should be turned over to public prosecutors.

I also believed that these principles had to be applied stringently at the IRS because of the vast public trust assigned to the agency. In fact, the modern IRS was reconstituted in 1952 to stamp out bribery and corruption. By abolishing political appointments, establishing independent investigators, and creating a powerful internal culture against political influence on cases of misappropriation of taxpayer funds, the reconstitution of the IRS had succeeded remarkably in creating one of the world's most honest tax administration agencies.

I met monthly with the treasury inspector general for tax administration and reviewed all significant cases of improper or dishonest action by IRS employees. The inspector general was David C. Williams, a committed, street-smart investigator with twenty-five years of experience watching over three major federal agencies. He periodically reported to me a few cases of dishonest behavior such as embezzlement, bribery, or collusion, all of which were publicly documented in his annual report. The numbers seemed proportionately fewer than when I had served on the audit committee of a well-run, medium-sized bank. There was no sympathy at any level in the IRS for such offenders.

Yet now we had new kinds of accusations, not of traditional bribery or corruption, but of mismanagement of employees and poor treatment of taxpayers. The complaints that surfaced in the Senate hearings created a snowball effect. Internal investigations and press stories multiplied in the aftermath of the first hearings, with more and more complaints surfacing. In this atmosphere, current and former employees saw an opportunity to get attention for long-held grievances and local feuds in IRS offices around the country. In one of my town hall meetings with several hundred employees in Houston, some employees used the open meeting to hurl accusations of discrimination, mistreatment, and retaliation against managers and co-workers.

The questions for me were "Who, really, are the bad people in the IRS?" and "What, exactly, are they guilty of?" Was this really a personnel problem that could be fixed by firing people, or was it the result of bad policies and neglect of festering problems over a long time?

Most complaints were about abuse of taxpayers and the mishandling of specific taxpayer cases. Members of Congress figured that it would be simple to find the person responsible for each of those cases and punish him or her. But it was anything but simple. By the time of the April 1998 Senate hearing, I was able to explain some of what I had found about the bad cases reported in the September 1997 hearing. Taking one example, I explained that the case, which went on for seventeen years, involved nine different organizational units in which major transactions went wrong. "And that is organizational units," I continued. "We really don't know how many employees it was. Many of these [mistakes] involved error-prone systems that contributed to the cause of the problem."[3]

Clearly, a problem of this kind was deeper and more systemic than the failings of one or two individuals.

If pinning blame on the individual employees who mishandled the cases was not practical, what about the managers who set the policies? One of the themes underlying many charges was that, by imposing quotas for enforcement statistics, IRS managers were driving employees to abuse taxpayers. On Christmas Eve 1997, I got the first internal audit report about the misuse of statistics. Newspapers in hot spots around the country translated the dry language of the report into headlines like this one in the *Houston Chronicle:* "IRS Offices Used Quotas, Audit Shows; Taxpayers' Rights, Law Took Back Seat to Money." The story reported that "Internal Revenue Service offices across the country have been improperly using statistical data to prod employees to collect more tax dollars. The [audit] found the agency pressured employees to achieve arbitrary tax collection goals by ranking the various IRS districts based on factors such as dollars collected per full-time employee."[4]

This first installment of fourteen thousand pages of audit and investigation reports indeed showed that the IRS was using enforcement statistics as its principal measure of success—a conclusion that should have surprised no one, since the performance statistics were widely distributed internally and externally. The very same enforcement statistics were prominently featured in the public presentation of the president's budget to Congress. They were submitted as the IRS's way of complying with the law requiring agencies to have quantitative performance measures. (Treasury Deputy Secretary Larry Summers got an angry reaction during the first Senate hearings, when he wrote a letter saying that all the enforcement numbers now found so objectionable had recently and openly been sent to Congress.)

There was no doubt that the IRS management had established far too narrow and unbalanced a focus on enforcement statistics. In general, customer service was poor and legitimate taxpayer complaints were ignored. Technology and business practices were horribly out-of-date. But who should be fired or punished for this unsatisfactory situation, which had developed over many years? During the previous ten years, there had been five IRS commissioners and two acting commissioners, four treasury secretaries, and three presidents, from two political parties.

Chairs from both parties had held dozens of congressional hearings about the IRS.

Standing for Objectivity and Fairness

The major thrust of the reform bill and the broad plan I had laid out for the new IRS was to solve its long-standing problems. I realized that a big test of my own leadership would be to get IRS employees, politicians, and the press to stop looking backward and to focus on making this plan work. Yet I had to resolve the allegations made by taxpayers and employees.

This dilemma of encouraging stakeholders to look to the future while the organization simultaneously tried to assign blame for past failings was one of the most intractable problems that I faced at the IRS. It is one that any leader must face when turning around an organization that has recently had serious, publicly reported, failures. It is truly a dilemma, because good and valid principles conflict. Insisting on accountability and total integrity is essential for the health of the organization and the confidence of the public. But maintaining a fair and factually based process for making decisions about people is essential to motivate them to achieve difficult goals.

I decided, first, not to be defensive but simply to listen to the accusations. This approach could be tricky. For example, in the April 1998 hearings focusing on sensational allegations of IRS abuses, one of the treasury political experts advised me to refuse to testify at this hearing if I had to follow the witnesses making the charges. She argued that I would seem ineffective and defensive, since I had none of the facts or privacy releases necessary for me to comment on individuals or cases. But I believed that refusing to testify would destroy my relationship with the committee and would make the public see me as unwilling to confront the problem. I worked out an understanding with Senator Roth, the committee chair, that I would agree to testify on the last day, after the other witnesses, but that he would make it clear that I was not expected to respond to specific allegations on the spot.

Next, I decided that I would not accept any allegation at face value, but I would commit firmly to gather the facts on every allegation and take action accordingly. In many forums, I made the same basic point I used to sum up at the Senate Finance Committee hearing: "Even though I am not commenting on the individual cases, from my point of view, any kind of mistreatment, of one taxpayer or one employee, is one too many. And I promise you that when we get the results of those investigations, we will act accordingly and take disciplinary actions where the allegations are substantiated."[5]

Having made that commitment, I had to make the process of arriving at these decisions bulletproof. The absolute worst outcome would be to investigate, to make decisions, and then to have them be so suspect that the whole process would start over again. The best chance I had to complete the process finally and fairly was to recruit people with unquestioned professional track records, and no connection to the IRS, to look at each complex situation thoroughly and to provide me written recommendations.

To advise on the marquee allegations of taxpayer abuse and imposition of improper statistical quotas, I recruited a panel of three senior executives from three federal agencies. Doug Browning, then the deputy director of the Customs Service, headed the panel. A career government executive with experience in an agency that dealt with the public, he was known as a straight shooter who could be counted on to do this distasteful assignment diligently. (Later John Layton, a former inspector general in several agencies, took on the big job of reviewing allegations against every field manager and employee.) Judge William Webster, former CIA and FBI director, and Michael Shaheen, the legendary former head of the Justice Department's Office of Professional Responsibility, assembled a major task force of experienced legal and law enforcement experts to turn over every rock and review every aspect of the IRS's criminal investigation division. Webster and Shaheen brought deep expertise in law enforcement and impeccable reputations for integrity to this sensitive assignment.

Why would such prominent people be willing to step into such a minefield? I had one recruiting pitch, which Killefer and Rubin at the Treasury Department supported. We said we were looking for hard facts, and we would take action based on their recommendations. Over and over again, accomplished people who were already busy with other jobs showed that they would help, if they thought we were serious about using their work to improve the IRS and to regain the confidence of the public.

Debating the Past Would Not Help Move the IRS Forward

It was not only politicians who tended to look back in anger.

The week after the incendiary April 1998 Senate hearing, I was meeting with a group of managers in Atlanta to talk about our new goals and modernization plans. But people don't want to talk about the future when they are seething about the past. They were angry that I had "failed to defend" the IRS by not taking on publicly the allegations that they believed were false or unrepresentative. I received this complaint over and over again in town hall meetings and e-mails.

I understood the feelings of IRS employees, but had to explain that arguing about allegations from the past would be a losing approach. Even if I could get the facts and the privacy releases needed to talk about an allegation, how effective would it be to argue publicly with someone with a grievance? It would be like telling a man who complained he was injured in a train wreck, "No, you weren't really injured, and even if you were, let's remember that we run a big railroad and deliver a lot of important freight."

We could only regain the confidence of the public by committing to make things better in the future and delivering on our commitments. We couldn't win a debate about the past.

The investigations and reviews dragged on for another full year, creating anxiety and sapping morale. Investigators interviewed thousands of employees across the country, spreading fear about what might happen. Month after month, meeting after meeting, I explained what we were doing to address the past problems fairly, so that we could focus on the future.

I told an executive meeting after one set of reports was concluded, "During the last year, we've had a heavy overhang in this organization in the form of audits and investigations. From the beginning I believed that we had to find a way to address these matters seriously, without sweeping anything under the rug, while being fair to people and without overreacting. Frankly, this has taken longer and been far more difficult to do than I could have ever imagined."[6] Finally we were nearing the end of this process.

Some members of Congress continued to beat the drum of punishment, because they and their constituents were not convinced the IRS would ever really change. They wanted proof, and one of their preferred metrics of success was, as one senator put it, "progress" in firing people. But gradually, most members of Congress and other stakeholders began to understand that major changes were under way. We began to regain their confidence by committing to make the IRS better in the future and delivering on our commitments. Taxpayers began to notice improvements in dealing with the agency. As it became evident that the IRS really was changing, the obsession with looking back and punishing the guilty was indeed easing.

The Ten Deadly Sins

Even after we had calmed the furor of the abuse allegations and assured employees of the fairness of our investigations, the clean-house climate complicated our efforts to move ahead with positive changes within the agency. Employees had particular difficulties with the provision of the 1998 IRS reform law known in-house as the "ten deadly sins." The provision required that IRS employees be fired if they committed any one of ten broadly defined offenses, a legacy of Congress's fear that only legal micromandates could change anything in the IRS.

In January 1999, when we rolled out the first training on this provision to our 100,000-plus IRS employees, they reacted with intense confusion and fear. It didn't comfort people to tell them that they were safe if they followed all the rules and procedures in eighty-three thousand pages of manuals. (Our clumsy examples, designed to make sure employees understood the importance of the provisions, exacerbated their feeling of betrayal.)

We soon corrected the examples in the training program and tried to calm employees by explaining over and over again that the provision only covered intentional violations. But even after the employees realized that they were not going to be fired for a foot fault, another anxiety became a real drag on everyday work: the fear of waiting in fear during months of investigation should anyone merely lodge an accusation.

One employee captured this problem in an e-mail to me:

> *I have been the subject of two Section 1203 [ten deadly sins] investigations in the past. Both of the investigations stemmed from allegations of harassment because I was successfully collecting taxes owed by the taxpayers. The taxpayers in these cases were not used to paying any part of their tax debts. For several years, they had been contacted by collection employees who took financial statements and later reported the accounts uncollectible. Both of these taxpayers were upper-income, self-employed individuals, one a psychiatrist, the other a CPA.*
>
> *I had the approval of District Counsel and my manager to take the collection actions. It took several months for me to be cleared of wrongdoing. In fact, it took longer for the investigation against me than it took for me to work the cases at issue. . . .*
>
> *For many employees, the fear of an investigation is nearly as important as the outcome. While my investigations were ongoing, I had frequent opportunities to reflect on my seventeen-year career with the IRS because I wasn't sleeping very well. It is simply wrong that no one has the authority to say, "the employee obtained the approval of District Counsel and his manager, close the investigation."*[7]

The employee concluded his message by pointing out that he could have avoided all this trouble simply by doing his job less diligently: "If I had simply followed past patterns and reported the cases as not collectable, I wouldn't have had to [lie] awake second guessing every case decision I made for months while the investigations were ongoing."[8]

For the rest of my term, I tried unsuccessfully to get Congress to modify this damaging, ill-considered micromandate, not by eliminating the list of the ten deadly sins but by giving more authority to the IRS to administer the penalties. Meanwhile, we did everything we could to get people thinking about executing the mission rather than looking over their shoulders.

Public Allegations, Secret Vindication

Imagine a television drama in which people report crimes in a town and numerous detectives spend years secretly investigating the crimes. At the end of the show, the mayor declares, with no further details, that the crimes have been solved and the guilty parties, if there are any, have been duly punished. No one following such a drama would be satisfied with this vague declaration of how it ended. Yet this is very nearly how the process of resolving allegations against the IRS works. Unless a case goes to court, strict privacy laws prevent the IRS from releasing the results of investigations or decisions on individual taxpayers or employees. Not even members of Congress, except the chair of one committee in each house, are allowed access to this information.

This unusual dilemma—of completing extensive investigations and then being unable to release the conclusions—made it all the more difficult to rebuild the credibility of the IRS. These circumstances showed the high price that an organization pays for lack of open communication with its stakeholders, even when there are good reasons for secrecy.

Over and over again, I received reports of exhaustive investigations and recommendations for resolving cases in which serious allegations had been made and reported publicly. In many cases, the result was simply that the allegation was false and no action was required. There was nothing I could do with such a report except feel happy and put it in a safe.

One allegation was so notorious that a dozen members of Congress demanded an investigation. Nearly a year later, the inspector general hand-delivered a numbered copy of a report to me. Over a hundred pages, it meticulously traced every detail of this case. Its conclusion: The case was handled entirely properly. The members of Congress who demanded this investigation could receive no information except that the case had been properly investigated and addressed. Naturally, they remained suspicious.

We tried to keep the public informed on the resolution of these cases as well as we could by releasing reports and statistics, but they were necessarily stripped of details. These releases included the following reports:

- A report by the Congressional Joint Committee on Taxation. Based on two years of investigations, the report found no grounds for allegations that the IRS had improperly audited certain tax-exempt organizations for political reasons.
- A GAO report covering some of the most serious allegations in the Senate hearings. It merely criticized the IRS for lack of good record-keeping, but said nothing about the findings on the allegations, which were provided only in another secret report.
- Judge Webster's four-hundred-page report of findings and recommendations on the IRS criminal investigation division. The report found no evidence of systematic abuses by IRS criminal investigators.
- A report of a year-long Justice Department investigation of one case of alleged retaliation. The investigation's conclusion on the merits of the charges could not be released.
- A summary of the findings about disciplinary actions taken in response to the panels that reviewed the charges of abuse of taxpayers and misuse of statistics by managers.

After all these investigations and reviews, the only significant finding of wrongdoing was that the top management of the agency, in its zeal for meeting the demands of its overseers for increased enforcement revenue, sometime bent the rules against the use of enforcement statistics to set goals and evaluate people. Under pressure to reach statistical goals, a few field managers and employees conducted seizures of property without following proper procedure. In response to these findings, nine executives (the highest rank in the civil service) received letters of reprimand, and one was suspended for thirty days. In addition, twenty-eight managers and ten frontline collection employees received reprimands. Although no one was terminated, several people chose to resign.

All the myriad other allegations, such as corrupt or improper audits, investigative vendettas against taxpayers, and retaliation against congressional witnesses, were found to be unsubstantiated.

What we learned is what we already knew.

The IRS's customer service task force, formed in response to the 1996–1997 restructuring commission, identified the source of many IRS problems in June 1997: "IRS performance measures are production driven, overvalue enforcement, focus on isolated steps, not outcomes, and may inadvertently encourage unfair treatment of taxpayers. However, getting rid of the wrong measures is only part of the solution; the other part is to put the right measures in place."[9]

Clearing Debris from the Path Forward

Whenever things go seriously wrong in a huge and complex organization, those taking over the leadership of the organization face the intractable problem of determining who was responsible for the failures of the past while mobilizing people to change for the future.

For the first two years of my term, I devoted a great deal of attention to resolving allegations related to past failures. We were listening to complaints, vigorously investigating allegations of wrongdoings, regularly publishing data about conclusions of investigations, and working on reducing the time to clear people of unsubstantiated allegations. At the same time, we were changing the IRS so it could do its job the way it should be done.

During this two-year period, the IRS and other agencies of government devoted immense resources and organizational energy to looking back and trying to affix blame for a wide range of allegations, some valid and most not valid. Some would argue that this process had some offsetting gain in assisting the positive changes that were under way. Maybe.

What was certain was that the IRS had sunk so far in public esteem that nothing short of a thorough investigation of all allegations would have served to end the debilitating cycle. But equally certain is that people cannot be motivated to achieve difficult goals by fear.

Fear and punishment are useful in deterring people from doing bad things. They are not useful in motivating people to accomplish good things. If they were, Iraq under the Saddam Hussein family, which brutally tortured soccer players when they lost a game, would have had the greatest soccer team in history.

The IRS had to do a better job of serving taxpayers, treating them right, and collecting the taxes that were due. This is a worthy, but very difficult, job to do well. Micromandates and fear of punishment would not solve the problem. What was needed was the right people, in the right jobs, motivated to achieve the right goals.

This is what the IRS reorganization was all about.

CHAPTER 10

Replacing the Furnace in the Basement and Calling It a Christmas Present

Reorganizing the IRS

IN 1979, WHEN MY SON and daughter were eight and nine years old, we bought a farm on Maryland's Eastern Shore of the Chesapeake Bay. We soon found that weekend farms are never-ending repair projects. In early December of the next year, the old furnace in the house broke and the verdict was clear—we had to buy a new furnace. No problem, I said to the kids. The new furnace will be our family Christmas present this year.

Nice try, but no sale!!

The riskiest decision I ever made at the IRS was to insist on a top-to-bottom reorganization as an early step in my overall modernization program. Organizational structure and technology are two of the most fundamental elements of a large organization, and they are the most expensive and riskiest to change.

I chose to work on organizational structure first. It was like the new furnace in the basement. It had to be done, but nobody would believe it was a Christmas present.

I knew that proposing a reorganization in early 1998, after the litany of criticism and charges hurled at the IRS, would draw derisive comments such as "he's just moving the boxes around" or "he's rearranging the deck chairs on the *Titanic*." People typically do object to such reorganization proposals. The changes require much time and money, they have no immediate benefit, and they require making dozens of controversial decisions that can set off nasty disputes. The short-term risk is high, because the disruption can cause mistakes along the way. The benefits, if they ever occur, are long-term and hard to measure.

With all the pressures on the IRS to show immediate results for taxpayers, why would we undertake a huge reorganization right away? Because there was no way to run the IRS as effectively as a modern business without organizing it like a modern business.

Back to the 1950s

The IRS in 1997 *was* already organized like a business, but one that was operating in the 1950s. Set up in 1952, the IRS organization replicated the pattern of large corporations of the time—companies like AT&T and IBM. In 1952, a long-distance phone call was an expensive event; there were no jetliners, commercial computers, fax machines, or e-mail; and most business activity was highly localized. The only practical way to manage a nationwide organization was to divide it up into small geographical units supervised by layers of management.

To wake up my audience at one large meeting, I read this quote from a report on why the IRS needed to reorganize:

> *The reorganization of the Internal Revenue Service is the culmination of a long series of actions taken to meet the responsibilities which have resulted from changes in the Federal tax system during the past decade;*
>
> *The heavy volume of recent tax legislation has strained severely the administrative forces of the Service;*
>
> *The tremendous expansion has already revealed many organizational and procedural weaknesses; and*
>
> *One of the outstanding management [consulting] firms in the country was engaged . . . to make a comprehensive analysis of the organization.*[1]

FIGURE 10-1

IRS Organization, 1998 (Simplified)

I showed the chart of the IRS organization at the Senate hearing in January 1998. The audience audibly gasped at its complexity. Forty-three districts and service centers each tried to do everything for every kind of taxpayer, while the regions and a big national office tried to coordinate.

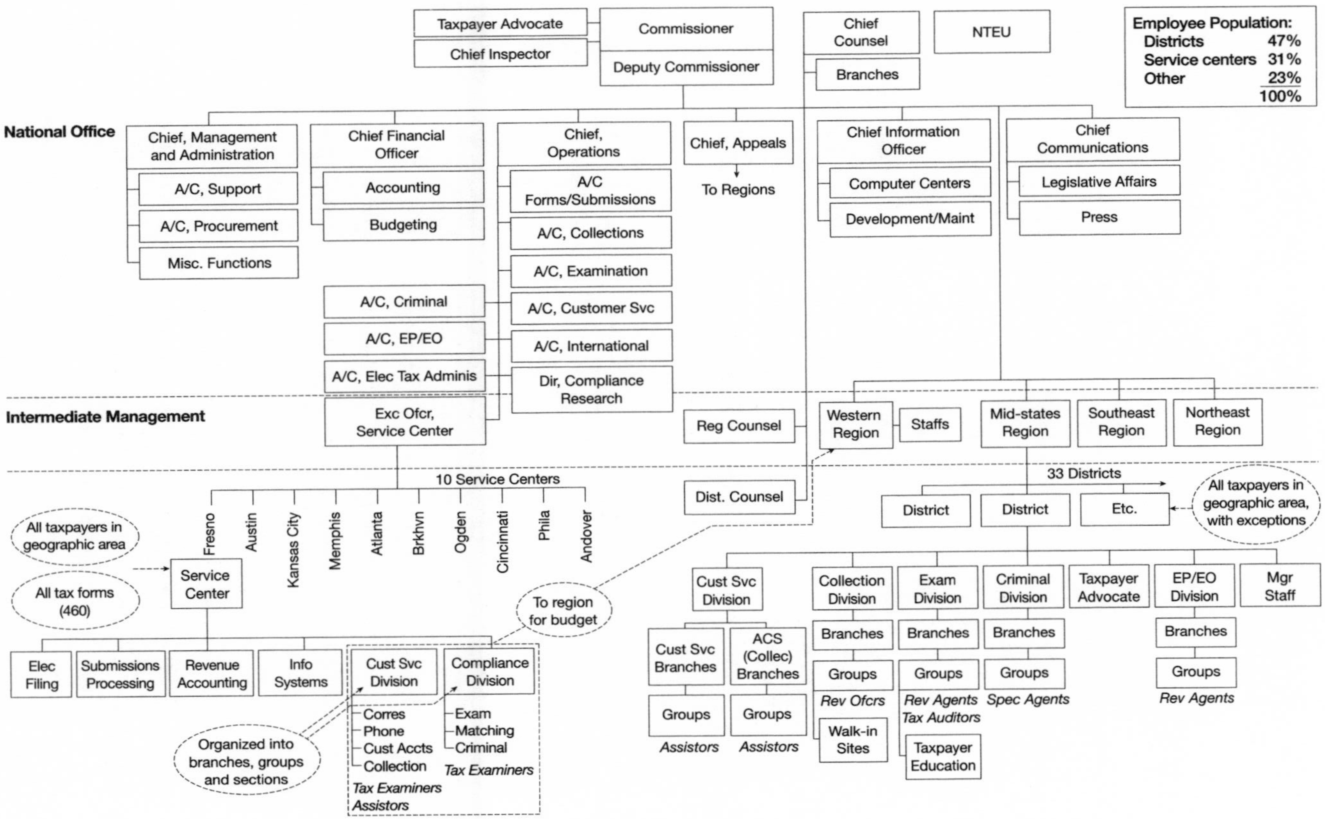

This quote was from the IRS's annual report—in 1952!

In the intervening forty-five years, most successful businesses had drastically changed their organizational models to meet the increasingly diverse needs of their customers, to streamline management, and to take advantage of both new technology and evolving management techniques. These companies reorganized into more decentralized business units with authority to meet the needs of specific groups of customers, cut out layers of middle management, and used technology to link and control the business.

But the IRS's organizational pattern had remained unchanged. Semi-autonomous local offices each attempted to provide everything for everybody, while a complex matrix of regional commissioners and assistant commissioners tried to coordinate and set policy. On top of this fragmented structure, hundreds of computer systems were layered in, one piece at a time, without any overall design. The organization was so complex and fragmented that when I showed a chart of it during my Senate Finance Committee testimony in January 1998, the audience emitted a noticeable gasp.

An Anchor on Progress

In my early visits to Capitol Hill, I met with then Senator John Glenn of Ohio, the former Marine test pilot and astronaut, who was accustomed to getting things done. He warned me that the four or five previous commissioners all had developed excellent plans to improve service and efficiency. But their plans were never implemented. There was something about the IRS, he said, that prevented good plans from ever coming to fruition.

Senator Glenn's assessment was correct, and a key reason was the IRS organizational structure, which both created problems and made it hard to solve them.

Service was inconsistent, since each local office did things differently. Implementing changes to anything, especially technology, took years and sometimes decades, because each local office had to decide how the changes might or might not apply to its way of doing things. It was hard to affix responsibility for anything, since many different managers often had part of the responsibility. If more than one organizational unit was involved in a taxpayer case, which they often were, delays and errors in resolving the case often resulted.

In one of my first visits to the IRS headquarters, I met Ron Watson, the IRS executive who was later so instrumental in improving IRS telephone service. He then had the title Assistant Commissioner for Customer Service. Talk about a hot seat! Everybody in Washington that summer was giving the IRS directives about customer service. Most of these flowed down to Watson, who had the near futile task of trying to make changes that would improve service.

Watson's biggest obstacle was the organizational structure he had to work through to get anything done. Notwithstanding his title, Watson was really only in charge of a staff at headquarters that made plans for phone service. All operations were carried out through twenty-five field sites that each reported up through separate layers of management. Each site had its own way of managing and even established its own hours of operation. Watson had no database to plan call workloads, since all the data was accumulated differently and kept locally at each site.

Watson was like a maestro who was trying to make beautiful music for the audience, but instead of conducting the orchestra, he had to send suggestions by letter to ten separate conductors, each of whom was conducting his own orchestra on a different part of the stage. No wonder the audience didn't like what it heard!

It wasn't only phone service that the organizational structure impeded. In one of my early trips, Bob Johnson, the executive in charge of the Southeast Region (comprising a quarter of the country), explained how he had worked around his own organization of geographically defined districts to deal with a situation in which no one in a particular district was qualified to audit a huge, multinational oil company. The need to spend a lot of time working around the organization was not going to make the IRS effective in overseeing huge, well-organized corporate taxpayers. Ironically, the corporate taxpayers didn't like the way things worked, either. Their biggest complaint was that IRS agents wasted much time on unimportant matters because they were assigned based on where they were, not what they knew. Hence, the agents often didn't understand the taxpayer's industry.

If the organization got in the way of dealing effectively with big corporations, it was no better with small businesses. On a collection call I attended with a veteran revenue officer, the owner of an auto body shop greeted the IRS officer like a longtime business acquaintance—which she was. Two years before my visit, the revenue officer had worked with the taxpayer over the course of a year so that he could file and pay all his returns. Once she had gotten the last check, which brought the taxpayer current, the case moved to another organizational unit—an IRS service center that had responsibility for collecting from the same taxpayer unless he became long overdue again. Now the case had come back to the revenue officer, because the check she had gotten two years earlier had bounced and the taxpayer had fallen seriously behind again. In any normal business, a delinquent customer who bounces a check would be back talking to the collection person responsible for the account in a matter of hours, not years. The revenue officer, of course, realized how absurd this was but could do nothing about it.

Several of the most gripping IRS horror stories in the press involved women whose husbands left them with tax debts stemming from returns that they had filed jointly. In response, Congress added complex tax code sections that in essence required the IRS to look back into a couple's broken marriage, decide who knew what about each line item on a four-year-old tax return, and then determine which spouse was responsible for the unpaid tax. If that were the only thing the IRS had to do, it would have been a tricky job.

Following the traditional IRS pattern, the flood of more than sixty thousand new innocent-spouse cases was at first simply distributed to dozens of IRS field offices and handed out to agents to work along with their normal audits. This process maximized the pain for everyone: The taxpayers received slow and inconsistent decisions, the agents were confused about how to handle these unusual cases, the cost and backlog was escalating, and Congress was getting complaints.

John Dalrymple was then the IRS career executive with the unenviable job of implementing the dozens of new taxpayer rights provisions in the 1998 reform law. Originally from Iowa, he had moved rapidly upward in the IRS, managing units in Minnesota and California before coming to Washington to run the operations staff in headquarters. In a job that required long hours, he somehow remained trim and fit. Since he never looked tired, people would give him more and more assignments. He had a comprehensive knowledge of the IRS organization, and he understood the problems the traditional pattern was creating in the innocent-spouse program.

I encouraged Dalrymple to solve the innocent-spouse problem but not to feel limited by the existing organizational structure. In doing so, he implemented an organizational model that demonstrated the power of two key principles that were to underlie the new IRS organization: external focus on understanding taxpayers' specific characteristics, and internal focus on the accountability of management for quality performance. Bypassing the thick geographic structure, Dalrymple designated one highly qualified manager to run the whole program, to talk regularly to outside experts and taxpayers, and to supervise one group of dedicated employees who could learn to meet the very special characteristics of innocent-spouse taxpayers. It was this kind of organizational pattern we needed to implement on a broad scale.

The Pattern Should Reflect the Purpose

In my first testimony on my modernization plan, in January 1998, I explained why we needed to reorganize the IRS: "The IRS organizational structure no longer enables its managers to be knowledgeable about and take action on major problems affecting taxpayers. Each of its 43 districts and service centers is charged with serving every kind of taxpayer, large and small, with simple or complex problems. There are *eight* intermediate levels of management between a front-line employee and the Deputy Commissioner."[2]

Privately I was voicing my concerns more directly: No sane and experienced businessperson would ever take the job of IRS commissioner if he or she thought that the agency would have to be managed through the existing organization. No one but the commissioner and the deputy was fully responsible for anything.

But fixing the organization, and especially changing its pattern, without breaking it was a risky and monumental task.

Structure is an important determinant of how an organization works, because people, money, and authority necessarily are managed through it. Structure determines who writes personnel evaluations, who awards contracts, and who decides which cases or projects to undertake, all important attributes of power. How this power is distributed greatly influences what an organization accomplishes. Matters of structure actually comprise a major part of the most important document in American history—the U.S. Constitution. The Constitution specifies how many branches of government should exist, how each is organized, and who has authority for what.

Because organizational structure can be such a powerful influence on performance, changing it significantly not only is hard and costly, but can also end up failing—the worst of all worlds.

Of course, the IRS reorganized all the time. Almost every year, the IRS would add or redefine the number of assistant commissioners at headquarters. In 1996, the agency completed a reorganization to reduce the number of districts from sixty-three to thirty-three. But such reorganizations don't change the pattern of an organization. And changing the pattern of an organization is what creates the big gains and the big risks.

If you ran a chain of ten hair salons, it wouldn't be such a big change to add one shop or to combine two shops into one. It would be a much more complex decision if you decided to make some of the shops specialize exclusively in serving men and others in serving women. Think of the new questions: Which shops do you pick for each category? Which employees have to be retrained, relocated, or let go? How do you pick the managers; should you bring in outside managers who have experience with specialized shops? Will all the shops have the same equipment? How will you redirect those customers who need to go to a different shop? More importantly, how do you keep people from getting confused and your company from losing business during the transition?

Fortunately, the IRS could draw from proven models in the business world for managing in a situation of diverse customers and diverse products. When local banks mainly provided checking accounts and small loans to individuals and local businesses, it was efficient to have a branch that did everything for everybody. Today, large banks have different business divisions, each of which serves different customers, from retail customers, to small and medium businesses, to large businesses. Each division has the right set of services, the right expertise, and the right locations to serve its customers. The local branch manager does not have to know about multicurrency lines of credit, and the global banking division does not have to worry about collecting on car loans.

In its final report, the IRS restructuring commission headed by Bob Kerrey and Rob Portman in early 1997 noted that these same principles could apply to the IRS: "Reorganizing into specialized units focused on taxpayer needs, rather than IRS internal needs, should better serve the American public."[3]

Internal IRS studies had also proposed reorganizing parts of the IRS into specialized units, but these studies faltered on the prospect of eliminating the geographically defined districts and service centers, which were the embedded power structures of the IRS. Each of these organizational units was set up as a mini-IRS, headed by a senior career executive with the title of director. These executive positions were the most prestigious jobs in the IRS. Those who held them, or aspired to hold them, usually opposed proposals that would diminish their power. In addition, an array of administrative staffs and union officials had grown up around each of these mini-IRSs, and they also had strong incentives to try to preserve them.

After reading all these studies and reflecting on my initial visits around the agency, I concluded that we needed to turn the IRS's major power structures inside out—to put the major focus of IRS organization on the taxpayers and what we did for them, rather than just where the IRS office happened to operate. Taxpayers are diverse, and therefore the services they require are diverse. The tax law is complex, but only a small part of it is relevant to most taxpayers. I thought that changing the organizational structure so that its primary focus was on responding to the specific characteristics of taxpayers would be one of the most powerful changes we could make to drive improved performance. It was an even more fundamental change than modernizing the technology, because technology supports, and indeed often locks in, the existing pattern of organization.

Remarkably, I got approval through the Treasury Department in a matter of weeks, and was able to launch the reorganization proposal publicly. I explained that my proposal was "to organize around the needs of our customers, the taxpayers. Just as many large financial institutions have different divisions that serve retail customers, small to medium business customers, and large multinational business customers, the taxpayer base falls rather naturally into similar groups. Therefore it is logical to organize the IRS into units charged with end-to-end responsibility for serving a particular group of taxpayers with similar needs."[4]

My written testimony was accompanied by briefing materials that showed that this reorganization would not be moving the boxes around at headquarters. It envisioned a top-to-bottom reorganization, eliminating the traditional districts, regions, and service centers across the country.

The heart of the proposal was to assign most of the operations in the IRS to four divisions, each of which would have responsibility nationwide for a set of taxpayers with distinct characteristics. The taxpayers for which each division had responsibility were grouped as follows:

- Individual taxpayers with only wage and investment income, comprising about 70 percent of all taxpayers, most with relatively simple returns
- Small-business and self-employed taxpayers, comprising individuals with business income and small corporations or partnerships, most with more complex returns
- Large- and midsized-business taxpayers, comprising the few thousand businesses with very complex returns
- Tax-exempt and government entities, which were governed by distinct sections of the tax code

Supporting these four operating divisions would be specialized functional units—criminal investigation, appeals, taxpayer advocate, and counsel—and two units to provide services to all the others, one for information technology services and one for other shared services such as facilities, personnel, and procurement. As part of the proposal, several intermediate layers of management, such as those in the regions, would

FIGURE 10-2

The New IRS Organization

The new IRS organization on October 1, 2000. Four operating divisions each had nationwide responsibility for a distinct set of taxpayers. One unit provided information technology services, and another provided facilities and other shared services for the whole IRS.

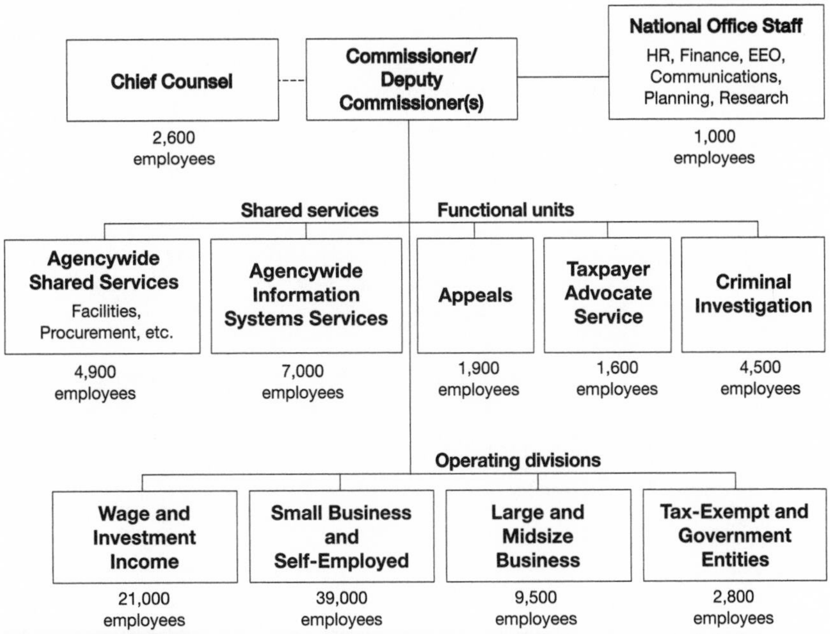

be eliminated, and the size of the IRS national office headquarters would be drastically reduced.

Although the proposal evolved as we studied its implementation, all the basic concepts remained intact, as the chart of the organization implemented on October 1, 2000, showed.

Reactions in Congress and the press were just as expected: Outsiders were positive about the possibility that the proposal might bring real change in the IRS, but skeptical that the change would ever really happen. "Lawyers and accountants here applauded the elimination of layers of management," wrote Albert Crenshaw in the *Washington Post*. "However, several cautioned that Rossotti might be taking on too much at a time when the agency has undergone an unprecedented public bashing."[5]

Bringing People into the Tent

Internally there was little of the backlash that so many outsiders imagined would occur. After the beating the IRS had taken for the previous two years, IRS executives and leaders of the employee organizations expected a new commissioner to propose changes. Their main concern was about what would happen next. They wanted to be part of shaping the all-important details of the proposals just in case the really surprising thing happened—that the proposals might actually be implemented.

Having laid out the concept for a major reorganization, my colleagues and I now faced three big challenges: making the right decisions on the thousands of big and little details; getting from here to there without breaking or getting shot down in the meantime; and making the plan work the way it was intended. Each of these problems held the distinct risk of turning the whole exercise into a disaster.

With help from Nancy Killefer, the former McKinsey consultant and my key ally at the treasury, and with expert advice from a team of consultants led by John Jones of Booz·Allen & Hamilton, we created a process that tackled all three of these problems. We realized that we might still fail, but not because we ignored what we knew would be hard problems.

The only way to accomplish such a pervasive reorganization was to get help from the people who knew the details—the people who were actually doing the work. But if we relied on those who knew how it was managed today, how would we get the fresh thinking we were looking for? Weren't people naturally resistant to change, wedded to the way things had always been done? As anywhere, some were and some weren't. The key was finding the people who wanted to be part of designing a new IRS, the internal changes leaders at the grass roots. If we could get these knowledgeable insiders to lead the design of the new organization, we could not only make more reliable decisions, but also begin to break down the skepticism and resistance from everyone else.

Outside stakeholders who dealt regularly with the IRS, such as taxpayer representatives, also had invaluable information about what worked and what didn't work. By seeking their help and input, we could improve the quality of the decisions and gain their support, or at least get more informed criticism, of controversial decisions that we would have to make.

The first step was to find a few brave souls willing to volunteer to lead the reorganization program. IRS career people had seen commissioners come and go, hearings that flare like Fourth of July fireworks and are forgotten just as fast, and bold plans announced and quickly watered down like a ten-cent cup of coffee. Volunteering to lead a reorganization proposal that was supposed to overturn internal power structures fortified over forty-five years was not an obvious, career-enhancing move. But with encouragement from Deputy Commissioner Dolan, two well-respected career executives, John Stocker and Jerry Songy, volunteered for a four-month assignment to work with the Booz·Allen consultants to study the validity of the reorganization concept and to develop a plan for the next steps.

By July 1998, four months after starting the first study, the IRS and treasury leaders agreed on a plan to proceed with the reorganization. We announced just a few key decisions: building the new IRS around the four divisions with end-to-end responsibility for a set of taxpayers, centralizing information systems, and drastically reducing the size of the national office. We publicly committed to work closely with all stakeholders, including the employees union and taxpayer groups, on the massive number of decisions needed to implement this new organization.

With Senator Roth's support, Congress included in the reform bill (which passed the same month) a provision that directed the IRS to reorganize along the lines of my proposal—a critically important step that instantly eliminated what could have been years of arguing with lawyers over what authority we had to change long-established structures.

In September 1998, we appointed the first members of the new top management team to manage the agency during the transition. If anyone in the IRS could hold it together during a tumultuous transition, it was Bob Wenzel. The visionary veteran had held almost every job in the

IRS and had often proposed changes that he could not get implemented. He took the job of deputy commissioner for operations. John LaFaver came into the IRS as one of the first outside senior executives, after a career modernizing three state tax agencies, to oversee the reorganization. He took the job of deputy commissioner for modernization.[6]

We knew that, of all the stakeholders that could most help or hurt the effort, one of the most important was the employees union, known as the National Treasury Employees Union, or NTEU. Almost 85 percent of IRS employees were represented by the union, and although it did not have decision-making powers, it had plenty of ways to throw monkey wrenches into everything if it chose. On the other hand, the union also had credibility with many employees—credibility that could help to overcome anxiety and resistance. In my first conversations with NTEU president Bob Tobias and Colleen Kelley, his deputy and successor, they saw the reorganization more as an opportunity than a threat, although they were skeptical about whether anything would really change. Tobias and Kelley joined our steering committee for the reorganization and helped recruit frontline employees as members of the dozens of teams that we set up to work out the details of the new structure.

Ground Rules for Decisions

In order to engage a large number of internal and external stakeholders as part of the decision-making process, while keeping the process orderly and efficient, we needed ground rules. We boiled these down to four:

No special-interest representatives: Although each person on a team had specialized expertise, such as in collection or phone operations, no one was supposed to represent any organizational unit or any point of view. By volunteering for the team, members were committing to develop the best possible solution for the IRS as a whole.

Sharing information widely: Information produced by the teams would be shared with people inside and outside the IRS, and comments would be solicited from the widest possible audience before decisions were made.

Strict limits on scope: Strict limits would be set on the scope and time frame of the each phase of the project. The number of decisions to be made was inevitably huge, and we wouldn't want to make any more decisions than were absolutely necessary to design and implement the new organization.

Fact-based, open decision process: An open but rigorous process would be followed for all decisions. Team recommendations would be supported by analysis and facts rather than solely opinions. Important or controversial options would all be presented to our steering committee. The team members would be invited to sit in on the steering committee sessions, and all decisions would be published. Everyone knew that I held the right as commissioner to make the final decisions.

Of course, each of these ground rules was tested by minicrises and near breakdowns of the process.

Confusion and opposition could readily be generated among employees or outside groups by the thousands of pages of documents that were being circulated within the design teams and outside stakeholders. At one point a firestorm nearly developed among the representatives of the small-business community when a document was circulated listing the numbers of enforcement staff in the new divisions. They interpreted this document as a sign that the small-business division was just a cover for a bigger enforcement crackdown on small business. But we heard about these objections right away, met with people to clear up confusion, and agreed to consider their views before arriving at final decisions. This front-loading gave us a better chance of gaining acceptance than would the practice of making decisions first and then trying to implement them in the face of determined opposition.

Team members were understandably skeptical that we would keep our commitment to making decisions based on facts and analysis, rather than the more traditional bureaucratic logrolling and secret deals. We were demanding that each of them abandon their long-held pet views and set forth honestly the pros and cons of each option. Would the senior management do the same? Although it was uncomfortable for even many of our senior executives to discuss controversial options with a relatively large group of people present, it was the only way to show that we were serious about making principled and fully informed decisions on matters that would affect the whole IRS for years to come.

After months of analysis, one team presented recommendations about how the ten big processing centers that do the initial handling of tax returns should be organized in the new IRS. But when the team reported to our steering committee, the recently appointed CIO, Paul Cosgrave, made an impassioned objection that the team recommendation would conflict with his plans for consolidating certain work at two computing centers. Although we only asked for more analysis, everyone in the room figured that the die was cast—their months of work would be overturned just because the new CIO didn't like it.

At the next steering committee meeting, with great trepidation but little hope, the team came back and showed with numbers that what the CIO wanted wouldn't save anything significant for the Information Systems Department and would disrupt other parts of the plan. Cosgrave graciously thanked the team for considering his suggestion and agreed to the original team recommendation. Stunned silence was followed by huge smiles.

Observing dozens of instances like this, the teams gradually beat back the cynics and encouraged those who wanted to make decisions based on facts and efficiency rather than bureaucratic politics.

Along the way, I got a surprising number of comments from employees. Some, like this one, came by e-mail:

> *Never do I remember a time when employees were given access to such high level information as we are now. The design teams are undoubtedly more creative as a result of employee inclusion. The change, albeit good, is difficult for some to accept. However, when we as employees are allowed to help structure the change that will affect our work life, it helps to ease the uneasiness and abate much of the fear that is often associated with change.*[7]

In two years, more than two thousand IRS employees volunteered to work on design teams, producing thousands of pages of options, analysis, and proposals. After dozens of steering committee meetings and decisions, the final product was a set of packages with charts, lists, and descriptions of every one of the eighty thousand full-time and forty thousand seasonal positions in the IRS. People joked that this was the first time in the history of the IRS that anyone actually knew what everyone in the IRS did.

Every employee received a customized letter at his or her home address saying which organizational unit and location he or she would be part of in the new structure. On August 21, 2000, I received my own letter. "Effective September 10, 2000," it read, "you will be realigned to: OFFICE OF THE COMMISSIONER within the National Headquarters organization. You are moving with your current work to the new organization."

The majority of frontline employees initially carried over their positions from the old to the new organization, with only their reporting relationship changing. Some new frontline positions were carved out of the savings resulting from the reduced layers of management and the elimination of intermediate headquarters.

Picking the Right Leaders

In the new structure, almost all of the two hundred executive jobs in the IRS, such as district directors in the field and assistant commissioners at headquarters, were abolished, and newly defined jobs in the operating divisions were created. The big challenge—and the big opportunity—in moving from the old to the new structure was putting the right people in these new executive leadership positions.

In my presentation of the modernization concept to Congress and the IRS work force, I described how we would "establish management roles with clear responsibility" to meet the needs of the taxpayers. I stressed that, since each unit would be responsible for a set of taxpayers with like needs, the management teams could be expected to become more knowledgeable about the needs and compliance problems of these taxpayers. Since the division leaders would have the authority to manage their work force with fewer management layers between the division leaders and the front line, the leaders would be able to communicate more effectively and to implement solutions to problems more quickly.

As part of the plan to fill these new leadership positions, I requested and received special authority in the IRS reform bill to recruit up to forty senior executives from outside the IRS, through streamlined procedures and with higher pay ceilings. Nothing I said or did created more anxiety in the top levels of the IRS. But I believed that nothing had more potential to change the way the IRS really worked.

In Boston, shortly after I testified on the special personnel authority, I spent an afternoon with about thirty executives sitting around a horseshoe table. Most of the conversation was routine and not very animated. Finally one asked, "Do you want to know some of the rumors that are floating around?" I said sure. "The rumor is that as soon as you get the new recruiting authority, you're going to fire half the IRS executives."

I answered that we had so much work to do running the IRS while we were reorganizing that we could hardly afford to fire experienced executives. "We just need a few people with some real-life experience with how other successful organizations do things—to work with the executives whose whole lifetime experience is inside the IRS," I said.

No one was ready to call me a liar right then, but the incident showed what people were thinking. My response, however skeptically received, was absolutely true. With the normal number of retirements, we had to increase our internal promotion of career executives as well as do external recruiting.

The IRS had long employed a very competitive and effective system to develop and promote a cadre of two hundred or so executives out of a base of one hundred thousand employees. Many were extremely resourceful at "working the IRS system" to get things done, often in spite of the structure and formal procedures. But their entire professional experience had been in the IRS. I believed that a few people with outside experience could make a tremendous impact.

An important advantage of the newly defined leadership jobs in the new organizational structure was that many of them were more comparable to executive jobs in other organizations. This made it possible to recruit outside senior people with relevant experience to work with the career executives. For almost two years, we recruited heavily and found exceptionally talented people with a whole career's worth of experience for major positions.

Larry Langdon, just retired as worldwide head of taxes for Hewlett-Packard, came in to head the division that dealt with large- and mid-sized-business taxpayers. Joe Kehoe, a successful executive with public accounting and consulting experience, headed the small-business and self-employed division. Each man had outstanding career executives as deputies who later succeeded them as heads of the units. John Dalrymple, the career executive who had managed the reform act implementation, took charge of the division responsible for most individual taxpayers and recruited an outside executive as his deputy. Evelyn Petschek, a lawyer with years of experience inside and outside the IRS, headed the tax-exempt and government entities division. Mark Matthews, a former prosecutor and defense lawyer, headed the IRS criminal investigation division. Cosgrave, the new CIO, had run several technology companies. Bill Boswell started the new shared-services division that provided personnel, facilities, procurement, and other support services to the whole IRS, after setting up a similar operation at British Petroleum.

The senior management team, combining people with experience outside and inside the IRS, was a unique experiment in the IRS and probably in government. The outside people were recruited entirely for their track records in management and had no reason to come into the government other than to try to make the IRS work better. As we expected—and indeed hoped—ideas clashed over how things should be done. But the shared commitment of everyone to the goal of making the IRS serve taxpayers more effectively helped convert the energy to progress. After their initial anxieties were calmed, the IRS executives became close teammates with the outside executives, and each gained from the experience of the other. In thirty-five years of working with management teams, I've never seen a group of people commit themselves more completely to a common goal than this group did.

Stress Point: Abolishing Two Thousand Senior Management Jobs

In the new organizational structure, about two thousand senior management jobs were abolished. About 20 percent of these jobs were eliminated outright, and the rest totally redefined so that they focused more specifically on producing quality work on taxpayer cases rather than on internal administration. Using the authority in the reform act, we defined these new jobs as pay-for-performance (known in the federal jargon as pay banding), in which seniority raises were eliminated in favor of raises based on meeting performance goals tied to the new balanced measures.

All this design was on paper. The hard part, and the scary part, was getting real people—those who wanted to manage in the new way—into these newly defined management jobs. This migration of almost the entire IRS senior management staff into new jobs posed an unprecedented opportunity but also tremendous risks. We could destabilize IRS operations and end up with people in jobs they were not suited for while losing good people who got discouraged in the process.

As they had time and again, the IRS leaders proved themselves far more adaptable than the conventional wisdom predicted. In about a year, with the help of two skilled personnel executives, Dave Mader and Ron Sanders, the IRS abolished all the old jobs, conducted a systematic evaluation and interview process, and filled the newly defined management jobs. We took extreme care to make the selection process open, to make decisions solely based on who could best do the job, and to involve respected career leaders, especially Bob Wenzel, in approving the decisions. We also used the authority in the reform law to provide early retirement options for those who did not wish to compete or who were not selected.

In addition to the complete overhaul of the senior management jobs, the IRS developed new or revised definitions of jobs. Numerous positions had to be redefined if we were to implement such new concepts as one-stop service in IRS local offices, a dedicated taxpayer advocate service, and an active marketing program to promote electronic filing and to deter gullible taxpayers from being sucked into tax schemes by promoters.

Fixing Deformed Norms

Reorganizing can also provide a means to unfreeze organizational norms that started for a useful purpose but became distorted and ultimately became an obstacle to quality performance. In the IRS, making a reality of one key principle—that managers must be accountable for the quality of their employees' work with taxpayers—required modifying some long-established beliefs and behaviors.

Former IBM chief executive officer, Lou Gerstner, in his book about turning around IBM, observed that successful enterprises develop powerful values and behaviors that often become more and more rigidly applied, to the point at which they "lose their connection to what the enterprise is all about." One of the basic beliefs set forth by Thomas Watson Sr. (IBM's legendary leader) was "respect for the individual," originally a positive value that built loyalty and commitment among IBM employees. But by the time Gerstner became CEO, this belief had evolved into things Gerstner believed "Watson certainly did not have in mind," like the notion "If your boss told you to do something and you didn't agree you could ignore the order."[8]

The IRS was a 99.44 percent pure example of Gerstner's astute observation. The agency had started with an important and hallowed principle—insulating employees from political influence—but had over forty years distorted the principle so extremely that managers became disconnected from the basic work of the organization, which was to handle tax cases.

The IRS was last torn apart in 1952, largely to stamp out corruption and political influence on tax cases. Appointments were abolished, and career managers were set up in a multilayered pyramid that led ultimately to the commissioner—the only remaining political appointee. A deeply held attitude developed throughout the IRS that any improper influence on a tax case should be rejected and reported to the independent inspector general. The purpose of the 1952 reorganization was achieved. Incidents of corruption cases became rare, and political influence on cases was unknown.

But the work of most IRS employees was to handle tax cases, and the role of managers was to supervise this work. Tens of thousands of employees were dealing daily with millions of taxpayers on matters ranging from routine account adjustments to audits of huge, multinational corporations.

As the Senate hearings and press stories demonstrated only too painfully, when cases were handled poorly or incorrectly, the consequences for taxpayers could be devastating. As I reviewed cases highlighted in the hearings and studied the internal statistics on quality, I realized with little doubt that quality problems were not just pernicious but pervasive. This was a serious failure of line management. And line management had to be responsible for correcting the problem.

Yet in the IRS, it had become the accepted norm that managers did not ordinarily talk to taxpayers or employees about the substance of cases, except for limited reviews by the lowest-level supervisors. While there was no formal prohibition against the managers' looking into the details of the cases that they had responsibility for, it was simply not within accepted IRS practice for them to do so. Most managers believed that getting involved with cases was not part of their jobs, and most employees considered it improper interference.

At a luncheon, the tax director for one of the largest U.S. corporations, which the IRS audited every year, told me of an incident in which an IRS agent misused a building pass. The tax director was so upset that he had called the IRS district director to complain, noting to me that this was an extraordinary action for him. Curious about this latter comment, I asked if he had ever before talked to an IRS manager, especially about his tax cases. He answered that in his decades as a corporate tax director, with IRS auditors on site almost continuously, he had never been visited by any manager above the lowest-level supervisor to discuss the cases he worked on with the IRS. The incident with the building pass marked the first time he had called anyone in IRS management.

The IRS was operating like a public accounting firm in which the partners responsible for the audits never met with the clients being audited, never reviewed the audit work papers, and never talked to the frontline auditors about their audits. How could such a firm sign off on the audits?

The valid notion of rejecting improper influence on cases had, over time, been distorted to become an abdication of essential management review and direction. The thick layers in the organizational structure effectively locked in this norm by increasingly isolating middle and upper management from taxpayers and frontline employees. Such norms had to change if we were to achieve our purpose of holding managers responsible for the quality of their employees' work with taxpayers.

Employees on the front lines—looking up from the bottom—often felt that they bore the brunt of the problems created by this steep pyramid of relatively disconnected managers. These employees reacted with faint hope, mixed with deep skepticism, that my reorganization proposal might change things. One of the most memorable communications of these feelings came to me in the form of a poem called "The Tower of Power":[9]

There once was a king of a district called XXX
Which was next to YYY and not far from ZZZ
His court was made up of SES'ers[10]
All loyal and true for he killed second guessers.

The king craved the limelight, national attention
He wanted his district in another dimension
Imagine his rage when a serf brought the news
That his district ranked low in the number reviews.

"I want more cases closed and increased dollar yield
And peons to spend much more time in the field."
He proclaimed to his minions from high on the hill
The subjects bowed low and succumbed to his will.

"Your majesty," they'd whimper, "we don't have the troops!
Your goals can't be met without jumping through hoops."
"I don't care how you do it," he grumpily said
"If I don't get my numbers then you lose your head."

So his minions went out and issued the cry
"Get into the field!! Bleed the taxpayer dry!
Give us seizures and closures and dollars per hour
So the king will be happy up there in his tower."

His soldiers went out and kicked taxpayer butt
Bank accounts seized, businesses shut
But the people complained that his soldiers were not fair
"Who cares about them!" said the nonchalant king.

As the carnage continued, a groundswell erupted
Taxpayers screamed that the joint was corrupted

Tabloids and news clips gave rise to a hoard
And it all came unglued when the pols jumped on board.

A hearing was given to give vent to the masses
Employees: disguised and behind dark glasses
Taxpayers came and told Kafkaesque tales
Of red tape, harassment, and threats of jail

"Dismantle them, fire them, bring back the rack!!"
Cried Gingrich, and Armey and Connie Mack
"Who is running the place? It sounds like John Gotti!"
To clean up the mess they brought in Rossotti.

So Rossotti came in and took a hard look
And did something that's not in the management book
Something so novel it gave quite a shock
To the king in his tower and the rest of his flock.

He studied the regions and districts and nation
Examined the structure that led to ruination
Visited sites (and this is the quirk)
Talked to the people who did the real work.

So what's in the future—it's anyone's guess
As the blame fixers fix the blame for the mess
Will history repeat with more of the same?
Will the king be allowed to continue the game?

Will a scapegoat be trotted out for the presses
A lamb to be slaughtered for past redresses
Or will meaningful change be allowed to take root
The responsible parties be given the boot?

If you're new to the game I can make you a list
Of promised "reforms" that have vanished like mist
I root for Rossotti but don't hold my breath
While the king and his cronies resist to the death.

Such bitter feelings that management was totally disconnected from the real work of the IRS with taxpayers, caring only about abstract statistics, were an enormous obstacle to quality performance within the old structure. Ironically, almost all IRS managers started as frontline employees and worked their way up. The reorganization was a way to eliminate these barriers and give managers a chance to again take charge of the real work of the agency.

Managing Money

Even if we could achieve our goals in managing people in the IRS, one crucial piece of the puzzle remained: managing the money. The IRS's ways of planning, budgeting, and managing its own resources were as complex and confusing as the organizational structure itself. Long lambasted as the shoemaker with holes in his shoes—the accountants who couldn't account for money properly—the IRS regularly received severely critical reports from the General Accounting Office. But I saw the IRS's most serious financial management problems as going beyond accounting.[11] They were a real obstacle to our overriding goal of improving performance across the board.

To make the new IRS work as intended, we needed a plan and budget that would answer the two big questions any management needs to know: What are we spending the money for, and what results are we getting for the money we spend? By aligning the budget and the new balanced measures of performance with the new organizational structure, we took a big step in answering these two questions, because the new organizational structure assigned responsibility for providing specific services to specific taxpayers. With such a plan in hand, we could then assign responsibility and monitor performance of the unit managers in achieving the plan, closing the loop between objectives, plans and resources, and organizational performance.

Most people wouldn't think of being handed a large budget spreadsheet as an exciting moment in life. But after struggling for three years with a nearly incomprehensible IRS budget, it was indeed a moment of excitement for me when our budget staff brought me a two-foot-square spreadsheet of the IRS organization and budget. The document showed all the major activities the IRS did, which organizational units were responsible for them, and how the budget was allocated to each unit for each activity. We now knew who was spending the money and what they were spending it for—all on one page (albeit a large page).

The newly organized IRS had four major operating divisions and several specialized and support divisions, far fewer than the 48-by-9 matrix of districts, centers, regions, and national staffs in the old structure. But no matter what the structure, there are always important problems that cross lines. To make the new IRS really work, the top team had to understand and commit to the overall plan as well as each person's unit plan.

The new planning and budgeting process was at the heart of developing this shared commitment. Just as we did with the reorganization, we worked out a systematic and open annual process, managed by Todd Grams, our talented new chief financial officer. The process exposed our whole senior team to the problem of how best to allocate our limited budget resources to achieve the maximum progress on our service and compliance goals. Clashes and arguments over priorities were natural, but the key was to get them out and resolve them as rationally as possible. The end product was a budget and performance plan that everyone understood and could commit to.

Good-Bye, Old IRS

Casey Stengel, the legendary manager of the New York Yankees, said that the secret to managing was never to let the four guys who hated you get together with the five guys who were still undecided. In January 2000, I felt good enough to kid an audience of several hundred tax lawyers, tax accountants, and assorted other IRS stakeholders that we were about to violate Stengel's rule by getting all these IRS watchers together at once. We had worked closely with all of them to plan the reorganization. Now that we were months from the implementation date of October 1, 2000, I wanted to discuss what was about to happen and to anticipate whatever transitional problems might arise.

My main purpose was to set the right expectations. Reorganizing the IRS really was like replacing the furnace in the basement—by itself it didn't change anything of direct interest to taxpayers or tax professionals. But it was an essential part of the foundation for progress. I summed up my message with a paradox:

> *Major changes to the IRS are taking place to improve dramatically the way we do business with you across the board. Yet, you will also hear that in spite of this massive reorganization, nothing has changed. The phone numbers have not changed and the revenue agent handling your case will be the same. IRS office locations don't change. Where's the change? Here's the answer. The new organizational structure merely enables us to put into place the leadership teams I introduced, and the tens of thousands of IRS employees they will lead. It enables us to give them the authority, tools and responsibility to make a difference. Over time, they—not the structure—will produce the real change in the IRS—the visible, tangible changes in service, compliance and productivity—that you and taxpayers across the nation so much deserve and will finally see. And that's no paradox. That's a promise we plan to keep.*[12]

In May 2000, we had our last annual management meeting with the old IRS still in place. The anxiety about refilling all the management jobs was sufficiently reduced that I could afford to tease the executive who years before had asked me if I had a secret plan to fire half of the executives. I pointed out that he had been given the worst job in the whole reorganization: assigning everyone new office space in the transition. In the evening, we had a short reception in which we cut up a "Good-Bye, Old IRS" cake with a "48" on it, for the number of years the old IRS structure had lasted.

Our greatest fear for the immediate period after the October 1, 2000, transition was that basic operations would fail: Employees might not get paid correctly, computers might not work right, papers might get misplaced. Worst of all, the upcoming filing season might be damaged.

Having planned for them, we were relieved to find that none of these really bad things happened. The IRS continued to function.

Other not-so-bad, but still unpleasant things did happen, however. Lots of ordinary and little matters that people throughout the organization took for granted either worked poorly or fell through the cracks, from ordering office supplies in small offices to processing routine personnel forms. People coped, but it wasn't what they had in mind. The need to learn new relationships with so many new people in new management jobs added to the anxiety.

By April 2001, despite progress on many fronts, the tolerance of many employees was stressed to the maximum. More fundamentally, the distraction of these internal administrative issues was hurting our ability to achieve our goals for improved operational performance. Some of the confusion spilled over to tax practitioners, generating complaints from outside as well as inside. To be true to our principles, as well as to address real impediments to performance, we had to acknowledge these problems forthrightly.

At a conference of executives and union officials in May 2001, we spent most of our time listening to problems reported from the field. Our senior management team vowed a special effort to fix these problems, putting together a priority list of improvements, much as we did in the early days of responding to taxpayer complaints. Still, it took about a year after the transition to the new organization for the noise to settle down. Had we planned these administrative items better, we could have settled down faster.

By 2002, most of the organizational transition was history and the new teams were focused on getting the whole work force engaged in improving performance. The IRS now had a budget that included performance goals with balanced measures rolled down in most cases to the lower field levels. We had a system of quarterly business reviews with each operating unit to monitor performance and adjust plans.

By early 2003, the IRS was achieving significant increases in most of the balanced measures of performance in service and compliance activities, despite flat resources. The all-employee survey showed strong increases in morale. IRS employee "engagement" ranked in the sixty-first percentile in Gallup's database of all public sector organizations, up from the forty-fourth percentile two years earlier.[13]

But when change is really happening—even good change—it almost always generates complaints. An employee in Dallas complained that her manager was behaving unethically because he was going out every week with his employees to visit taxpayers and review cases! Ironic as it was to receive this complaint, at least it showed that at least some managers were getting re-engaged with their employees and taxpayer cases.

It will take years before the full results from the reorganization of the IRS are realized. But one thing was clearly different when I left office in November 2002: The IRS was structured not just to make good plans but to carry them out—to support the overriding goal of improving performance on both service and compliance objectives.

Dozens of improvement projects were defined in the annual plan with milestones and budgets. In a period of about eighteen months, a major project to improve quality in operations involving over twenty thousand employees and millions of taxpayers cases was designed, piloted, and implemented and started showing measurable results.

Major enforcement initiatives involving civil, criminal, and legal IRS resources were rolling out against promoters and taxpayers who engaged in corporate tax shelters, hid income in offshore bank accounts, and used phony trusts to underreport income.

The newly appointed chief counsel, B. John Williams, had seen the IRS from every angle over a distinguished career as an IRS attorney, Justice Department official, tax court judge, and attorney in private practice. In March 2002, he gave his assessment to a gathering of corporate tax executives: " 'Transformation' is an overused word. As one who observed corporate transformations from the outside, I confess to having had substantial doubt about whether I really understood what the word meant. I will say, however, that it does accurately describe the difference between the IRS twenty years ago and the IRS today. The IRS today is a different institution and its potential for offering the public a valuable service has been enormously enhanced by the structural changes."[14]

The new furnace was in the basement. Now it was time to renovate the house. This meant changing all the basic IRS operations—from processing returns to tracking down taxpayers who didn't report what they owed—so that the operations worked more efficiently and effectively. To this end, the IRS needed to crank up one of the biggest, riskiest, and most important technology modernization projects anywhere.

CHAPTER 11

You Want More Money After Wasting $4 Billion on Computers That Don't Work?

Modernizing IRS Technology

THE IRS'S MARTINSBURG, WEST VIRGINIA, computing center is a first-class building in every way, including the sculpture outside, which displays the names of all the U.S. presidents and treasury secretaries written in binary code. In August 1999, I attended a dedication ceremony for a new building housing the center. Senator Robert Byrd of West Virginia gave one of his trademark speeches, all from memory, which included a historical account of the overthrow of Charles I in the English revolution and connected that event to the king's effort to usurp Parliament's authority to collect taxes. Inside the modern building, the computer equipment is also modern—thanks to money spent in the tax system's modernization program of the early 1990s.

But, incredibly, the modern equipment in this modern building was operating on an antiquated software system written by IBM in an obsolete computer language of the 1960s. The records of every taxpayer in America were stored on *tapes* that were updated once a week—starting every Saturday and ending every Tuesday. Every night, files still known internally as "good tape" would be transmitted to Martinsburg and accumulated for the weekly update. Around the country dozens of other systems would use this data about taxpayers to try to give employees the information they needed to do their jobs. (Up until the late 1980s, reels of magnetic tapes were physically flown back and forth to and from Martinsburg. By the 1990s, the data was transmitted over leased data circuits.) The computing center even had automated equipment to find and load the thousands of tape cartridges that contained the master file. It was the most advanced system in the world for doing something that should no longer need to be done—finding data on magnetic tape files.

From the day I agreed to accept the job as commissioner, I began working on how to accomplish the daunting task of completely rethinking and replacing the IRS's technology systems. The extent of the problem was stunning.

When we took inventory for the Year 2000 conversion, we found no fewer than 130 separate computer systems essential for the functioning of the tax system, running on 1,500 mainframe and midrange computers from twenty-seven vendors and comprising about eighteen thousand vendor-supplied software products and fifty million lines of custom computer code. These were connected through three wide-area communications networks, many stand-alone dedicated circuits, and 1,182 local-area networks. Although the IRS employed about 120,000 people at peak season, the agency had in its inventory over 200,000 end-user computers, partly because many users needed more than one computer to access the numerous incompatible systems and databases.

There is an old joke about an economist traveling with some engineers. They all fall into a deep hole. When the engineers could not come up with a way to get out, the economist says, "No problem; we'll just assume a ladder." The IRS had fallen into a deep hole, with no way to assume a ladder. It was totally dependent on very old systems that had to be completely replaced. But its systems needs were also very big and very complex. Very big, plus very complex, plus very old was a formula for a very long, very expensive, and very risky program to climb out of the hole.

And that was before you got to the politics.

For starters, there was the clamor in the press. At the time Rubin and Summers were recruiting me for commissioner, headlines like this one in *USA Today* were screaming: "After Eleven Years, $4 Billion, IRS Computers Don't Work."[1]

As the press focus on IRS problems intensified, Republican political strategists saw opportunities. They featured the IRS's $4 billion computer fiasco in their fund-raising letters beginning in 1996 and extending well into 1997.

The Treasury Department—taking serious flak for allegedly not overseeing the IRS properly—saw not only the real problems of a failed technology program, but also political problems for the administration. In the spring of 1997, the treasury pushed aggressively for improved management of IRS's technology modernization programs and began to move rapidly forward on a huge prime contract to modernize IRS's technology.

Then there was Congress, which had its own grievances about the IRS's technology problems. The thicket of complications on the Hill had first been made clear to me in December 1997, in what I remembered as my "green cloth meeting."

On the way to my first visit to the House Appropriations Committee, Floyd Williams, the IRS's legislative director, described the people I was about to meet. Williams had started working on Capitol Hill as a page and knew every character there as well as he knew his own family. Michelle Mrdeza was the committee's key appropriations staffer for IRS business, and Williams briefed me on her: Legendary for knowing her business in detail, Mrdeza forgot nothing that had ever been promised by agency heads, and she suffered no fools. She had recently been featured in the *Wall Street Journal* in an article about how much power appropriations staffers wielded over agency budgets.

When we arrived at the massive office building, which was named after House Speaker Sam Rayburn and located on Independence Avenue, we descended to the basement conference room of the committee. There Mrdeza and other staffers were seated around a large table that was covered, like a billiard table, with green felt cloth. After a few pleasantries, Mrdeza and her staff launched into the failure of the IRS's tax systems modernization program, which after seven years had been terminated in 1996. In their view, this failure had been not merely a waste of huge amounts of taxpayer money. It was also personal. They had believed in what IRS management had told them, they had gone to bat to get money, and then they had found out that it was frittered away. They felt that they had been burned. "Do you realize that you wasted four billion dollars?" they said in an incredulous tone.

Trying to get us all on a less tense footing, I pointed out that I hadn't yet had time to waste anything, because I had just gotten there. I added that I couldn't promise to succeed at everything we tried, but I would promise to level with them. They wished me well, but it was clear that nothing had done more to destroy congressional confidence in the IRS than the agency's failure in trying to modernize its essential computer systems.

Such initial visits to Capitol Hill convinced me that to most people in Washington, talk about IRS technology was just strange words, big numbers, and wasted money. I needed to find some way to help people understand what was really at stake for taxpayers.

Getting People Aboard—Literally

By the following April, I came up with a low-tech device for getting our point across—a rented bus. I invited congressional staffers who worked on IRS matters on a road trip to learn more about the IRS's technology problems. Capitol Hill is pretty deserted at 6:30 A.M. on a Monday morning, so we had plenty of room to park the bus on Constitution Avenue. We boarded the bus and left Washington with about twenty Capitol Hill and Treasury Department staffers in tow.

The first stop was MBNA in Wilmington, Delaware. I had worked with MBNA while at AMS and knew Charlie Cawley, the CEO. I knew that MBNA had some of the best customer service in the business and that the company had exploited technology to provide it. Cawley, a highly successful former banker, entrepreneur, collector of antique cars, and slightly paternalistic CEO, graciously agreed to provide our group a tour and briefings.

Nothing makes abstract words come alive like seeing people doing real work with customers. Cawley's team took the group to observe MBNA customer service representatives as they fielded customer phone calls in immaculately painted rooms with neatly arranged and fully equipped workstations.

An elaborate call-management system planned and allocated phone calls so effectively that more than 95 percent of the calls were answered in twenty seconds. Each representative had immediate access to every relevant piece of information about the customer's account and could make adjustments with a few keystrokes. In the section where disputes over charges were handled, every piece of correspondence from customers was imaged and routed by computer for resolution. The only piece of paper in sight was the menu in the beautifully arranged employee lunch area.

Leaving MBNA at noon, the bus headed north to visit the IRS service center in Philadelphia. My special assistant, Adrienne Griffen, who had carefully planned every detail of the agenda to maximize its impact, arranged for a box lunch on the bus so that we could visit Philadelphia and still be back in Washington by dinnertime. (This sensible idea showed how government rules sometimes make it hard to do even the simplest things. After weeks of discussion, Griffen finally got an official legal opinion taking several pages to say—yes, we could serve a box lunch on the bus.)

The IRS service center was housed in a huge, flat forty-year-old building, which was often fighting a leaky roof, on a highway north of downtown Philadelphia. Originally set up to receive and process tax returns, the center had expanded to include scores of diverse tasks, such as answering millions of incoming taxpayer phone calls and letters, as well as collecting overdue taxes. At the time of the congressional visit, more than four thousand employees were crammed into the building, many working at desks almost as old as the building. Most of the desks were bought before employees used computers, so the furniture was too small to hold the computer monitor and the huge paper manuals that the employees needed to do their work. Ingenious employees devised makeshift solutions such as placing wooden boards over open file drawers to create work space. Paper lay everywhere, on carts, on desks, and in cabinets of all kinds standing around the huge open floor.

Just as at MBNA, the managers took the congressional group to sit next to employees who were answering phone calls and letters from taxpayers. The employees would often look up some things on the computer, look up other things in the paper manual, and make computations by hand on little calculators. To adjust the taxpayers' accounts, the employee would have to enter a sequence of five-digit codes that were listed in still another large manual.

One employee explained a case in which a taxpayer required an adjustment to the taxes owed. The employee made the adjustment, but got a second letter back from the taxpayer before the adjustment had even shown up on the computer system (a routine delay since the main tax files were updated only once a week).

Another employee explained that the paper manuals they referred to were often out-of-date because of changes in tax laws and regulations. When new tax rules were issued, as they were almost weekly, they were typed on paper inserts that took weeks or months to reach the frontline employees, who then had to insert them into their manuals by hand.

The IRS's ancient systems made it slow, expensive, and sometimes impossible to do business correctly, since almost every IRS employee depended on information from the systems to do the job. An observer did not require a degree in computer science to see why taxpayers who called MBNA in the morning and the IRS in the afternoon were likely to be disappointed by the IRS, no matter how hard the agency employees tried.

Bad Systems, Bad Results

People in business didn't need a bus ride to grasp the drastic nature of what I was facing at the IRS. When I explained to private-sector colleagues what the IRS depended on to run the $2 trillion tax system, mouths literally dropped open. Frank Salizzoni, an experienced and successful business executive who was then chairman of H&R Block, had some good ideas on things the IRS could do to promote electronic filing. When I explained the reasons the IRS could not take him up on his suggestions, supplying a few details about the IRS's computer systems, he simply stopped short. After a surprisingly long silence, he replied, "I didn't realize. Just let us know if there is anything we can do to help."

I had received my own shock on my first day in the office, when I thought it would be nice to send an e-mail to all IRS employees. The staff just smiled—there was no IRS e-mail system. I could send an e-mail to others in my Washington office, but all the other offices had their own e-mail systems, or had none at all.

On visits to call centers early in my term, I saw countless examples of the impact of such inadequate systems:

- A taxpayer who was owed a refund changed her address before receiving the check, but delays built into updating IRS systems meant the IRS employee could do nothing to prevent the check from being sent to the wrong address.

- An accountant representing a business taxpayer had sent in the necessary authorization from the taxpayer, but that authorization was not electronically accessible at the location the accountant had come to, so his question went unanswered.

- A taxpayer received a notice rejecting the exemption for her son as a dependent because of a simple transposition error in the social security number, but to fix it the employee had to use separate spreadsheets to calculate the adjustments and enter numerous codes—all while the taxpayer waited on the phone.

Slow, old systems also reduced the collection of delinquent taxes. In August 1999, I was traveling with a revenue officer who had inherited a collection case after another agent had completed an audit of a businessman who owed taxes for several S corporations. The revenue officer got the case with virtually no information about the work done by the previous agent—no case notes, no agent reports, not even the name of the agent who had done the work. The taxpayer disclaimed any knowledge of overdue taxes, saying he had given a check to the previous agent. As we walked out of this taxpayer's office, I knew that collecting these taxes would take months of work and would probably be unsuccessful.

The cost of such system failures was tremendous. The IRS's old technology and old ways of doing business imposed the equivalent of a huge tax increase every year on honest taxpayers, who spent more time and money dealing with the IRS than they needed to. And honest taxpayers were effectively making up for the taxes that with modern systems could have been, but were not, collected from others.

A Bad Combination: Size, Complexity, and Age

But why was the IRS still in this predicament in 1997, and why was it so hard to get out of it? Modern information technology of every sort was readily available, and most successful companies were increasing their service and productivity every year with the help of this technology.

Certainly part of the problem was the agency's sheer size. In technology terms, the IRS is big—really big.

No other organization in America conducts financial transactions with every adult individual every year over his or her entire lifetime—not to mention the taxpayers' estates when they die. Similarly, no other organization in America conducts financial transactions with every business every year, and often every month, of its business life—continuing even if the business goes bankrupt. The IRS does both—and adds in every pension fund and almost every charity as well.[2] This activity requires massive record keeping that must be as accurate, to the penny, as any bank's records. None of this activity could possibly be done without computer databases and computer software systems.

Sheer size makes any computer-based business system more expensive and more difficult to design, implement, and operate—often disproportionately so. On the basic level, larger numbers of users and greater volumes of data to be processed and stored require more machines, circuits, and software, each of which requires time and money to buy, install, and maintain. But bigger systems are also more unforgiving and more complex. If you make a mistake entering your monthly expenses on your PC, it may be annoying, but you may be able to recover just by reentering the data. If you are the IRS, however, you may find it astronomically expensive (if not impossible) to recover if there is an error in processing 130 million tax returns after the refunds have been sent out. Therefore, you must implement very thorough and expensive methods to cope with such possibilities. Add to this the fact that the number of potentially significant errors multiplies with size and increases the complexity of guarding against them. Finally, if you are the IRS, you must assure the security of taxpayer records while providing access to all who need access inside and outside the agency.

Size alone, however, does not explain the IRS's technology problems. There are businesses that have successfully coped with business systems of comparable scale. One package delivery company has a database as large or larger than what the IRS needed, and some banks and phone companies have larger networks of employees connected to systems.

The IRS has to contend with one more level of monstrous complexity: the ever-changing tax code.

The tax code and the attendant IRS regulations amount to tens of thousands of pages of dense prescriptions—prescriptions not only for how to compute the tax due from an individual or a business, but also for how the money is to be collected. IRS staff must understand these millions of rules well enough to define them with extreme precision so that the prescriptions can be properly programmed in the computer software systems used by the IRS to process returns, correct errors, and collect amounts due.

When the rules change, the systems must change. And Congress changes the tax code almost ever year. In 1999, the tense year just before the Year 2000 high-wire act, eight hundred changes had to be made in IRS systems because of tax code changes alone. Even one error in one change might result in incorrect processing of returns, wrong refunds, or failure to collect the right amount of taxes, not to mention potential errors in accounting for $2 trillion.

Complex as they are, however, the systems problems created by the tax code are not impossible to solve. The IRS itself has in fact kept its many systems up-to-date with the changing tax code—not perfectly, but with relatively few truly significant tax code errors. A number of commercial vendors provide software that accurately prepares individual and business tax returns. Almost all professional tax preparers depend on commercial software to prepare tax returns.

The sheer size of its operations and the complexity of the tax-code-mandated business rules mean that the IRS must operate in a very difficult and risky zone in the world of business computer systems. But it is not an impossible zone.

One more factor, however, enormously increased the difficulty of solving the IRS's technology problem. This factor was reflected in the dropped jaws and widened eyes of every expert I talked to about the problem.

No organization as big as the IRS and as utterly dependent on computer systems had ever fallen so far behind. Any private-sector business that fell nearly so far behind the competition would long since have either gone out of business or been acquired. I knew of no real precedent for the IRS situation—a huge financial organization that, for its essential work, depended on complex information systems so fundamentally deficient that nearly everything from the ground up had to be replaced.

How Such an Important Agency Fell So Far Behind

One of many ironies about the IRS is that it got into this pickle in part because it was once *ahead* of its time in using computers to do business. Paradoxically, many technologically pioneering organizations eventually lose their edge, and even fail, because they wait too long to adapt to change. The initial technology can become so essential and so old that it becomes almost unbearably costly and risky to replace. In the private sector, this may kill the business. In the IRS, it created the extraordinary situation I inherited.

In the 1950s, the IRS had experimented with using punch-card machines to process tax returns. But the use of machines was limited by the IRS's lack of authority to require taxpayers to put unique identifying numbers on returns. Returns were just filed in local offices by name and address, with no central file. In 1961, Commissioner Mortimer Caplin got permission from Congress to require social security numbers on individual returns. The IRS then put out a twenty-three-page document soliciting bids from the nascent computer industry. IBM won the bid and successfully implemented a software system to maintain a master file of every taxpayer's account on magnetic tape—a real breakthrough at the time.

A retired IRS executive, Bill Smith, told me about how he selected the location for the IRS's first central computing center in 1960. Because of Cold War worries about a nuclear attack, the center had to be at least fifty miles from Washington. Smith and another IRS executive drove south into Virginia and then turned north along the fifty-mile radius, looking for sites. They stopped for lunch at a greasy spoon in West Virginia, where they heard about a nearby site in a town called Martinsburg. Looking at the site after lunch, they decided it was good enough. So they stopped looking and went home in time for dinner. Ever since, the IRS's taxpayer master file has been in Martinsburg.

To feed the central master file in Martinsburg, the IRS set up ten processing centers around the country in the 1960s and early 1970s to key-enter some of the data on the returns. In the early 1970s, the IRS successfully built its first online system, quite an advanced project for the time. (I was amazed to learn that none other than Bob Wenzel, who became deputy commissioner in 1998, had been the manager of this project.) This Integrated Data Retrieval System took limited data out of the master files each week and sent it back to the ten processing centers, where employees could get access online to the data in their location in order to answer letters and phone calls.

Like a precocious child whose later life was totally molded by his or her early success, the IRS information systems became more and more constrained by those first systems.

Year after year, decade after decade, the IRS modified its taxpayer data systems by adding computer code to accommodate the ever expanding tax code and the increased volume and variety of tax returns. Clever programmers under pressure found dozens of ways to jury-rig the system to get around limitations. For example, they used a data field set up for tax dollars to enter the taxpayer's zip code. (Postal zip codes did not exist when the system was designed.) By the late 1990s, these systems had been pushed far beyond the limits of their designs and the 1960s software technology used to implement them. And only a tiny number of people in the IRS understood the accumulated tricks and intricacies well enough to fix problems or make changes.

As information technology advanced during the 1980s and 1990s, people throughout the IRS's far-flung organization identified ways to use technology, beyond just basic record keeping, to make their operations more efficient.

It is almost always cheaper and faster to build a small system used by a small group of people than to redesign a network of systems that involves many more people. To meet the demands for fast implementation with limited funds, the IRS built dozens of systems to do specific jobs for specific groups of people—one collection system to allow employees to collect by phone, another to eliminate paperwork for field collectors, another for agents who examined returns, another for appeals officers, and many more. Some systems operated only in certain offices or sites, where enterprising managers figured out ways to implement quick and dirty systems to solve specific problems. One service center director even implemented a rudimentary electronic interchange system with local tax practitioners.

Since almost any IRS system needed data about taxpayers' tax filings and payments, these dozens of new systems passed data back and forth with the master files and the service center systems—resulting in a dizzying maze of systems mixed together like the strands in a large bowl of spaghetti.

All along, some people at the IRS recognized that this patchwork approach was inadequate. As far back as the 1970s, the IRS made proposals for more comprehensive systems modernization, but these were not accepted by Congress. Finally, after a near breakdown of processing in the 1985 filing season, Congress approved the IRS's ill-fated tax systems modernization program, which started in the late 1980s. This program built some successful systems, such as a very productive system for matching documents like W-2s with tax returns, and it brought in some necessary new hardware. But it failed to lay out how all these many systems should fit together, and it did nothing to modernize the most basic data systems still operating on the design and technology of the 1960s. Considered a $4 billion failure, the program was finally killed in 1996 by the Treasury Department.

When I was sworn in as commissioner in November 1997, I inherited not just this legacy of failure, but also a major initiative to replace the recently canceled tax systems modernization program. This initiative, which I feared was flawed and premature, was intended to start an altogether new program for a coherent modernized system—and to award a fifteen-year, multibillion-dollar contract to manage it.

President Roosevelt had reassured the public in the Great Depression with the words "there is nothing to fear but fear itself." But I couldn't reassure anybody, and certainly not myself, that there was nothing to fear about another IRS technology modernization program costing the taxpayers billions of dollars.

I believed that it made no sense to launch this big program in 1997. The IRS just wasn't ready. First we had to focus every bit of management capacity on our immediate customer service problems, on implementing the mandates in the 1998 reform bill, and on our internal reorganization. And at the same time, we had to fix the Year 2000 problem.

I managed to get the release of the request for proposal (RFP) for selecting a prime contractor delayed until early 1998, and then I had stalled as much as I could on moving the program forward. By mid-1999, I had done as much as possible to see that the conditions for success were in place. Then, we had to acknowledge the difficulty, manage the risks, and forge forward.

Managing IT Before Replacing IT

The first and most obvious question about technology in the IRS was, Who was managing the IRS's vast array of computer hardware, software, and networks?

Following the pattern of IRS organization, each major unit managed its own information systems. There were officially fifteen information systems departments, plus many other subgroups with dedicated information systems staffs or contractors. The chief information officer (CIO) was only directly in charge of the national office systems and had only loose coordinating authority over the rest.

Because there were so many organizational units that bought and managed computers, the IRS relied on equipment and software from almost every vendor in the industry. It was like a Noah's Ark of technology: In captivity we had an example of nearly every hardware and software product ever produced. But this diversity of products was no joke, since it massively increased the complexity of making changes and fixing problems. Fixing the Year 2000 problem turned out to be a huge $1.3 billion project in itself, much of which was directly related to the age and diversity of hardware and software products installed in the agency.

Before we could successfully manage a big program of new technology, we had to manage the technology we already had, since the new and the old would have to coexist for many years. We would have to fundamentally change the IRS organization and technology while carrying on vast and vital operations. In one speech, I compared the IRS's systems problems to living in a very big, old house with a large family: "It's been renovated so many times that your guests need a guide to find the bathroom. Occasionally the toilets flush when you turn on the lights. The good news is that you know how to redesign the house. The bad news is that you have to live in it while the work goes on."[3]

My first major move in the IRS reorganization was to redirect its major information technology (IT) departments to report to the CIO, Paul Cosgrave. After a successful career in several technology companies, Cosgrave agreed to come into the IRS in May 1998 at a time when the political crossfire on IRS technology was at its peak and the morale of the staff was at its lowest. His was a true act of patriotism. By the time Cosgrave returned to his home in New York in 2001, he had taken control of the IRS's fragmented IT organizations, navigated flawlessly through the Year 2000 date change, supported the reorganization of the rest of the IRS, and launched the new business systems modernization program.

John Reece, also an industry veteran who had been CIO at a major insurance company and at Time Warner, succeeded Cosgrave and completed the reorganization and standardization of the IRS operations. Reece completed these steps while overseeing the implementation of the first projects in the new modernization program.

Through all the turmoil, Toni Zimmerman—an IRS executive who started in human resources but knew more about the agency's IT organization than did anyone else—was the glue that held the place together.

The centralization of responsibility for the agency's IT activities had immediate benefits in executing the successful Year 2000 program and in imposing technology standards across the IRS. Centralization reduced the number of overlapping vendor products and created for the first time IRS-wide basic services like e-mail and voice mail. By 2001, the IRS had achieved such standardization of its desktop and laptop computers that the agency was able to conduct a single reverse auction over the Internet for seventy thousand computers, obtaining prices far below previous levels. But it took four years to weld the IRS-wide information systems activities into a truly integrated organization providing service to the whole IRS.

Rethinking IRS Information Technology

Managing the IRS business systems modernization program required the reorganization of more than the IT activities themselves. We were not out to change the way the IRS's IT worked. We were out to change the way the IRS worked. We deliberately named the program Business Systems Modernization, with stress on *business.*

In the slang of the computer industry, we did not want to "pave the cow paths"; we wanted to find new and better paths.

A computer system in a business organization is a codification of the way the organization does its work. The IRS had three different collection systems—all of which could have data about the same taxpayer—because it had three collection organizations, each of which worked in a somewhat different way to collect money from taxpayers. (One organization collected by mail, another by telephone, and a third by personal visits from revenue officers.) The agency had large data-processing systems in ten locations because it processed paper tax returns in those locations a certain way. These systems helped the employees in these organizations do their jobs the way the jobs were defined when the systems were built, but they also limited the way the jobs could be redesigned in the future.

In successful public and private organizations, there were plenty examples of how most of the activities done by the IRS—from answering inquiries, to auditing, collecting, and resolving disputes—could be done faster, more efficiently, and more accurately with modern technology. Indeed, people in the IRS knew of and often had proposed radically better ways of doing business. They knew that it should not take two years for a revenue officer to get a collection case involving a high-risk business taxpayer. Nor should a customer service representative have to digest four pages of detailed instructions and codes to correct a simple transaction like a payment applied to the wrong taxpayer account.

In 1997, CIO Arthur Gross made a real contribution to IRS technology modernization by producing the IRS's first comprehensive technology blueprint. Nevertheless, it was also largely built around, and limited by, the IRS's old organization and ways of doing things. Changing these basic attributes of the agency was a matter beyond the capacity of any CIO.

Making any changes in the way things were done across the whole IRS had been extraordinarily difficult because of the fragmentation of the organization. Even if people in headquarters decided on something new, it could take years for the parties to agree on the details, and even longer to adapt a new system to all the local practices on how business was done. Even after a new system was developed, implementation across the IRS could take ten years.

For the IRS to be successful in modernizing its business operations and technology, the agency would first need to reorganize itself into fewer units, which could thus manage operations more consistently across the whole country. The overall IRS reorganization, implemented in October 2000, was therefore a critical step for the Business Systems Modernization Program as well.

Another critical step was to lay out how the new IRS organization would operate in the future across the whole agency. In 2001, the IRS produced the first set of documents specifying how the basic business processes of the IRS—processing returns, providing customer service, and carrying out compliance activities such as auditing and collecting—should operate to take advantage of new technology. Building on the earlier blueprint, this enterprise architecture also covered basic technology topics such as managing taxpayer communications and maintaining consistent, secure, taxpayer data. But most important, the entire top leadership of the IRS was personally involved in developing this picture of a radically transformed agency. If updated regularly, the IRS's enterprise architecture will be a tool for many years to make the IRS's technology investments fit together and pay off.

Precarious Procurement

Preseason training is always necessary, but no football team knows whether it can win until the real season starts. This adage was equally true of the implementation of major new systems at the IRS. We couldn't just plan, organize, train, and write playbooks. We eventually had to go out on the field. We knew the first games would be a learning experience, but we had to do everything possible to prevent season-ending injuries.

A key step was selecting the IRS's prime contractor and getting it started with the right goals and agreements as to what it was to do. Here there was a conundrum that anyone who ever hired a contractor to renovate a kitchen can understand.

You know you want an efficient kitchen with modern appliances at a price you can afford. But lots of decisions still have to be made. What, then, is in the contract? What are you responsible for, and what is the contractor responsible for? Do you hire a separate kitchen designer to select the appliances and to lay out the kitchen, or do you rely on a contractor who claims to know all about kitchens? Who draws up the plans, and how detailed do they have to be, before you agree on the price? If you pick the contractor before you complete the design, how do you know you're getting a competitive price? Who pays if the cabinets have to be rebuilt because the plans didn't properly allow space for the plumbing? Is it your fault because you approved the plans, or the kitchen designer's fault because he or she drew up the plans, or the contractor's fault because it's a contractor's job to coordinate the subcontractors? What happens if you have to stop the contractor's work every afternoon while you use the kitchen to cook dinner for the family? Above all, what happens if you build the kitchen and it takes you longer to cook than it did in the old kitchen, because the design is inefficient? Isn't that why you paid good money for an experienced kitchen person—to tell you how to design an efficient kitchen?

No wonder even kitchen renovation projects often take longer and cost more than expected. And nobody claims that kitchens depend on sophisticated, fast-changing technology.

Work on the process for managing the new technology modernization program began even before I took office, as the Treasury Department pushed forward with an RFP to select a prime contractor. Because of the IRS's previous problems with modernization, all parties agreed that the IRS should rely on the private sector as much as possible. Under the plan developed by the Treasury Department, the IRS would hire one prime contractor to manage the whole thing under a fifteen-year contract, rather than hiring lots of contractors just to provide technical personnel or do specific projects. The theory was to find "one belly button to push" when things went wrong. But this plan presented the IRS with the same conundrum as the person renovating his kitchen—only a million times more costly and risky.

The IRS was hiring the contractor to design the kitchen as well as to build it. Although the agency had general goals for modernizing its basic ways of administering the tax system, and a general blueprint for the architecture, there were no specific designs for specific projects. These would have to be developed in manageable pieces because the program was far too big to do all at once. Until there were decisions and designs for particular projects—and thousands of decisions would be required in the design for each project—the contractor could commit to nothing specific. If the contractor faced no specific commitments, the IRS would take all the risk while giving a fifteen-year monopoly to one contractor.

In my first meetings with the teams of contractors that were planning to bid, it was clear that the prospect of getting a long monopoly on a big chunk of IRS business, with no specific commitments required, did not trouble them at all. Nor, in truth, would it have troubled me when I was in the systems contracting business. But as the buyer, the prospect troubled me a lot. If management accountability was to be a key principle in the new IRS, it had to extend to contractors carrying out this key program.

We revised the procurement as much as we could to provide for ongoing competition among subcontractors and to make it clear that we expected the contractor to assume some of the risk for delivering projects with business results. But making this accountability for results work in practice remained one of the hardest problems in managing the program.

Launching the Program

Having stretched out the process as much as possible, by the end of 1998, we were nearing the point at which we were going to have to award the prime contract. On the Tuesday before the 1998 Thanksgiving weekend, we cleared the calendar for a six-hour brainstorming meeting with people who I knew understood what we were about to undertake. In addition to Cosgrave, I invited Larry Levitan—a recently retired top executive from Andersen Consulting (now Accenture) who was advising Cosgrave and me.[4] Also joining this group were several veteran IRS information systems experts—Bob Albicker, Tom Lucas, and Curt Turner—who fully comprehended the problems with IRS technology. We focused on making sure we worked on the right problems, in particular finding a way to get out from under the 1960s master file. No previous plan even addressed this issue in any practical way. Having not thought of an acceptable way to replace the master file, previous modernization programs just tried to build around it. We all agreed that this could not continue—we had to free the IRS and all of America's taxpayers from their bondage to a 1962 system. Lucas and others came up with some promising ideas on how to replace the master file in manageable increments, and we agreed that studying this would be one of the first tasks given to the new contractor.

We also agreed that we were still not ready to start up the program on a large scale, but could start some relatively low-risk projects that would be a good learning experience. We awarded the prime contract to Computer Sciences Corporation in December 1998, but for another whole year, we mainly did planning studies and small-scale design work.

Performing for the Greek Chorus

By early 2000, we were ready to begin larger-scale work on a few projects, starting with a system to help improve telephone service for taxpayers. For this we needed money. For money we needed approvals. As the first significant request for funding went forward, we exposed the unique anatomy of the IRS situation: the almost comical number of steps required to approve funding; the conundrum of fixing responsibility on a contractor whose job was both to recommend and to implement; the intrinsic difficulty of replacing pieces of the IRS's ancient technology while the technology continued to support vast operations; the legacy of distrust from previous IRS failures; the Greek chorus of IRS critics, not all with the best of motives, ready to chant whenever there was a problem, "There they go again."

Trying to get anything done in this situation would have challenged the patience of a saint—and we were short of saints at the IRS. In fact we were even short of nonsaints who were able to run the program. We slowed down again and worked on beefing up the IRS's own program management office. By 2001, we had recruited and reassigned senior executives to form a much deeper IRS team. Fred Forman, one of the

FIGURE 11-1

This cartoon in Government Computer News *depicted the press's view of the mess we faced when we ramped up the business systems modernization program in February 2000. We had to start more slowly than what an earlier plan had called for.*

Source: Posted with the permission of Washington Technology, copyright Post Newsweek Tech Media. All rights reserved.

leaders who built AMS with me, came to the IRS and headed the program. Jim Williams, a procurement executive with outstanding leadership skills, managed the day-to-day activities.

No matter what we did, we knew we were going to have to do it with lots of people watching. After the uproar over the earlier "$4 billion fiasco," none of the many IRS overseers and approvers was going to be again accused of inadequate oversight of IRS modernization. Two sets of auditors, one from the Treasury Inspector General and one from the General Accounting Office (GAO), worked full-time auditing the modernization program—sometimes showing up to audit a project before it started! Funding required approvals at various points from the IRS Oversight Board, the Treasury Department, the Office of Management and Budget, the GAO, and two congressional committees.

The only way to manage this reality was to share everything as it happened—the good, the bad, and the ugly—acknowledging problems as they happened but also showing that we were acting to solve them. One way we did this was to invite representatives of the various oversight groups to sit in on our key meetings such as our top-level steering committee meetings.

The program-steering committee meetings often grew so large that people lined the walls of the narrow conference room, while others waited in the hall for their turn to present. The meetings took on the feel of a construction project where one guy was down in the hole digging while three guys stood around the edge writing on clipboards. It was often uncomfortable, but it was penance for past sins.

As we entered one of these meetings in the spring of 2001, we were supposed to be delivering the first new systems—small by IRS standards although large for almost anywhere else—and were scheduled to begin large-scale work soon on other systems. As usual, a large cast was assembling for the meeting. And everyone knew that most of the news was bad.

The reports began. The first system to be delivered was slipping another month. People disagreed over whether the design of the taxpayer database was complete enough to proceed to large-scale programming. A GAO report criticized the lack of control over changes in the designs. Another project was projecting to cost more than expected for the completion of the design. The IRS operating divisions were having trouble supplying the requested number of experts and were complaining that the contractor staff had not learned enough about their operations.

Everyone knew that backing off the widely known plan would fire up the critics to predict that the whole modernization program was heading for disaster. Nevertheless, the entire IRS senior management team at the meeting supported a substantial slowdown of the program to reduce the risk and to make sure that all the deliverables were done right. Levitan, now chairman of the IRS Oversight Board, summed it up: "You called a time-out." It was the kind of decision that management must sometimes make to manage risk in any big program.

Although it imposed an enormous burden on our managers, the open access we provided to the numerous oversight groups did pay off when we had to make hard decisions concerning the program, as well as when we were requesting funds. At least the overseers understood the facts and the real reasoning for the decisions we were making, rather than speculating about, and potentially magnifying, the problems

A Partnership or a Deadly Embrace?

By the spring of 2002, the first two technology modernization projects—a system to manage the IRS's toll-free phone service and a small system to calculate corporate taxes for IRS examiners—had been successfully delivered. Other projects were progressing—not perfectly, but at least in the right direction. The management of the program had matured noticeably.

Then the tremors of an earthquake begin to shake the whole edifice. The prime contractor reported that the date for the first installment of the new taxpayer database would slip, and the company had no reliable new date. Costs would clearly mushroom, and no one knew by how much.

The problem was not a simple schedule slippage of a programming project. The contractor had omitted essential pieces of the design. A year earlier, we had deliberately delayed the start of programming to ensure a quality design. How could we now find out that the design was so deficient? This time we had to do more than react to the immediate problem. We had to insist on assigning responsibility for the extra cost and use the bad experience to galvanize everyone to fix the underlying causes.

When two companies enter into a business venture, it is often described as a partnership—meaning that each party needs the other to succeed. In the IRS program, the IRS was the kitchen owner and it needed a more efficient kitchen. The IRS needed its prime contractor, Computer Sciences Corporation (CSC)—the kitchen designer and builder—to renovate the kitchen successfully. For its business success, CSC also needed to keep the IRS a continuing, satisfied customer.

When things go well, the partnership moniker is a good description of such a relationship. But when things go badly in a complex, long-term venture, such as IRS modernization, the relationship can seem more like a deadly embrace. The parties are so dependent on each other that neither can withdraw without doing damage to themselves.

By 2002, the IRS and CSC had worked for three years to resolve the ambiguities in the complex relationship and thereby to clarify responsibilities. Methodologies, sign-offs, task orders, review meetings, and all the other customary tools had been used. Yet we now had a real problem, not only with a project but also with the relationship. The problem that CSC had reported with the taxpayer database project—which had been the subject of special care—raised the unwelcome but unavoidable issue of whether we had a partnership or a deadly embrace.

Such an issue can only be resolved at the highest level of each organization. On the IRS side, my top modernization management team and I, together with Levitan from the IRS Oversight Board and Teresa Ressel (Killefer's very able replacement at the Treasury Department), dug into the facts and assessed the situation. We shared our facts and conclusions with CSC, agreeing to consider any new facts or analysis, but making clear that the issue had to be resolved on the merits. From CSC, CEO Van Honeycutt and his two top executives, Pete Boykin and Paul Cofoni, without defensiveness or rancor, also dug in to review the facts.

Over several weeks, we arrived at an agreement that clearly affixed on CSC most of the responsibility for the additional cost. Equally important, we agreed on a plan to address the underlying problems. Under this plan, we would replace some managers in the program and place more emphasis on the contractor's understanding of the details of IRS operations.

Lots of Progress, but Lots Left to Do

As I left the IRS in November 2002, the IRS's technology program was a lot better than I had found it, but it was still a work in progress. We knew who was in charge and what we were spending money on, and we had some key performance measures in use. Product standards, asset inventories, and formerly missing basic services, such as e-mail and nationwide access to at least limited taxpayer data, were in place. Many more taxpayers could file and do business electronically with the IRS. Security over data and facilities was far better. The agency was using a meaningful architecture for the future of business operations and technology to guide modernization. Some new systems had been delivered and were helping to improve service in the 2002 and 2003 filing seasons and to provide new software tools to some IRS compliance employees.

One big accomplishment I most hoped to see, the first move of taxpayer records off the ancient master file, was not done when I left office in November 2002. This big event was announced by the IRS in July 2004.

The IRS has an immense ongoing opportunity to improve its effectiveness by taking advantage of improved business practices that are enabled by ever evolving technology. With intense top management attention, constant modernization can succeed, but it is difficult and risky. Occasional setbacks along the way are likely. The IRS must catch up and must never again be allowed to fall so far behind.

Some Lessons

The IRS technology story holds some clear lessons for any large business or public agency.

Above all, no organization that depends on information for its key functions can afford to stay mired in seriously outdated systems. To do so threatens the continued viability of the organization. Catching up becomes extraordinarily expensive and risky.

Most organizations will occasionally need to undertake comprehensive modernization programs—not only to take advantage of business opportunities but also defensively, to avoid being overtaken by others using new technology more effectively. Small, limited investments affecting the fewest number of people and the shortest time frames will always seem more attractive than bigger projects. Most of the information systems investments an organization makes should be of this small, fast, focused kind. But when larger investment proposals come forward, they cannot always be deferred. The serious long-term consequences of becoming irretrievably obsolete cannot be ignored.

Top managers must recognize that important systems modernization programs almost always involve changing the business as well as changing the technology. If there is no business change, there is probably no business gain. It is not like building a missile or another piece of equipment. It is changing the way people work and, often, the way they work with customers.

Relationships between the players in a business systems modernization program need to be thought through with great care. Such programs inherently involve several key players—the business operators, the technology managers, the program managers, and the outside systems integrators and product vendors. These players should have shared incentives and accountability for the success or failure of the program.

Qualified leaders are the scarcest and most essential resource for the success of a major business systems modernization program. Many valuable and necessary tools, techniques, and processes are available to help structure and manage such programs. But no procedure or methodology can be mechanically applied to produce a useful result.

Finally, large business and technology change programs challenge a fundamental cultural characteristic of an organization: its willingness to face up to problems. Just as the military says that no battle plan survives the first contact with the enemy, no major business and technology modernization program can be successful without regular adjustment. When the reality is bad news—whatever the reason—there are two paths: Cling to the desired but increasingly unrealistic plan until it crashes irretrievably, or face up to reality and make practical adjustments, without overreacting, along the way.

During my time in office, the IRS gained plenty of experience facing up to bad news—and not all in the systems field.

CHAPTER 12

The Cover-Up Is Worse Than the Crime

Averting and Managing Crises

Suspicions of IRS cover-ups of abuse and mismanagement were never far from the surface in the Senate Finance Committee hearings in 1997. The stunning picture of IRS employees testifying anonymously behind screens because they claimed fear of retaliation conveyed the message that the IRS was an organization ready to use its power to suppress the truth.

After describing his view of IRS abusive practices in the collection division, Anonymous Witness No. 1 summed up his key point: "Does the IRS cover up abuses? The answer is, yes. If the pubic ever knew the number of abuses covered up by the IRS, there could be a tax revolt."[1]

The press, as might be expected, picked up the theme. *Newsweek*'s cover story in October 1997 accused the IRS of "wielding its awesome power under a cloak of secrecy."[2]

Over and over again in government and business, people fail to learn that the cover-up is almost always worse than the crime, often with dire consequences. Arthur Andersen, the world's largest accounting firm, collapsed in 2002 when it was found guilty of a classic cover-up—obstructing justice by improperly destroying documents in the Enron scandal. The public and the jury could more easily understand a story about people shredding documents when government investigators were on the way than they could a charge that accountants misclassified the debt of offshore special-purpose entities.

I could make few specific promises in my own confirmation hearing, since I had no prior experience with the agency. But years of experience in the computer systems industry, where things go wrong every day, taught me that you can't fix problems you don't know about—and you won't hear about the bad news soon enough unless you emphasize that you want to hear it. So I said in my testimony that, while it would take years to solve the problems of the IRS, in the meantime I was committed to "open, honest communication" inside and outside the agency. Internally, I stated this repeatedly as one of my key principles in running the IRS. It was also a positive way of saying that we wouldn't indulge in or tolerate cover-ups.

Senator Bob Graham of Florida tried to encourage me on the subject by telling me how Eisenhower perked up his staff during the Battle of Bulge, when the Allies were surprised by a massive German counterattack. Eisenhower told the staff that this move was sure to end the war, because the half million German soldiers whom they couldn't find before were now out in the open. The senator recommended that I look at the IRS the same way.

Senator Daniel Patrick Moynihan of New York felt so strongly on the subject of openness that he had written a book on the bad consequences of too much secrecy in government. He was glad to hear me talk about open communications at the IRS, but he was skeptical that a large bureaucracy would reveal anything unfavorable until it was finally compelled to.

Risking Embarrassment to Duck Disaster

As it turned out, we had plenty of opportunities to prove that we could admit mistakes and embarrassing incidents, starting my first month on the job.

At this time, the public outcry for finding who was responsible for the alleged abuses at the IRS was at its peak. The Senate Finance Committee investigators were hot on the trail of accusations from employees and taxpayers around the country. In one of my internal meetings on the subject, somebody mentioned that a videotape of a training session for revenue officers could be "problematic."

Whoa! Tape recordings. Smoking guns. Cover-ups. It seemed as if all the ingredients were being assembled for a spicy scandal stew à la Washington. The chefs in Congress were certainly ready to stir it, and the press was hungry to eat it. Just what the IRS needed. Just what I needed.

I figured the only thing worse than the IRS's having a smoking-gun videotape at that moment would be for the press or Congress to expose it. We couldn't let that happen. I got a copy of the videotape and took it home over the weekend to watch it, fully aware that now this potentially explosive item was squarely in my own lap.

Watching the tape, I could only wince at the ready-made sound bites it contained. The instructor tells the class his purpose is to instill in them the "enforcement mind-set." He tells them that their "niche" is to be the ones who "take no prisoners." Certainly embarrassing stuff, especially in the atmosphere of the time. The press could use the sound bites to build a television drama designed to enrage a public already adequately enraged about the IRS.

But evidence of a crime? No. The instructor was careful to say that all IRS guidelines must be followed. In substance, it was just an inappropriate pep talk. The big risk would be the appearance of a cover-up if we seemed to be concealing the tape from Congress when we knew it was investigating this very issue.

I had already been chewed out once by political advisers at the treasury for sending information to Congress without a long clearance process. But I figured that holding on to this tape while treasury people debated about it was like sitting on a ticking time bomb.

The next week, I sent the tape along with some routine material to the Senate staffers who were working on this stuff. We never heard anything about it again. One pseudoscandal averted.

Besides dispelling external accusations of cover-ups in the face of investigations, I viewed internal communications as a vital part of the change process. People throughout the agency knew things that I should know about problems in the agency, but information could be filtered—or stopped—as it moved through the layers of management. Having an outlet for their views also provided people some relief from the stress of the relentless external criticism and massive internal change.

A key part of my first message to all IRS employees was on this topic:

> *An important part of teamwork is honest and open communication with each other and with Congress and the public. We cannot solve problems that we do not acknowledge.*
>
> *As an initial step, I plan to spend as much time as possible over the next two months meeting with you and especially learning about the front-line work in the districts and service centers. I invite you to send me your views on matters that you think will be helpful to me in learning about the IRS and how it can work better.*[3]

Over the next five years, I received thousands of comments and messages from employees. Some were just gripes, but many were valuable in helping me and my top management team understand more concretely how things were working. What was most important, our encouragement of this informal message flow was the signal that management wanted to know what was really going on, good or bad.

When we finally began to roll out an IRS-wide e-mail capability, the informal communications flow became a lot easier. I could read the accumulated employee e-mails whenever I had a free minute with my laptop.

One day, an agent who audited large corporations sent me a message about what she felt was a long-standing error in the way the IRS treated the taxes on its own employees who received reimbursement for travel expenses. It seemed implausible that the IRS would be making such a mistake. Maybe it was a local problem or an isolated case. But figuring it was worth looking into, I passed the message to Bob Wenzel and suggested he get someone to check into it.

I could usually tell immediately when IRS people were coming into my office with seriously bad news. A few weeks after I forwarded the employee's message to Wenzel, a group with stone faces filed in very quietly, taking seats around my table as though they were sitting in church waiting for a funeral service to start.

Wenzel broke the news. The employee's e-mail was right. For perhaps ten years, the IRS had been failing to follow its own published rules on how employers must handle taxes on employees who were traveling on company business to a location for more than a year. In such cases, the employer was required to treat these reimbursements as taxable income, imposing employment taxes and withholding, and the employee was required to report the income on his or her tax return. The IRS had failed to comply with any of these rules for thousands of employees every year. Worse yet, most of the employees involved were the most highly trained agents, who tended to work for long periods auditing large corporations on-site.

At first impression, these facts presented a real horror story for the IRS. The public and Congress regularly expressed outrage at reports of even minor tax compliance failings by IRS employees. Failures of tax compliance by IRS employees were even included among the "ten deadly sins," the reform act's list of offenses for which employees must be fired. Now we had a situation of large-scale, systemic noncompliance by IRS management and thousands of its most highly trained employees.

But that was only the first impression. The situation got worse.

The specific tax rule that had created the problem was an unpopular one that affected many of the taxpayers being audited by the very agents who had not been properly taxed. These circumstances could only fuel the outrage and raise the obvious question of how such a problem could have persisted for so long at the IRS. And there was no quick fix for the problem, since the back taxes would have to be laboriously calculated each year for thousands of employees and based on information that could only be obtained from each employee. Then there were the state taxes. We would have to work with most of the fifty states to pay the back taxes owed them. All this would keep the issue alive for months, if not years, while we worked with the problem. Finally, there was the little problem of the money to pay the taxes, plus interest, none of which, of course, was budgeted.

It was an extreme example of the kind of self-inflicted wound created by an organization unwilling to face up to bad news. Obviously, someone, sometime, had noticed this problem before. But after it went on for a while, it was such a messy problem that no one addressed it, which only made the problem worse. Now we had to deal with it.

We immediately set up a task force to figure out how to calculate and pay all the back taxes and to make sure that we handled the issue correctly in the future. We worked out the best process we could for employees to file the necessary returns and pay the taxes. We communicated what we were doing to all the interested parties, including the employees union, the inspector general, the Treasury Department, and the key congressional committees.

The silver lining in a very dark cloud was that we found the problem and were fixing it ourselves. It was not uncovered by an audit, a press story, or a congressional investigation. This fact alone was so powerful that, to my surprise, the problem never became a major public issue. Another good lesson about facing up to bad news.

Admitting a Mistake

We were not always successful in catching our own mistakes before they blew up, however.

Among the deceptively simple mandates in the reform law was a provision requiring the IRS to notify a taxpayer before it contacted third parties, such as banks or employers, about the person's tax return.

The intent of the provision's sponsors was straightforward—to save the taxpayer potential embarrassment by giving him or her a chance to provide information before the IRS asked someone else for it. But, as written, the provision covered *any* contact by the IRS about a taxpayer. A dozen different kinds of contacts covering millions of cases were covered by this mandate. One revenue officer asked me, "What do I do if no one answers the apartment door when I'm trying to collect money? Can I ask someone walking by in the hallway if so-and-so still lives here, or do I have to first notify the person I haven't been able to find that I'm contacting the neighbor to find him?"

Under crushing pressure to implement the numerous mandates in the reform law, the IRS staff came up with a solution to this seemingly simple but broad third-party-notice requirement. It drafted a standard flyer to be included in every one of the millions of letters sent to taxpayers about an exam or a collection case, saying that the IRS "may need to contact third parties. Third party contacts may include, but are not limited to, neighbors, employers, employees and banks. We may use these contacts to help us determine your correct tax liability, identify your assets or locate your current address."

As word of this flyer got out, it created an uproar. A law intended to save taxpayers embarrassment over normally rare third-party contacts in audits instead was creating a fear that the IRS was planning mass waves of contacts with anyone the taxpayers knew.

Sponsors of the original provision, including Senator Kit Bond of Missouri, who was chair of the Small Business Committee, were not only outraged, but also suspicious that the whole thing was a plot by the IRS to undermine the reform law. "It appears that the IRS has decided to dust off its old, subversive tactics with this daunting notice," said Bond.[4]

Now that the problem was out there, the question was what to do.

There was no doubt that the IRS's simple, if offensive, flyer complied with the law. In fact, the treasury lawyer who worked on the provision intentionally provided for a broad, generally worded, notice. Some of our own lawyers recommended that we stand by our position, a stance that some congressional staffers, who understood that the IRS flyer complied with the law, fully anticipated (even while they geared up to savage us for doing so).

We concluded that the best course was to admit publicly that the flyer was a mistake and to ask outside tax professionals and key congressional players to help us find a reasonable solution. We especially wanted to take away any basis for the charge that the IRS was deliberately defiant, and we wanted to share the burden of coping with the law's maddeningly deceptive difficulties.

"We made a mistake, and we're going to fix it," I told the Associated Press. "This third-party notice does not represent the first-rate service we must give taxpayers."[5]

As I found over and over again, most of the IRS's severest critics were willing to suspend disbelief and give us a chance to work with them. When we did so seriously, two things happened. First, they began to get over the idea that the problem was caused by bad intentions and they started to focus on practical solutions. Second, they began to understand the real trade-offs and difficulties that often constrained solutions.

For months, our third-party-notice task force labored over the issue. Ably led by Beverly Babers, a talented lawyer who worked on special projects, the task force consulted with tax practitioners and Senator Bond's staff to devise a far better, although still not perfect, solution to the notice problem.

From this and many other experiences, we developed a slogan to summarize the approach that worked best in dealing with stakeholders: "Engage, then decide." We tried first to share information and options with affected stakeholders before making a decision; then we tried to make a clear decision. The contrasting approach, "Decide, then explain," meaning to decide secretly and then to try to explain the decision to the people affected, usually didn't work.

Saying No—Regardless of Who Is Demanding Yes

I always tense up a little when driving on the long, high bridge over the Chesapeake Bay, on my way from Washington to my farm in Maryland. I usually don't use the cell phone on the bridge. But when the car phone rang at 6 P.M. on Tuesday, July 3, 2001, I picked it up. As I drove onto the bridge, I started to register the heart-stopping information I was hearing, trying my best to keep my hands steady on the wheel.

Ninety million taxpayers who were expecting to receive special tax refund checks of up to $600 might not get them until weeks or months later. Getting this money out to stimulate the drooping economy was the highest-priority program in the newly elected Bush administration and was the highest-visibility project in the IRS. And now it seemed about to crash.

Computer production runs had already started. A bug in the program apparently slipped through the testing and was found only by an auditor reviewing paper notices already printed. All we knew was that there seemed to be an error in the computations for some taxpayers. No one could tell what the delay might be until we could find the problem and fix it in the ancient computer codes of the IRS master file.

The problem showed, only too obviously, the frightening vulnerability caused by the IRS's continued reliance on the forty-year-old master-file software. We were working on replacing this software through our modernization program, but for now we were still depending on it. The tax code provision directing the special refund—seemingly simple—actually contained subtleties that reduced the amount of the refund based on how much the taxpayer had paid and whether he or she had used certain tax credits. Only four programmers understood the part of the master-file software that implemented these provisions, and only one was fully qualified to make the most sensitive changes.

But the problem also showed the resourcefulness that IRS employees used to overcome these problems. Calling people in to start round-the-clock work on the problem, the IRS team, led by our crack trouble-shooter, Dianne Grant, found out that the key programmer had taken a printout of the code with him to the beach just in case something came up during the production runs. By the time the members of the team assembled on the morning of July 4, they had already begun to pinpoint the problem. Amazingly, by the time of an 11 A.M. conference call, we could make a reliable decision on how to proceed. The problem affected only about 0.5 percent of the taxpayers, and we would have to send these few taxpayers a corrected notice explaining their refund. But, since the checks themselves had not yet been cut, we could send all taxpayers their correct checks with no delay.

It was a close call, but in the end, the IRS sent correct checks for over $34 billion to eighty-four million taxpayers in a matter of months.

Little did I know that this crash project to send out eighty-four million checks was going to be the easy part.

Before we even finished sending out all the checks, Congress was working on still another tax bill to send out a second round of checks to about forty million taxpayers who didn't qualify under the provisions of the first law for the full amount of the special refund.

By now it was October 2001, only three months before the IRS had to start processing tax returns in the coming tax season. The terrorist attacks on September 11 and the anthrax mailings created unprecedented problems in protecting IRS facilities and employees. These events also created new demands for assisting taxpayers affected by the attacks. Because of extra work from the special refund and hundreds of other tax law changes, preparations for the filing season were mostly in red status, meaning that we were at high risk of a delay in the start of processing in January. We were reduced to trying to recruit retired programmers in an attempt to stay on schedule.

With the help of Treasury Assistant Secretary Mark Weinberger, we appealed to congressional committees to help us develop a practical plan for this second round of special refunds. We came up with an option to get the extra money out to taxpayers as they began filing returns the following year—only a few months later than the draft bills floating around Congress. We sent letters to the senators and members of the House and prepared briefings for the committee staffs. But we also made it clear that there was no practical and responsible way to get another round of refunds out by Christmas, which had suddenly become the Capitol Hill rallying cry.

I knew we were getting into dangerous territory when one of the most aggressive committee staffers said he wanted to personally interview the IRS programmers to find out why they couldn't work faster. We invited all the interested committee staffers to meet with the IRS experts who were handling the intense preparations for the upcoming filing season, including implementation of the tax code changes.

To underscore immediately how seriously I took this matter, I arranged for the meeting to be held in a conference room right next to my office. The room was so packed with staffers from the Hill, the treasury, and the IRS that some people were standing against the walls and in corners. I came in the side door from my office, quickly greeted everyone, and sat down at the table, with people crowded around and behind me.

The aggressive committee staffer immediately showed us what kind of meeting this was going to be. In response to my polite attempt at preliminary small talk, he snapped, "We're here because we can't understand why the IRS can't issue these refunds on the schedule the Congress wants."

Trying to be as positive as possible, I replied that our job was to do what Congress wanted and that we had done that in everything Congress had asked. In this case, we had been trying to figure out the best way to get out the refunds as quickly as possible. This required a series of steps that must be followed in a project like this. I handed out a summary of the time line of steps we had taken on the last special refund and asked our expert to run through it.

Thirty seconds into the explanation by our expert, the staffer who was dominating the meeting grew red in the face, leaned across the table, and moved from being merely hostile to abusive: "We want the refunds out this year, and we want you to tell us how to do it, not that you can't do it. Why is the IRS spending all this time explaining why you can't do something, instead of finding a way to do what we want done? We don't care if there are errors, we don't care if it is 99 percent. We just want to get something out, and if there are some errors, we'll tell people not to worry about it."

One of the IRS people noted that taxpayers would be confused if some of them started getting checks just before they expected their regular refund checks in the filing season.

"We're not worried about that," the staffer snapped. "Nobody will care as long as they get more money. And maybe a few morons out there won't get the word that another check is coming, but we can't make policy worrying about a few morons."

By now, there was deadly silence in the room. People were looking down at the table or the floor. But the staffer wasn't finished. He moved on to making a threat: "And if you talk about the filing season, you better have a perfect filing season, because if we don't get what we want, we will be expecting perfection, and you will hear about it big time from us if anything goes wrong. If you would do this for us, we would tell the inspector general not to bother you, but if you don't do it, you can expect to hear from the inspector general regularly at our request."

At this point, I stopped the discussion. "We really want to be able to give you and the Congress what you want," I said quietly. "We don't like at all being in the position of saying no at this meeting. It would be a lot more pleasant meeting for us if we just saluted and said, 'OK, we'll find a way to do it.' But sometimes we also owe the Congress our best judgment, even when it is not what the Congress wants to hear." I ended by stating plainly where we stood. "Our view is that it is not a realistic possibility to get forty million more refunds out before the end of this year and that any attempt to do so will pose serious risks for the tax filing season and millions of taxpayers."

By the time Congress adjourned for the year, the issue had died a natural death because Congress never could agree on a bill. Had we agreed to the committee's demands that we make an all-out effort to get ready to send out refunds by Christmas, we would likely have created a major problem for taxpayers by delaying the start of processing in January, and would have done so for what turned out to be a proposal that was never even passed.

(The aggressive staffer did, however, try to make good on his threat. We got a copy of a request containing three pages of detailed questions, from the staffer to the treasury inspector general, for an audit to find any errors the IRS made in issuing the special refunds the previous summer.)

This episode shows another dimension of the importance of honest communication, no matter how tough the going gets. In this case, the essential but unwelcome communication was from the IRS upward and outward. Just saying yes was not a responsible option, regardless of who was demanding it.

The Real Test

The sky was a perfect blue, the water on Long Island Sound was calm, and the air temperature was ideal at 8 A.M. in Port Jefferson, New York. I was sorry I was only walking across a parking lot to a conference with about seventy-five managers from the IRS's campus in nearby Holtsville. I would rather have been taking a long walk along the harbor.

By 9:30 A.M., I had finished my part of the meeting and was ready to drive to the Holtsville facility when my special assistant, Joanne Sullivan, stopped me. Two planes, she said, had just crashed into the World Trade Center.

Over the next hour, the situation changed minute by minute. At first I thought we should go over to the IRS center and at least do a town hall meeting, but I soon realized that this would not be possible. Within an hour, as we heard of the attack on the Pentagon and the evacuation of the White House, we were able to cobble together a conference call with Bob Wenzel, Dave Mader, and Mark Matthews, our criminal investigations chief who was in contact with the other law enforcement agencies. We decided to close all but a handful of IRS facilities around the country and send all employees home. We also sent out an all-employee message stressing our commitment to their safety and asking them to check voice mail the next morning for another update.

As we watched the unfolding situation on television, the horrible magnitude of the events of the day sank in. Planes were grounded around the country. No one knew how many other attacks might come or what form they might take. Carol Landy, the executive in charge of the IRS center on Long Island, told us that many employees were in shock and in tears as they left the building, partly because many had friends and relatives who were in or near the World Trade Center. We began to think that we would have to keep the whole IRS closed for at least the rest of the week, until we could get some better idea of the threat. When we heard that President Bush was going to speak to the nation that night, we scheduled another conference call for after his speech.

In his short address, President Bush said that the government would be open for business the next day. His tone conveyed that we could not let this event, massive as it was, stop the country from functioning. This made our decision easy. Within ten minutes, I sent out an all-employee message, referring to the president's speech and saying we would reopen for business the next day. There would be special attention to security, I stressed.

I left Long Island at 5 A.M. the next day in a car driven by two special agents. It was eerie to drive through Brooklyn on highways nearly deserted except for emergency vehicles. Crossing the Verrazano Narrows Bridge, we could see the smoke from the World Trade Center fires in the distance.

On the cell phone the whole way to Washington, the questions were multiplying faster than the answers. They didn't stop when we got back to the IRS building. Our number one priority was finding out the status of the hundreds of employees who worked in or near the World Trade Center itself. Miraculously, all but a few were accounted for, but we wanted to track everyone and communicate to our New York employees the exact situation.

Employees everywhere wanted to know what we were going to do about security. As we were discussing security issues, people were shuttling in with messages about other urgent problems: The airlines were not able to make their excise tax deposits. The Office of Management and Budget wanted numbers on the cost of our security upgrades that day. A bomb threat was called into the IRS New York midtown office. The White House wanted every law enforcement agency to contribute trained people to be sky marshals, starting immediately. Tax practitioners were calling every line at the IRS, plus my personal lines at home, frantically asking for relief from filing deadlines.

The IRS deals every year with local disasters such as floods, hurricanes, and earthquakes. Usually the president declares a disaster in certain cities or counties. The IRS then extends filing and payment deadlines and provides special assistance to taxpayers in those geographic areas. Immediately after September 11, IRS managers tried to follow these procedures. But within hours it was clear that they wouldn't work.

Taxpayers all over the country were affected because people traveling were stranded, accountants' offices in New York were destroyed, and planes were grounded, preventing people from getting back to their records at home or in offices. Victims on the crashed airplanes, visitors to New York, and workers at the Pentagon might have lived anywhere. We did not want to force victims of the attacks, who had suffered such grievous losses, to worry about taxes. Yet, not every taxpayer, even in New York City or Northern Virginia, was affected. Treasury Department representatives started worrying about a financial crisis if the tax receipts dropped drastically at the same time the bond market was shaky. Taxpayers and their representatives frantically wanted answers.

We knew we had to announce some relief immediately, and we knew we couldn't get all the details right in a matter of hours. On Thursday, September 13, we put out an announcement extending some deadlines and promising to revise our guidelines after getting feedback.

On Friday morning, Treasury Assistant Secretary Weinberger and I decided that we needed to get knowledgeable taxpayer representatives together with the IRS and treasury to discuss options and get their support. Within two hours, people from all the key tax groups—accountants, lawyers, small- and big-business representatives, charities—showed up at the IRS to give us their suggestions on how we could provide relief to all who needed it without making the government insolvent. The gravity of the situation overcame all other factors and caused people to do their best to give specific, well-considered advice. They came up with various options, including a short delay in the immediate deadlines for filing and payment for everybody in the country, followed by more fine-grained relief for those more directly affected.

That afternoon we put out revised instructions in accord with what the representatives of the tax groups recommended. We called the representatives of the tax groups back to ask that, in the national interest, they advise their clients to use this broad relief only if necessary and not just as a cash-flow device. They all agreed.

For the next two months, we kept up the dialogue with the many stakeholders and rapidly resolved dozens of specific issues, such as identifying the victims who were entitled to special relief legislation passed by Congress, defining how charities could be set up for the victims, putting up a special victims hot line, and working on solutions for businesses whose tax records were destroyed. Our communications channels with taxpayers and tax professionals were tested as never before. With few exceptions they stood the test.

Coping with Catastrophe

Because of the very special impact on employees in New York, Wenzel and I made several visits there to deal with practical issues like finding space for employees whose offices were destroyed. Mainly, though, we listened to the concerns of employees who had gotten out with minutes to spare or who had seen people jumping out of windows. Wenzel also visited most of the ten processing centers to get direct feedback on local problems in protecting against bioterrorism and other threats. Sadly, we also attended the funeral of David Bernard, an IRS agent who was killed by falling debris from one of the twin towers.

Within days of the attack, the IRS offices in lower Manhattan were back in operation. By early January, we completed urgent preparations at all the essential facilities to protect our employees and our operations. Employees continued to work with minimal effects on productivity. Our communication approach had helped the organization recover from the first impact of the catastrophe.

Even in normal times, the IRS receives a regular flow of suspicious packages in the avalanche of incoming mail. Most are hoaxes, but some are serious enough to require shutting down a large facility. In 2000, during peak season, we had had to shut down one of the IRS's largest processing centers because of an envelope containing an apparently harmful chemical. These events caused huge traffic tie-ups and tremendous anxiety among employees, one of whom was a pregnant woman who went into labor prematurely.

The September 11 terrorist attacks, followed a month later by the widely publicized incidents of letters containing anthrax sent to government offices, stimulated an upsurge in threats and hoaxes, some of which required shutdowns of large processing centers. A puff of white power emitted from an envelope led to the shutdown of the IRS center near Cincinnati on October 10. Even when there was no need to shut down an entire facility, local newspapers gave prominent coverage to every incident that might be a sign of an attack.

"The FBI was investigating Tuesday the contents of a letter containing a suspicious substance at the Internal Revenue Service center," reported the *Kansas City Star* on October 24.[6] "The shadow of anthrax fell briefly over yet another federal agency yesterday while the Internal Revenue Service anxiously awaited test results on an employee at its sprawling regional service center in Northeast Philadelphia," reported the *Philadelphia Inquirer* on October 30.[7]

Every scare at an IRS facility multiplied the anxiety created by the terrorist attacks and the anthrax incidents. Every employee knew that the IRS would soon be receiving trailer loads of mail at each center every day as taxpayers filed returns in the upcoming filing season. Shutting down for even a few hours could wreak havoc with the tax system. Yet, we had to assure ourselves and our employees that we were not taking risks with their health and safety. Resolving this dilemma became a dominant issue in the minds of our whole top management team, because we had no clear answers.

Wenzel and a security task force were working day and night, consulting with experts in and out of the government, on how to protect our facilities and employees while continuing to operate. Colleen Kelley, the new president of the employees union, and her staff worked closely with the task force as they developed practical options.

Through almost daily messages, we reported to the whole work force what we were doing, what we were considering, and what the facts were about the threats and hoaxes in various IRS locations. By January, when the mail started flooding in, the employees understood that the essential preparations were in place. The filing season went smoothly.

Over my five years at the IRS, we encountered dozens of mistakes, setbacks, potential disasters, and problems big and small: delays in computer modernization, unexpected problems in fixing Year 2000 programs, glitches after the reorganization, inspector general and GAO reports about IRS failures, taxpayer returns shredded by the employees of a lockbox bank, backlogs in processing certain taxpayer claims. The list is long and will continue to be long.

In any big, complex organization undergoing as much change as the IRS was experiencing, life is never smooth, decisions are not always proven right, and progress is uneven. The only common theme we developed to deal with this reality was to own up to it and to promise honest, two-way communication with the people who had an interest in what we were doing. Our practice of sharing information as we gained it, even when it was sometimes incomplete or subject to change, allowed us to maintain a regular flow of communication, rather than allowing speculation to build while we remained silent.

But following this policy goes against the natural grain. It often seems safer and easier to wait to communicate: Wait until we've got more information; wait until we're more sure of what we're going to do; wait until we've settled certain issues; wait until some other event has passed; maybe wait and see if the problem just goes away. For all these reasons, or just from pure inertia, we would sometimes fail to follow our own policy about open communication or would just go through the motions rather than truly engage with people. The results were almost always bad. "Engage and decide" really does work better than "decide and explain."

CHAPTER 13

Why People Think the IRS Picks on the Little Guy and Lets the Big Guy Get Away

Making the IRS Effective at Enforcing Compliance

"IT IS WELL KNOWN that the average person has to pay his taxes, while it is the rich people who get away with not paying," said a well-spoken caller when I visited the Diane Rehm radio show shortly after I became commissioner. Continuing in a matter-of-fact tone, he asked, "So now that there is a captain of industry as IRS commissioner, how can we be sure that the rich people won't now get away with even more?"[1]

I knew that many people in all walks of life held the same belief that this caller did—that the IRS picked on the little guy and let the big guy get away. And recent press reports were feeding this widespread belief.

The taxpayers who testified about mistreatment by the IRS at the televised Senate hearings were not big guys. One was a small construction contractor, another a medical professional, and a third a priest.

If anyone who heard these taxpayers' stories missed the point, follow-up television stories hammered it home. Quoting Jennifer Long, the IRS employee who had testified at the 1997 hearings, NBC correspondent Lisa Myers reported: "Long says she almost never is told to audit anyone rich. Instead she is sent out to pick on the poor or defenseless."[2]

Leading publications published front-page stories, such as these in the *New York Times,* that harped on this theme:

> "Reducing Audits of the Wealthy, IRS Turns Eye on Working Poor" (December 15, 1999)
>
> "IRS More Likely to Audit the Poor and Not the Rich" (April 16, 2000)
>
> "Affluent Avoid Scrutiny on Taxes Even As IRS Warns of Cheating" (April 7, 2002)

The IRS sent millions of notices each year to individual taxpayers about errors in their returns and sometimes called them into the office for an audit. Hearing and reading stories about rich people and big corporations getting away with cheating on taxes led many people who got these notices to wonder, Is the IRS just picking on people who can't fight back?

I sometimes witnessed incidents that aggravated such perceptions. In one office audit—a sort of abbreviated audit for relatively simple returns—I listened as a taxpayer who worked part-time as a freelance engineer met with an IRS auditor. As the auditor reviewed the taxpayer's records, it became clear that the IRS had made a clerical error that caused this return to be selected for audit. But once the IRS agent looked at the return, he also found a small taxpayer error, which would require the payment of a couple hundred dollars in additional tax. The agent patiently explained why he was not permitted to ignore this error, and added that the tax code would let the taxpayer get the money back in the following two years. Visibly upset, the taxpayer launched into a series of complaints about how the IRS makes life hard for small businesspeople.

A few famous people reinforced popular perceptions, with memorable lines about how taxes were for other people, but not for themselves—that is, not for the rich ones and smart ones. A billionaire real estate and hotel owner, Leona Helmsley, who was convicted of tax evasion, was quoted by her housekeeper as having said, "Only the little people pay taxes."[3] Myron Scholes, a Nobel Prize–winning economist who devised intricate tax-shelter strategies for a failed hedge fund, doubted that there were people who would *not* go to extremes to avoid paying taxes. "No one actually *pays* taxes," he reportedly snapped disdainfully.[4]

These cynical comments came to light only when the cynics were caught. As a result, the comments seemed even more memorable because they had the cachet of an important secret that was only accidentally revealed.

Finding Out the Truth

I realized soon after taking office that these public perceptions were more than mere resentments of the tax collector. And they had far more serious consequences than just an image problem. The American tax system is based on the willingness of all citizens to calculate and pay the taxes they owe, based on the understanding that, if they don't, the IRS will intervene. If the IRS is thought to ignore rich and powerful taxpayers who don't comply, the most basic principle of the tax system is undermined.

The compliance aspect of the IRS mission is to find out which taxpayers may not be filing, reporting, or paying what they legally should and, where necessary, to use its enforcement authority to make them comply. The words *compliance* and *enforcement* are often used interchangeably when referring to IRS activities. More precisely, compliance with the tax law by taxpayers is the IRS purpose, while enforcement by the IRS (such as seizing property, making assessments in audits, or doing criminal investigations) is one of the tools to achieve compliance. Referring to the IRS mission as enforcement is like saying that the mission of a police department is making arrests—a much easier task than its true mission of stopping crime.

I knew that it made no sense for the IRS to have ignored the big guys and picked on the little guys. More than two-thirds of the income tax is paid by high-income individuals and large corporations. IRS employees who worked on big taxpayers generally had higher salaries and more prestige than those who worked on small taxpayers.

And government agencies are very sensitive to bad press coverage. So why did so many people think the IRS focused on the little guy and let the big fish get away? How much of this perception was myth, and how much reality?

To answer this question I didn't need dark conspiracy theories or complicated statistics. The truth was that the IRS approach to enforcing compliance with the tax law was just as out-of-date as its organizational structure, its customer service, and its 1960s-era technology. In its compliance activities, the IRS was like a police department that was giving out lots of traffic tickets while organized crime was running rampant. The public's perception was not entirely a myth. The IRS did not intentionally pick on the little guy, but it was increasingly ineffective in performing the compliance aspect of its mission.

The business world is filled with examples of once successful companies that declined, or even went out of business, because they failed to adapt their strategy to changes in the economy. Downtown, general-purpose department stores declined as specialty stores, suburban malls, and big-box retailers better met the varied demands of many kinds of retail customers. Banks that could not provide the range of services demanded in the current market were acquired by other banks that could.

The IRS also made strategy decisions. It decided what categories of taxpayers were most seriously not complying; what errors, devices, or methods noncompliant taxpayers were using to reduce their taxes; and how tax-sheltering devices were being spread or promoted. The agency then decided what compliance techniques—ranging from warning letters to criminal investigations—would best combat each kind of noncompliance, and how the limited staff resources should be used to get the best results.

But the IRS did not adapt its strategy to the current economy. Over twenty years, the economy grew and changed dramatically, but the IRS compliance strategy failed to keep up.

Year after year, the IRS handled compliance the same way. Each district office and service center assigned its available staff of compliance employees to do as many of the same kind of audits or collection phone calls and visits as they could. When staff was growing in the 1980s and early 1990s, this meant doing more of the same. When staff declined because of budget cuts, it meant doing less of the same.

National projects would be established from time to time to focus on a special compliance problem—such as transfer pricing by multinational corporations—but the implementation of these projects was often watered down by local executives. If a local office started a good program to focus on a problem it encountered—like large banks using certain tax-shelter devices—the good program spread very slowly, if at all, beyond the office where it started. A lack of updated market research on what was really happening out in the taxpayer base hampered any attempt to make informed strategy changes throughout the agency.

By 1997, this failure to keep up with a rapidly changing economy made the IRS's compliance activities increasingly off target—often missing the most serious problems while spending valuable resources on less important ones. And the agency's failure to use modern auditing and collection techniques made the work that was done far slower and less effective than it should have been.

Obsolete Practices, Ineffective Enforcement

The IRS had ignored the dramatic increase in the 1980s and 1990s in the number of people with high incomes. The agency continued to manage its audit program for individuals as though incomes were still distributed as they were in the early 1980s.

One morning in 2001, I was meeting with a group of tax lawyers from the bar association. Such tax professionals who meet regularly with the IRS tend to be those with an interest in the tax system as a whole. They are often very helpful in explaining what is going on in the real world, and in pointing out problems with how the IRS is working. In this case, the lawyers also had a more direct interest in making the IRS more effective—they were losing market share to other lawyers and accountants, who were aggressively promoting tax shelters to their clients.

One of the lawyers acknowledged that the IRS was starting to fight corporate shelters in an organized way. But he wanted to know why the IRS seemed not to be doing anything about the very high income individuals who were also using these phony tax devices.

I noted that the IRS, until it reorganized in 2001, had put no focus on this segment of the taxpaying population. In managing its examination program, the IRS divided individual tax returns into classes by size of gross income. By 2001, 65 percent of the individual income tax was paid by taxpayers with income over $100,000. While the IRS still defined several income classes for returns with income under $100,000, it had only a single income class for all returns with incomes over $100,000, thus providing little information to manage audits on the taxpayers who now owed 65 percent of the tax. Even the well-informed lawyers in the room were stunned into silence. One said in astonishment, "$100,000 is your highest income class! My God, that's what we pay a first-year law associate."

Although the lack of resources had steadily diminished the number of audits the IRS could do, the audits the IRS was doing were often not the right ones, because of obsolete selection methods.

One morning, I went out with an IRS agent in Boston on an audit of a medium-sized construction firm. On the way over, I asked the agent why he had been given this company's returns to audit. He showed me a one-page paper form that an IRS reviewer had used to select the return for audit. Two checked boxes on the form conveyed that the likely problem was in the cost of goods sold. No other information was provided.

The audit was to be conducted at the offices of the taxpayer's accountant, a thirty-person accounting firm in business since the 1930s. We were met in a conference room with all the documents neatly laid out in piles. The accountants had put together spreadsheets cross-footing every one of the taxpayer's construction contracts with the financial statements and the tax return. All costs were clearly documented, and the results showed lower-than-average costs of goods sold and higher-than-average taxable income—the opposite of what the IRS selection form had implied. Within a half hour, it was apparent that this audit didn't need to take place.

When we met with the senior partner in the firm, he proudly said that in the last thirty-five years, it had not had an audit with the IRS that ended in disagreement with his work. From the work papers we had just reviewed, we could clearly see why this was true. The good-natured senior partner was pleased, but I was not. The IRS was wasting its resources and his time doing such audits.

Almost a quarter of the audits of individual tax returns were producing *no change,* meaning that the return was correct as filed. And audits of many more individual and corporate returns found only modest technical errors. The IRS used statistical formulas to select returns for audit. But the research data needed to feed these formulas was last updated in 1988, and the formulas themselves were still based on techniques developed in the 1960s.

The situation reminded me of the complaint Yogi Berra supposedly made about a restaurant: "The trouble with this restaurant is that the food is lousy and the portions are too small."

Bogged down in decade-long hypertechnical audits of large corporations, the IRS was missing the epidemic of tax shelters that had spread in the 1990s.

The IRS's practice was to audit annually the tax returns of the twelve hundred largest corporations in the United States, because of the large amounts of income they earned and the complexity of calculating their tax. But the average large corporate audit was not finished until five years after the return was filed. Some cases took even longer. Then, any unresolved issues would go to the IRS appeals office, which typically would take another two to three years to resolve the questions—and that's assuming it didn't go to court.

When I became commissioner in 1997, many IRS auditors were still working on corporate tax returns for tax years in the 1980s. I joked to the IRS people on these cases that they weren't auditors, they were archaeologists. They were digging out records and trying to make sense of transactions that had long since been forgotten by most of the people who worked on them.

But this long and sometimes unproductive time spent on auditing and appealing very old tax returns was no joking matter. Many issues in these long cases ended up with little or no additional tax paid, because they involved relatively technical legal issues that were eventually settled by the appeals office for small fractions of the amount in dispute. While our best-trained agents were being consumed with these old and sometimes routine cases—spending a decade arguing about how many years should be used to depreciate railroad equipment—some of these same taxpayers were failing to pay billions by using obscure and intricate tax shelters on current returns. And big accounting and law firms were busy spreading these shelters to more and more corporations, with little interference by the IRS.

The IRS was largely overlooking an ocean of money hidden in business entities for which the owners, rather than the businesses themselves, are supposed to pay the tax.

During a visit to Seattle, I met with an agent who was working on audits of twenty taxpayers who were using the same scheme to reduce the income reported on personal income tax returns. All were medical practitioners who received most of their income from insurance payments. Each taxpayer set up a trust and assigned most of his or her insurance payments to be received by the trust. The trust, with its own IRS-assigned identification number, filed a return with the gross income received from the insurance, usually amounting to well over $100,000, but paid no tax. (Partnerships and certain types of trusts and corporations are allowed by law to pay no income tax directly; instead their income is supposed to be reported by their owners on their individual returns.[5] These are known as flow-through entities because their income flows through to its owners.)

The medical practitioners showed salary income of $10,000 to $20,000 on their individual 1040 tax returns, with no itemized deductions. These returns were too small and simple to require much payment of tax—or to trigger any interest by the IRS. The taxpayers counted on the IRS not to make the link between the trusts and the individuals who owned them—and without the link the taxable income would just magically disappear. In this case, the local agent did make the link because an honest taxpayer told the IRS about the accountant who had advised the taxpayers to set up their trusts.

But this case was an exception. For years, the IRS had run no organized program to focus on the links between flow-through entities (trusts, partnerships, and S corporations), which paid no tax themselves, and their owners, who were supposed to report the income. The flow-through entities reported the net income to the IRS on information documents (usually a form called the K-1) similar to the familiar W-2 statement that employees receive from their employers. But unlike W-2s, the IRS had no program to computer-match these twenty-three million documents to the returns of the individuals who were supposed to report the income.[6]

Meanwhile, the amount of money coming into these flow-through entities was growing to almost unimaginably huge proportions. By the year 2001, over seven million entities reported more than $6 trillion of gross income and more than $800 billion of income flowing through to owners. Millions of these business returns showed *net losses* on hundreds of billions of gross income—a lot of people doing a lot of work just to report that they were losing money. Yet the IRS audited only a tiny percentage of these entities—one out of every 255—and few agents were trained to follow these intricate relationships.

Promoters of all stripes—ranging from small accounting firms to outright scam artists—were advertising on the Internet to sell schemes that used these flow-through entities to hide income. But the IRS had no systematic program to identify the promoters or the taxpayers who were buying their schemes.

Continuing the traditional approach of selecting one individual return and auditing what was on the return, the IRS was a bit like the man who was walking around in circles under a street lamp late at night. When a police officer asked the man what he was doing, he replied that he was looking for his watch. The officer asked where he had lost the watch. The man replied that he had lost the watch in the middle of the block but the light was better here at the corner.

The IRS, however, was not just failing to find a lost watch. It was essentially overlooking a vast sector of the modern economy.

The IRS was allowing its most powerful enforcement tool, its criminal investigators, to be increasingly diverted away from tax crimes.

In California, I met with a small team of IRS criminal investigators, auditors, collectors, and lawyers who had caught up with a particularly abusive taxpayer who was making a fortune operating clinics for workers' compensation cases. He had accumulated four houses and lived lavishly, but by his use of various false devices, he had reported no income at all—for his businesses or for himself—for years. Acting on a tip, the IRS team began investigating. When the taxpayer realized the IRS was on his trail, he tried to leave the country. The IRS team was able to put together enough information to get legal authorization to seize the taxpayer with $3 million just before he crossed the border. But cases like this, in which the criminal investigators worked on important tax cases, were becoming the exception rather than the rule.

The IRS criminal investigators, known as special agents, for years have been known as the most effective financial investigators in the world. Although expensive and time-consuming, criminal prosecution is the most effective deterrent available for tax evaders, many of whom are white-collar professional people who do not expect ever to be spending time in jail. Because they are among the few IRS enforcement actions that are not secret, criminal prosecutions also can be publicized to explain to the public the risks of evading taxes.

Yet, the number of criminal tax cases investigated by the IRS had been declining for years. Why? Because its criminal investigators were working on nontax cases that they thought were more interesting. These cases were brought to the agents directly by local U.S. attorneys, and in the absence of effective direction from IRS management, the agents chose the cases they considered more glamorous, such as chasing drug dealers.

Judge William Webster, in a report that I requested after the 1998 Senate hearings, documented how the IRS's criminal investigation component had suffered from "mission drift." A smaller and smaller proportion of the IRS's very limited criminal investigation resources were being devoted to investigating tax crimes, and cooperation with the IRS's civil enforcement divisions had fallen to minimal levels. With no effective central management, in many areas of the country, criminal tax cases were considered low-priority, boring work—an attitude that the special agents sometimes explicitly conveyed to their fellow IRS employees.

The IRS was like an army that failed to use its heavy artillery to support the infantry in battle because the artillerymen preferred to fight in a different war.

Even when the IRS knew that a taxpayer owed money, its obsolete methods of collecting debts were so slow as to be often ineffective.

Collecting overdue debts is not rocket science. The most important principle is simple—the longer you take to start collecting, the lower your chances of getting the money. If you wait too long, even honest debtors may not have the money to pay.

Statistics on commercial debt collection show that the chances of collecting what is due are 93 percent after one month of delinquency, 28.4 percent after one year, and only 12.5 percent after two years. Yet a year or two past the due date is when the IRS's revenue officers—the best and most expensive collectors—would typically start working the case.

The IRS collection process had not changed materially since the early 1980s, when the agency implemented a telephone collection system. But even then the overall system was never redesigned, leading to a

FIGURE 13-1

Debt Collection over Time

Widely known statistics show that the likelihood of collecting a debt declines rapidly as it ages. At twenty-four months, the time when IRS revenue officers typically got their collection cases, the probability of collecting was already down to 12.5 percent.

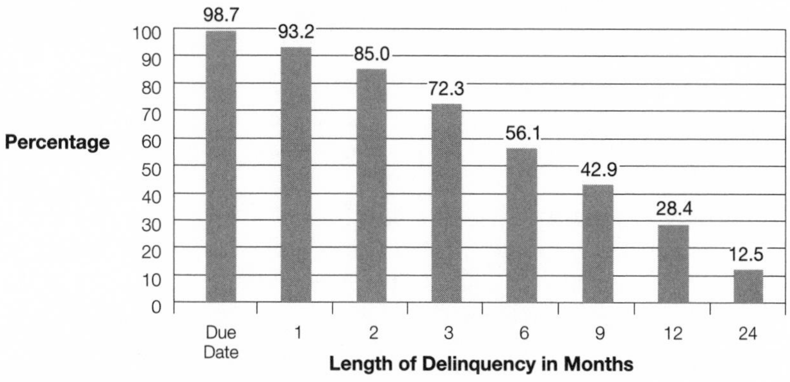

Source: Commercial Law League of America

complex, linear, and slow process in which first letters, then telephone calls, and finally visits would be used for nearly all delinquent accounts.

As with customer service, the IRS compliance strategy remained frozen because it was so deeply embedded in the old organizational structure and technology of the IRS. Under these structures and systems, consistent changes of any kind were slow and expensive. The ancient technology made it difficult even to add a few more high-income categories to the systems used to assign audits. The fragmentation of the organization and technology locked in slow and inefficient operation of routine activities such as audits and collections. In addition, because of the rigid, obsolete grading and pay system, the best agents could not be routinely assigned to audit high-income individuals. With no effective structure for managing criminal investigations, local preferences could divert the IRS's most powerful deterrent away from tax crimes. Finally, inadequate financial management provided little meaningful information on how money was really being spent.

Beyond these structural limitations, other factors contributed to the obsolete compliance approach. The narrow performance measurement system led to a counterproductive focus on the number of enforcement actions, rather than the IRS's effectiveness in fostering compliance. Promoters were largely ignored, and there was no systematic process to warn the public about common errors or tax schemes. Published guidance on technical tax issues was often years behind, while IRS agents wasted time auditing taxpayers on poorly understood issues. Lack of systematic communication with tax practitioners failed to tap this valuable source of information on what errors by taxpayers were most contributing to noncompliance, while lack of up-to-date research made the IRS statistical formulas for selecting returns to audit inaccurate.

Statistics or Not, the IRS Had to Change

Clearly, the painful changes the IRS was making in nearly every important dimension of its operations were every bit as necessary to tax compliance as they were to customer service. But I knew it would be hard to sell the unprecedented idea that the IRS could actually improve its effectiveness in compliance while dramatically turning around its treatment of, and service to, taxpayers. The challenge was convincing people inside and outside the IRS that the change would eventually work, while the statistics during the transition showed results going down.

When companies make big, wrenching changes, they usually suffer big, presumably temporary, drops in financial results, often booking huge restructuring costs that temporarily drive the bottom line far into the red. The IRS had no single bottom line and the government has no method of booking financial charges to recognize the reality of past mistakes or neglect. But the IRS still published its notorious enforcement statistics. When these statistical standbys began to drop, the inevitable buzz in the press and on the Hill began. In the spring of 1999, the *New York Times* reported that "IRS tax collectors, under intense pressure from Congress to be nicer to taxpayers, have drastically scaled back efforts to collect unpaid taxes, newly available statistics show."[7]

It was important but difficult to refocus our compliance managers and employees on taking enforcement actions when appropriate and to clear up the confusion created by the reform law's micromandates. In March 2000, for the first time in IRS history, we gathered every field collection manager in the IRS together for a week-long training session. The rumor throughout the agency was that we were calling the collection managers together to kick butt for the falling statistics. To make the atmosphere even worse, I was quoted in the press before the meeting as saying that our collection managers were "confused."

In the large, ornate ballroom of the Palmer House Hilton in downtown Chicago, six hundred IRS collection managers crammed into every available space, including the balconies surrounding the floor. Immediately I ticked off reasons why any reasonable person—including me—would be confused after being in the eye of the congressional storm, the target of two years of investigations, and on the receiving end of a flood of micromandates: "I would guess that about half of the stuff I deal with leaves me confused. So the question is, How do we learn to resolve the difficult and often confusing reality we face? We need to work together as an organization to clarify, learn, and move forward. That's what we're here for."

Once everybody realized that the meeting was to be a problem-solving session—and not a scolding—we spent a good part of the week working through practical issues and case examples, such as when to take an installment agreement and when to seize property. The collection managers began to realize that we wanted them to take enforcement action when needed, but not just to produce statistics. No one wanted to go back to the time when, as one person told me, a revenue officer could come to a manager with a collection case in which the taxpayer had brought clear proof that the whole overdue amount was an error, only to have the manager respond, "That won't help us with our numbers; tell him to pay up and claim a refund."

A CEO undertaking big and costly changes had better have some powerful supporters—board members or key stockholders—who are willing to see the changes through the tough times. I was fortunate to have this support from the three treasury secretaries I served under—Bob Rubin, Larry Summers, and Paul O'Neill. From my first meetings with Rubin and Summers (then deputy secretary), I acknowledged that some of our enforcement statistics would drop as we went through the

FIGURE 13-2

IRS Performance Trends

I used this chart to explain to Secretary Paul O'Neill in March 2001 how IRS performance of its compliance activities would first decline—because of the micromandates in the reform bill and reduced resources—and then would increase to surpass previous levels as the benefits of the modernization program were realized.

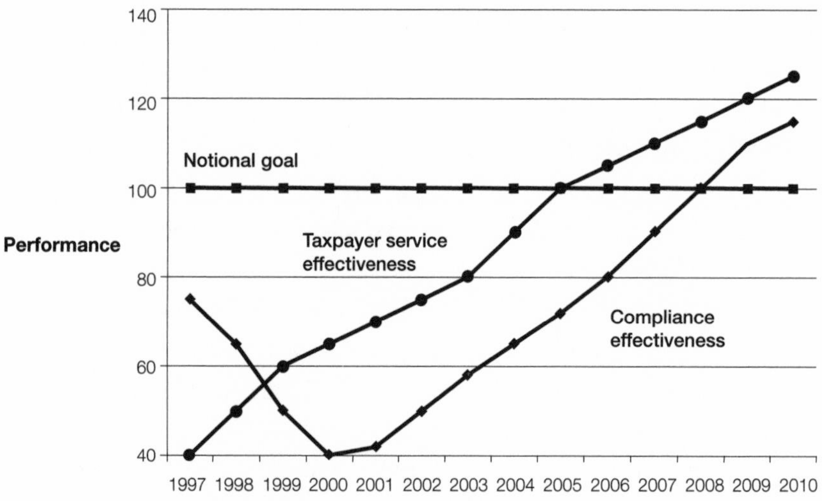

changes. When O'Neill came into office in 2001, I even presented him a time line showing my assessment of how the effectiveness of IRS service and compliance activities would first drop, and then surpass, previous levels.

Fitfully but steadily the clouds cleared, the focus returned, and the numbers followed. In March 2003, the inspector general reported that "while collection statistics have not returned to their pre-1998 levels, most of the downward trends were reversed in the last two years." The report added that "the use of collection enforcement tools, including liens, levies, and seizures, all increased substantially from fiscal year 2000 [to] fiscal year 2002."[8]

Attacking Designer Tax Shelters

The biggest gain would come not only from turning around traditional statistics but in making the whole compliance program more effective. The world had changed, and now the IRS was finally getting in position to deal with the new world—one in which seemingly respectable accounting firms, law firms, and investment banks packaged tax shelters for big corporations and wealthy individuals.

New York is the financial engineering capital of the world, so I had not been surprised on my first trip to the New York office in December 1997 to hear from IRS agents and lawyers about a court case in process against AlliedSignal, Inc. This industrial conglomerate, according to the complaint, had tried to shelter $400 million in capital gains generated in 1990 by the sale of a subsidiary company. The convoluted scheme involved a partnership set up between AlliedSignal and two temporary foreign corporations arranged to be in offshore jurisdictions, where they were not subject to corporate income tax. In a series of prearranged, rapid-fire transactions, the partnership bought $850 million worth of notes and sold them for different kinds of "indefinite installment" notes covered by a special tax rule. Supposedly, these transactions created a big gain for the tax-free foreign corporations and left AlliedSignal with a big tax loss to offset against its domestic gains. The net result was big fees shared by the promoters, a big tax savings for AlliedSignal, and a big loss for honest American taxpayers.

In the early 1990s, Merrill Lynch offered the same shelter to other *Fortune* 500 companies with large capital gains.[9] The IRS's New York office was auditing some taxpayers who had bought into this particular shelter, but the IRS then did not know all the taxpayers who had bought into it or others like it nationwide.

I was a little more surprised in a trip to North Carolina a few months later where I met with an agent who had become expert in another kind of tax scheme that was being heavily used by banks and other corporations to shelter income taxes almost at will. In a complex series of heavily papered transactions, the U.S. corporation leased a big fixed asset, like a city hall in Germany or a municipal rail system in Switzerland, paying up front most or all the amount to buy the lease. The foreign local government, however, would not get the money. Instead, the money was held in escrow to avoid any risk of the U.S. corporation's not getting paid back. The foreign local government would then lease the asset back from the corporation, using the funds in escrow to make the annual payments and, ultimately, to unwind the whole transaction. The American corporation essentially invested some borrowed or spare cash in a safe escrow account, booked significant tax savings on the relatively fast write-offs on the paper lease, and the foreign local government—not being subject to tax—took a nice fee for its troubles. The honest American taxpayer was again the loser.

The local IRS expert believed that one corporation had conducted in three years almost a hundred such lease-in/lease-out transactions. (This kind of transaction was dubbed LILOs and was pronounced like the character in the Disney movie *Lilo and Stitch,* but was not nearly as amusing.) The tax savings for this one corporation were possibly reaching $1 billion, and each transaction was a nightmare of paperwork to unravel.

Meanwhile, at the treasury and IRS headquarters in Washington, we were getting plenty of direct feedback from taxpayers and tax lawyers about abusive shelters. The treasury's numbers were showing corporate tax payments slowing, while corporate profits reported to their shareholders reached record levels.

Although the individual work of the field agents and lawyers was remarkable for its skill and dedication, the IRS could never win just by

FIGURE 13-3

Gap Between Corporate Income and Reported Income

Treasury data showed the ever widening gap between the profits that corporations were reporting to their shareholders (book income) and those they were reporting to the IRS (taxable income) during the 1990s.

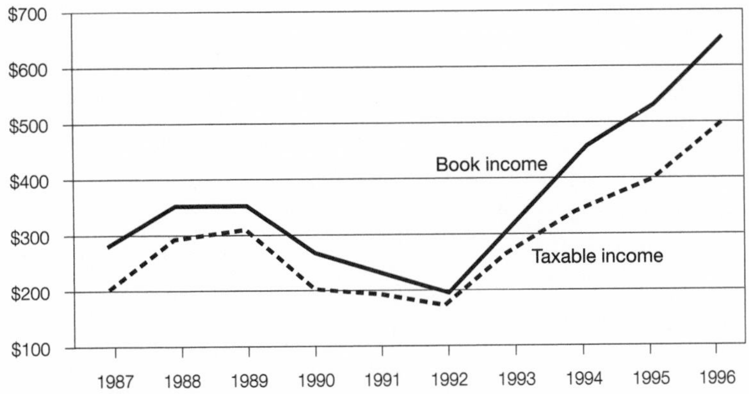

playing a one-on-one defense with huge taxpayers who were being sold phenomenally complex prepackaged schemes by fast-moving global banking and accounting firms backed up by million-dollar-a-year tax lawyers. The IRS was like a retailer that left each of its stores to fend for itself against competitors that were far better organized. In early 1999, Deputy Secretary Summers began pushing hard for a more comprehensive strategy—exactly what was needed, if not exactly what the IRS was yet well equipped to carry out.

But as our new organization came into operation in 2000, our large- and midsized-business division, which now managed the audits of all large corporations, was finally able to take on the tax-shelter problem with a coordinated strategy, working with the IRS counsel and the treasury staff.

There was noticeable shuffling and rustling in the audience when I announced at a meeting of four hundred executives in October 1999 that the IRS was starting a major initiative to find and stop abusive corporate shelters. Every major corporation had a high-level executive in charge of its taxes. I had talked regularly to these executives, who gave me a real sense of what was happening in the corporate tax world. Many of them were not happy about the phony tax-shelter deals, but when they turned the offers down, the aggressive promoters would sometimes go over their heads, taunting the CFOs about paying a higher effective tax rate than their competitors were paying. These executives, whether or not they participated in phony tax shelters, knew that this initiative was going to be the start of a big battle.

Not that we didn't occasionally kid about it. In one speech, I joked about an IRS agent who read his child the bedtime story about Cinderella. When the little girl heard about the pumpkin turning into the golden coach she asked, "Daddy, when they got that golden coach, was that ordinary income or a capital gain?" Someone in the audience immediately shouted, "It was a capital gain, of course." I shot back, "See, you tax guys count it as a capital gain even before checking what the holding period was."

The IRS tax-shelter strategy, as with all good strategies, was to use better knowledge of the market, more powerful tools, and more focused resources to be more effective—not just to do more of the same. In the new strategy, we would use long-dormant legal authority to require taxpayers and promoters to disclose potentially abusive shelters, and would focus more of our audit resources on these shelters. Working with the Treasury Department, we would also more quickly issue special legal notices warning taxpayers that specific shelters were not acceptable.

Larry Langdon and Debbie Nolan, who headed the large- and midsized-business division, set up a special hot line for taxpayers to report anonymously on shelters, established an office of highly skilled professionals to analyze them, and appointed executives to track down and fight each particular shelter. They began experimenting with newer analytical software to find shelters in corporate tax returns. And they began the arduous process of revamping the traditional audit process to allow for faster attention to high-risk areas.

The new IRS strategy—publicly endorsed by Summers in February 2000—drew big attention in the press and in the corporate community. Much as product announcements by big technology companies sometimes temporarily freeze the market even before the new product is delivered, the IRS announcements on tax shelters began to affect the market for these devices. Within months, several major corporations came in to settle on big transactions, only one of which the IRS audit teams had already found. By getting the information on these deals, including the names of the promoters, the IRS began to build a web of information on what was really happening in the market.

We found that these tax shelters had spread from large corporations to wealthy individuals. As more and more individuals realized paydays in the hundreds of millions, or even billions, from exercising stock options and selling companies, the promoters offered these wealthy individuals complex schemes to delay or drastically reduce the tax on these huge amounts of income. Sometimes the promoters were the same accounting firms that had audited the corporate books. In other cases, the promoters got leads from banks and investment banks. At the peak of the boom, most individuals who realized a large gain were being offered ways of sheltering the tax on it. As the IRS disclosure requirements and promoter audits proceeded, we began to get specific information on the thousands of individuals who bought into these complex shelters.

Despite stonewalling by some promoters and some other setbacks, the IRS's strategy gained momentum, because there was finally a sustained effort to manage its execution. The agency began for the first time in years to go to court to enforce summonses for records listing tax-shelter clients.

B. John Williams, the new chief counsel, energized the counsel's office to fight the promoters that resisted disclosure. Williams resurrected a tool so powerful it had rarely been used since it was authorized by the Supreme Court in the 1980s. The tool was the requirement of taxpayers in certain abusive circumstances to produce the work papers used by their accountants to accrue tax reserves on their financial statements. Williams worked closely with Langdon and Dave Robison, the head of the Appeals Unit, to develop nationwide coordinated legal positions on some of the most important tax shelters.

In August 2001, Merrill Lynch became the first promoter to settle with the IRS on disclosure of all the tax shelters it had sold. Later, the IRS announced settlements with PricewaterhouseCoopers and Ernst & Young.[10] These settlements were important because they provided the IRS the first systematic information about the many variations of shelters devised by big promoters, and information on who was buying them.

Other promoters continued to claim in court that various privileges allowed them not only to sell tax shelters but to keep them secret from the IRS. But apparently some of the promoters that sold these devices to their clients on the basis that the IRS would never find the shelters—and if it did, would never do anything about them—were not so confident when it came to their own taxes. Some promoters that had eaten their own dog food—using their own devices to shelter their own income—quietly filed amended tax returns, paying tens of millions of dollars of back taxes on the huge fees they had made selling these shelters.

The IRS's information on who was promoting and using these abusive devices grew rapidly. By November 2002, the agency had identified more than twenty-five hundred specific abusive transactions, which represented over $50 billion in taxes not paid. The information kept pouring in. Our experts believed we had just started to tap the mother lode.

In mid-2003, the IRS reported that 268 summons had been issued to obtain lists from promoters and that over four thousand shelter exams were completed or in progress.[11]

Finding Money in Tropical Isles

In March 2002, widespread press coverage of an unusual IRS enforcement action began to lay out one of the schemes promoters had been selling to enable taxpayers to flat-out hide income—or so they thought. "IRS Seeking Visa Records," the Associated Press headline proclaimed.[12]

In this case, we went to court to obtain records from Visa to help track down people who were using offshore banks in tax havens to hide income from the IRS. We also announced that we were already using records from MasterCard for this purpose, and that American Express had agreed to turn over records for accounts located in Antigua, the Bahamas, and the Cayman Islands. Getting these credit card records was a real breakthrough, because we could link them with the taxpayers' tax returns to find out how much income they were failing to report.

Promoted to a much wider audience than the more complex designer shelters sold to large corporations and superrich individuals, this offshore scheme relied on a simple credit card issued by a bank in a tax haven to solve one of the old problems with hiding money offshore—

getting the cash back. Setting up trusts or corporations in the tax haven country to stash cash from a U.S. business, the taxpayer would then use the offshore credit card, issued in the name of his or her foreign entity, to charge purchases or draw money from an ATM. How would the IRS ever know?

The IRS started to know because Joe West and Dan Reeves, two exceptionally resourceful agents in New Jersey, worked doggedly for years to find a way. West, a revenue agent with experience investigating fraud cases, and Reeves, a computer audit specialist, carefully studied a single criminal case against a banker. The case revealed that thousands of U.S. taxpayers were using his bank in a tax haven to hide income. This finding led them to suspect that the practice might be widespread. They then came up with a creative way to penetrate the promises of secrecy offered by tax haven countries: using records of U.S.-based processors to find taxpayers with offshore credit card accounts.

Eventually obtaining a court order to force MasterCard to produce a limited set of transaction records from a few tax haven countries, West and Reeves identified thousands of American taxpayers who were using these cards regularly to draw on hidden bank accounts—to pay for everything from airline tickets, to boat purchases, to filling up at the local gas station. People in all walks of life were doing it—rock stars, CEOs, engineers, authors, professional athletes, even law professors.

People using MasterCard accounts were by no means alone. Promoted over the Internet and by word of mouth, the scheme offered a deal for everyone. A simple Google search of the Internet in October 2003 for "offshore tax savings" produced over fifty thousand entries with enticing offers like this:

> OUR COMPLETE OFFSHORE PACKAGE
>
> *Going offshore should be simple and affordable. Accordingly, EDG has put together the Complete Offshore Package that includes* everything *needed to go offshore and maintain complete financial privacy. The Package includes an offshore company (IBC) complete with nominee directors and shareholders (if needed), an offshore trust, offshore bank account, offshore online brokerage account and offshore mail forwarding service. The Complete Offshore Package is $2,500.*[13]

West and Reeves had created a breakthrough with their pioneering work using credit card records. Their initial work showed that the problem was big enough to justify a major enforcement effort by the IRS. Dale Hart and Martha Sullivan, the executives in charge of civil enforcement, and Mark Matthews, the head of criminal enforcement, worked together to implement a nationwide strategy to find the promoters and taxpayers who were using such techniques to hide income offshore. A coordinated strategy was essential to handle the large number of important but complex cases, many of which involved recalcitrant taxpayers. Criminal investigation was the best technique for nearly all promoters and for many individual taxpayers, who all too willingly participated in schemes to hide their income. Civil audits and penalties were appropriate for many more. And the team worked out a limited voluntary disclosure initiative for taxpayers willing to pay all taxes, interest, and some penalties in exchange for helping the IRS track down promoters.

A Scheme for Every Market Niche

In most businesses, new products and services will emerge to fit every market segment in which there is money to be made. So it is in the tax business. Most taxpayers can't afford complex tax shelters or offshore bank accounts. But promoters are ingenious at finding, in every income bracket, market niches of taxpayers who are all too gullible, or all too willing, to avoid taxes by buying a tax scheme tailored to their situation.

For years, promoters had been peddling to African Americans a scheme based on the false notion that the tax code contained a special tax credit to pay reparations for slavery. The promoters would charge a fee to prepare a tax return claiming a refund for a phony credit, usually $40,000 per person.

In 2000, this scheme started to spread rapidly, and in 2001, the IRS received about eighty thousand of the refund claims, which totaled over $3 billion in fake claims. The IRS caught and stopped 99 percent of them, but a few did get through. These checks from the IRS in turn lent credence to the false claims of the promoters.

The IRS developed a strategy of aggressive publicity on television and in local newspapers and cooperated with local political and other community leaders to warn African American taxpayers that there was no slavery reparations credit. This education strategy, combined with prosecution of promoters, quickly reduced drastically the number of slavery reparations claims by early 2002.

But we knew that variations of this scheme, and others still to be invented, would continue to be marketed by unscrupulous promoters. In February 2003, as the tax season ramped up, the IRS published a "dirty dozen" list to warn taxpayers of the most popular tax schemes. In addition to slavery reparations, the list included a scheme supposedly allowing individuals to deduct most of their personal expenses by setting up phony home-based businesses, and another telling retired people how they could file for a refund of all the social security taxes they had ever paid.

Clamping Down on Wealthy Corner-Cutters

Tracking down promoters of schemes like offshore credit cards to hide income, or phony slavery reparations credits to claim refunds, is extremely important. But it was only one part of the job of finding people who were underpaying their taxes. The IRS also needed a strategy for finding underpayment of taxes on the *trillion dollars* of income received by upper-income taxpayers from their businesses. The IRS had an especially weak understanding of the wealthiest taxpayers, almost all of whom owned all or part of businesses. Fewer than 2.5 percent of the returns of individuals with income over $1 million were audited, even though these taxpayers owed almost as much tax as the one thousand largest corporations, 100 percent of which were audited every year.

We needed a whole new strategy for this critical part of the taxpayer population. With the new organization in place, we finally got one.

It was devised by Joe Kehoe, Dale Hart, and Martha Sullivan, the leaders of one of the diverse teams that we had formed to manage major parts of the IRS. After thirty years as a public accountant, management consultant, and senior executive at PricewaterhouseCoopers, Kehoe came into the IRS in 2000 to head the small-business and self-employed division, the largest single unit in the new IRS. He was just as amazed as I was to find out how far behind the times the IRS auditing practices were, often startling his staff with blunt comments about them. Kehoe's deputy, Dale Hart, had started her career as an auditor in Brooklyn and had held compliance jobs all over the country, but had never before served at headquarters in Washington. From the field, she had seen first-hand how the IRS could go seriously off-track chasing enforcement statistics, and now was determined to make the IRS compliance programs attack the right problems. Martha Sullivan was one of the few IRS career attorneys ever to transfer to a top-level line job in the IRS, taking responsibility for all the compliance activities in Kehoe's division.

In February 2002, after months of planning, they proposed to me a radically new plan for revamping the entire compliance program for individuals with business income. The plan shifted IRS priorities in two major ways. First, we would divert much more of our audit staff to auditing individuals with incomes over $100,000 and even more to those with incomes over $1 million. Second, we would change the focus of audits from checking the items that these taxpayers reported on their returns, such as whether their deductions passed muster, to finding income that was not reported at all on the return—such as income stashed in partnerships or corporations controlled by the taxpayer. The idea was to look for the big money that was not being taxed, rather than just what was easiest to check.

Although the ideas behind this plan seemed like common sense, implementing them required a multiyear program of retraining agents, establishing new audit selection formulas, paying greater attention to the complex links between individuals and their many businesses, and setting up close coordination with tax-shelter experts, attorneys, and criminal investigators. To illustrate the challenges of the new approach, the team presented me with a diagram showing the links between one wealthy individual and his business interests. It had twenty-five boxes representing different corporations, partnerships, and trusts—some located outside the United States—and dozens of lines crisscrossing the page, showing the links between them. Auditing one such individual could take ten times as many staff hours as an average audit of an individual return would take, and required much more advanced skills.

Since the IRS had no additional staff for this plan, implementing it also meant making hard decisions on where to take the resources from. It meant that many individuals and corporations that should have been audited would not be—a highly undesirable situation. But we knew that with the new plan, the IRS would be doing a better job of using its limited resources, by allocating more of them to the most serious cases of noncompliance.

If It Sounds Too Good to Be True, It Probably Is

More effective targeting of taxpayers who were hiding income was a critical part of the strategy. But the larger objective was to stop people from buying into such schemes in the first place. Every taxpayer prevented from going down the wrong path was saved from incurring big penalties or jail time. And the IRS was saved many resources that could be applied to those who failed to heed the warnings.

As part of the reorganization, the IRS established its first systematic program of warning taxpayers and tax professionals about both ordinary mistakes and schemes offered by promoters. A key part of the strategy was working with trade and professional groups, which had far more credibility with their members than did the IRS alone.

One morning, our taxpayer education group arranged a meeting for me with the executive directors of two dozen specialized medical societies. With Matthews from the criminal division and Hart from the small-business division, we discussed how promoters go to medical meetings and try to lure doctors into their schemes to hide income. Many of the participants agreed to publish articles and alerts in their newsletters, with real examples of doctors who had been ruined by buying into these schemes. One such article appeared in a February 2002 issue of an American Academy of Otolaryngology publication, headlined "Unscrupulous Trust Promoters Target Medical Profession."[14]

In business, publicity, advertising, and dealers are often far more efficient methods of reaching customers than are one-on-one direct sales. We were now applying this principle in the IRS, where communications, education, and partnerships with organizations such as associations were becoming a key part of the compliance strategy.

Good Intentions, Bad Results

Serious tax compliance problems were not limited to high-income taxpayers and corporations. The IRS had long been criticized by Congress for incorrect payment of refunds of the earned income tax credit for low-income taxpayers. This program offered to low-income working families a cash credit in the form of a refund based mainly on the number of children they supported. By 2000, more than eighteen million returns—about one out of every seven filed—were claiming this credit. Of the $30 billion the IRS paid out, studies showed that about 25 percent, amounting to $7–8 billion per year, was paid in error.

No matter how well intentioned, any government program that year after year pays out billions in error is a fat target for critics. In 1997, Congress had passed a special appropriation for the IRS to reduce incorrect payments under this program. For five years, the agency tried all the conventional techniques—prosecution of tax preparers who prepared returns with false claims, education programs for taxpayers, and audits of hundreds of thousands of returns claiming these credits. Although these audits usually involved nothing more than a letter requesting documentation that the child lived with the taxpayer during the year, they were still counted in the published enforcement statistic, giving rise to accusations that the IRS was unfairly targeting the working poor. "The Internal Revenue Service sharply increased audits of the working poor last year," the *New York Times* reported in March 2002, "while reducing to record low levels those of the highest-income Americans and big companies."[15]

By 2002, it was clear that the traditional strategy was not working. Even while the IRS garnered bad press for doing too much auditing of the poor, the error rate in the program stayed high and the number of erroneous dollars paid out increased year after year. It was the quintessential example of a well-intentioned but poorly operating government program.

The essence of the problem was that the program used a traditional process, designed to *collect* money from people who had enough money to pay taxes, to *send out* money to people with few resources. Once the money was sent out, it could not usually be retrieved. All a local tax preparer needed was the name and social security number of a child under eighteen, and the preparer could file on a computer in a few minutes a return that would very likely cause the IRS to send the taxpayer a check averaging $1,600 in three to six weeks. Even with four hundred thousand of these returns stopped and audited—the most the IRS could do with the money appropriated—millions of incorrect returns got through. Ironically, although this process didn't stop most of the bad refunds, it did impose a real burden on thousands of honest taxpayers whose refunds were stopped for up to a year until they could be audited.

The program nevertheless resisted fixing. Supporters and critics of the program were in an uneasy standoff, which effectively allowed the unsatisfactory status quo to continue. Advocates for the poor and their congressional allies saw the program as a way of distributing money to low-income people quickly and cheaply, and opposed anything that they thought might interfere with the flow of money. Critics of the program in Congress were not entirely unhappy with the opportunity to get regular headlines criticizing the IRS for sending out billions in wrong refunds, but were leery of taking strong action against a program helping poor workers. And then there were the small groups of economists, in the Treasury Department and Washington think tanks, who had spent whole careers studying the program; these experts seemed to be all too willing to study its problems forever while finding fault with all the proposed solutions.

With the support of Secretary O'Neill, an IRS and treasury task force in 2002 developed a practical proposal, based on extensive analysis, to fix the real problems with the program. The key change would require about a quarter of taxpayers who wanted to file an earned income tax credit claim—those for whom IRS data showed that the risk of an error was highest—to send supporting documentation to the IRS in advance. By using this and other information to screen refund claims, the IRS could reduce the number of erroneous refunds paid by billions of dollars a year while also reducing the risk of delay for some taxpayers with correct claims. By greatly reducing the error rate, these changes would also reduce the long-term political vulnerability of the program.

In 2004, it was still an open question whether the IRS would be able to overcome the forces for the status quo and be allowed to implement its plan to fix the program.

Auditing a Few to Avoid Auditing Many

Apart from a few special areas such as the earned income tax credit program, the IRS did not know how many dollars of taxes were not paid that should have been. It did not know who was failing to pay taxes. And it did not know why these people were not paying. Once a leader in using statistical techniques, by the late 1990s the IRS was using data so old that a large fraction of returns selected for audit should not have been chosen, and many that should have been selected were not.

Historically, to gather data to measure how much tax was and was not being paid, the IRS conducted extremely intensive line-by-line audits on a large random sample of taxpayers. Known as the Tax Compliance Measurement Program, these audits were popularly derided as "audits from hell" or "an autopsy without the benefit of dying." People who had undergone such audits decades ago often could still recall the details—finding birth certificates to prove when the children were born, trying to find receipts for minute expenses like postage, even trying to prove how much cash they put in the church collection basket each week.

In 1995, the IRS had proposed another round of 150,000 hyperintensive audits to gather data. The uproar was so fierce that the program was stopped cold, leaving the IRS with nothing but its increasingly out-of-date information from the 1980s.

To me, the dilemma was obvious as early as 1997. Without meaningful current data on who was and was not paying what was owed, the IRS would become increasingly inefficient, ineffective, and burdensome. But the traditional method of gathering this data was the third rail of tax politics—touch it, and you die.

Meaningful measures of tax compliance were not only critical for managing the audit program. They helped keep the whole focus of the IRS on solving the right strategic problem—getting people to pay all the taxes they owe. The drift toward an ever narrower focus on enforcement statistics had been driven in part by the simple fact that statistics were available to measure enforcement, while numbers measuring tax compliance were not available. The IRS had become like a business so focused on the quotas for its sales force that it became distracted from the basic purpose of its whole sales and marketing program—to increase market share as efficiently as possible.

Beginning in 1999, I asked some IRS experts to begin thinking of more efficient, less intrusive ways of getting the data we needed. By 2001, Keith Taylor, an innovative IRS executive, and Mark Mazur, a brilliant economist who recently joined the IRS as head of research, came up with a new proposal that required far fewer and far less burdensome audits to get the data needed. After many meetings with Congress, tax professionals, and small-business groups, we convinced most stakeholders that the IRS had developed a truly better way of getting the critical information to manage the tax system. Secretary O'Neill gave us the go-ahead, and by late 2002, the program was under way.

Big Opportunities Ahead

Years of work still remain to make IRS's compliance programs work as well as they can and should.

Meaningful information on which taxpayers are failing to pay what they owe is just starting to be available. This information, together with improved statistical techniques now available in the private sector, holds great promise for pinpointing which tax returns—and which issues on them—need attention from the IRS.

By completely revamping its collection process to intervene much more quickly with precisely the right technique—letters, phone calls, or visits—when taxpayer accounts become delinquent, the IRS can collect billions more tax revenue and can reduce the burden on taxpayers from interest and penalties.

The IRS can also make audits more effective and reduce the burden on taxpayers by revamping the audit process so that it begins more quickly. Other improvements to audits include making all the relevant data available to agents before they start an audit, more rigorously focusing the audit process, and greatly accelerating the resolution of issues through appeals.

More precisely targeted taxpayer education and warning programs can reduce the numbers of taxpayers who make common errors or buy into phony tax schemes. Developing effective partnerships with industry and practitioner groups will also help in this effort.

The agency can save itself and taxpayers much time by more quickly issuing notices and other technical guidance on murky tax issues and emerging tax schemes.

These and many other improvements can increase the effectiveness of the IRS's compliance programs while protecting taxpayer rights and reducing taxpayer burdens. However, nearly all these major potential gains will require investments in technology and business reengineering. All of them depend on recruiting and retaining high-quality, well-trained professional people as well as technology.

Well-run businesses understand that changing the way business is done is an essential and continuing part of staying competitive, not an occasional exception to business as usual. Managing continuous change to stay current with the economy and to improve the agency's internal processes is just as important for IRS compliance programs as for a business that intends to stay competitive. Success requires a long-term commitment to rethinking the way business is done and a willingness to invest in people and technology.

Even if, over the coming years, the IRS is very successful in continuing to improve its own effectiveness, these improvements can contribute only part of what American taxpayers need and deserve—a fair and efficient system for collecting taxes. Regrettably, the tax system has been steadily deteriorating since the early 1990s, at great cost to all honest taxpayers.

CHAPTER 14

The IRS Can't Fix the Tax Code and the Budget

What Honest Taxpayers Should Demand

"WHAT DO YOU REALLY THINK, Commissioner Rossotti?"

Politicians and reporters used endless variations of that question to try to get me to take sides in the latest political fight about the tax code or the president's budget proposals. And why shouldn't they? A quote from the IRS commissioner on the tax code or the budget would be good for at least a debating point in a speech or a paragraph in a news story.

But one of the most important decisions the leader of any organization makes is which fights to take on. In business, if you take on the wrong competitors in the wrong markets, you can ruin your business. In government, if you take on the wrong political controversies, you can ruin yourself and accomplish nothing.

From my first day as commissioner, I knew that the job of overhauling the IRS would inevitably involve as many controversial issues as anyone could possibly handle. To resolve them, I would need as much support as I could muster in the administrations for which I worked and in Congress. Stepping into politically charged debates about the tax code or engaging in public disputes with the administration about its own budgets would serve only to gratify the cynical reporter who asked me early on if I was taking on a suicide mission.

I wasn't on a suicide mission. I was on a mission to make the IRS perform better for taxpayers.

So I adopted a personal policy for my term in office: I would not talk about the merits or demerits of the tax code, and I would publicly support the administration's budget for the IRS. This policy worked. For five years, I enjoyed broad support for the IRS modernization program, under two different presidential administrations and from both political parties in Congress. As a result, the IRS was able to implement the array of changes described in this book, and it began to turn around its performance.

Improving the IRS is important, because the agency administers and manages the vast tax system that allows our democracy to function. It makes a difference how well the IRS executes this role. But no matter how much the IRS improves, it alone cannot make the system fair to honest taxpayers.

In my last report to the IRS Oversight Board, I broke my own guidelines about talking about the tax code and the budgets. Despite my inherently optimistic nature, I felt compelled to say without exaggeration that, when it comes to the tax system, America is winning the battle but losing the war.

Ultimately, the American people will have a tax system only as good as they demand from the president and Congress. But in the last decade, the presidents and Congress have not been giving Americans what they deserve. Instead, the elected leaders have consistently made politically expedient decisions that are leading to a steady deterioration of the system, to the enormous detriment of all honest taxpayers. How?

First, the president and Congress decide what tax laws are passed—and under both political parties, they have been passing more and more laws that place increased burdens on honest taxpayers and the IRS.

Second, the president and his agents in the Office of Management and Budget effectively control the resources the IRS has to administer these laws—and under both political parties, the administrations have been steadily shrinking these resources.

Since the early 1990s the president and Congress have been making these hugely contradictory decisions year after year. As a result, an enormous and growing amount of tax that should and could be collected continues to be left unpaid. In 1999, taxpayers failed to pay about $277 billion that they should have paid. The IRS was able to follow up and collect about 17 percent of this amount, leaving about $230 billion uncollected.[1] This vast amount of unpaid tax is growing every year.

Every honest taxpayer in every income bracket—from the $30,000-a-year wage earner to the $1 million-a-year businessperson—is in effect paying a 15 percent surtax to pay for these free riders. This free-rider surtax has nothing to do with the endless popular debate over whether the tax code benefits or penalizes rich, middle-income, or poor taxpayers—it just lets *every* honest taxpayer at *every* income level proportionately subsidize taxpayers who are not paying what they owe.

Even the free-rider surtax is not the biggest reason honest taxpayers should care about the continuing deterioration in the IRS's capacity to administer the tax system. The American tax system works only because most people honestly pay what they owe *without* intervention by the IRS. As the number of people cutting corners on taxes increases, so does the number of their friends and business competitors who start to think, "Everybody else is doing it and getting away with it, so why not me?"

Capitalizing on this attitude, promoters and some tax professionals continue to sell a wide range of schemes to taxpayers in all brackets. These schemers base their practices on the simple premise that they can probably get away with it. And millions of taxpayers continue to take them up on it. Already, about six million taxpayers surveyed say that they will cheat as much as they can get away with.[2] Many more say that they will cheat a little.

There is no reason to expect that millions more will not follow in their footsteps if the entirely contradictory trends since the 1990s continue—increasingly complex tax laws, and fewer and fewer resources for the IRS to administer them. Tax revenue called for by the tax code will be paid by a smaller and smaller fraction of taxpayers, and the revenue shortfalls will add to the already huge budget-deficit projections. The eventual consequences of such a downward spiral for our country and our economy are intolerable.

That does not mean the situation is hopeless. It was possible to make the IRS work better and the agency continues to improve; likewise, it is possible with practical steps to make the whole tax system work better for honest taxpayers in every tax bracket. The necessary practical steps are easy to understand. They have all been proposed before and would not require far-reaching legislation: The president and Congress must simplify a few key provisions of the tax law, outlaw tax shelters, and provide the IRS with the resources to do its job.

Tackling the Tax Code

Everyone who talks to the public about taxes tries to find a good way to get across the almost unimaginable size and complexity of the tax code. The late Senator Moynihan of New York sometimes carried around to interviews a book containing the text of the latest tax bill. It was the size of the Manhattan telephone directory, and he thrust it out to show how physically thick the latest tax bill was. Others complained that the tax code was longer than the Bible.

Preparing for a hearing, I once asked IRS tax experts to tell me how many pages the tax code really has. Weeks later, they came back somewhat sheepishly and advised me against citing any particular number of pages. They said the experts could not agree how many pages the code actually had and that any number I cited could be attacked by other experts as incorrect. (I'm not making this up.)

One big reason the tax code has so many pages, whatever the exact number, is that almost every page is a compromise over whose constituents are going to get, or not get, a tax break, and how much that tax break is going to "cost" in lost tax revenue.

The messy political process of changing the tax code does not happen just once or only rarely, like amending the Constitution. Instead the process has become nearly continuous. Every year, the president in his annual budget submission proposes tax law changes, and Congress passes tax bills, some large and some small. The few big showy provisions, like reduced tax rates or bigger child credits, get a lot of public attention. But there are usually dozens of smaller provisions tucked away in bills, many of which are ways of providing breaks or incentives for particular groups of taxpayers—people who adopt children, businesses that invest in certain kinds of energy production, people who save money for college tuition, and so on. The possibilities are endless.

As I was preparing for my confirmation hearing, I came across a provision providing a break for energy produced from certain kinds of "biomass." I wondered what this meant. One of the IRS legislative people explained that this tax break applied to the use of material less euphemistically known as chicken shit—a provision popular with the poultry farmers on Maryland's Eastern Shore.

Lobbyists and members of Congress work for years waiting for the opportunity to get their special provision into whatever tax bill looks as if it is moving. At the end of the congressional session, when tax bills often move, lobbyists act like refugees from a war zone, fighting to get the last seat on the last plane out. They crush in the hallways outside meeting rooms. Ultimately, the language of the bills is agreed on by staffers representing the key committee members and the treasury tax policy office, often working in the middle of the night to produce an inches-thick document. Senator Moynihan was fond of pointing out that no member of Congress ever read one of these bills before voting on it, and no one person really understood what was in it.

The differing political philosophies of Republican and Democratic presidents affect which tax breaks are proposed and who may benefit from them, but the bipartisan constant is this: Every year, a stream of tax code changes is proposed, and some are passed.

Who can defend such a complex and ever changing tax code? Few people even try (except for passionately defending their own favorite tax break, or "incentive").

Yet only once in the last fifty years—when President Reagan in 1986 threw the full weight of his presidency behind it—has a major tax code simplification bill that eliminated many special breaks and reduced rates actually passed. Almost immediately after the 1986 act, the trend toward putting more and more special breaks into the tax code began, and it shows no sign of slowing down. On the other hand, any broad proposal for simplification runs headlong into a dilemma: Tax code simplification would either increase taxes on millions of taxpayers by eliminating their special breaks or would cost hundreds of billions in lower tax revenue in a period when huge deficits are mounting. Perhaps that is why no such broad simplification proposals were sponsored by any presidential candidate in the 2004 primaries or general election.[3]

Perhaps someone, someday, will come up with an ideal, simple system that enough people can agree on for raising $2 trillion per year so that the existing tax code can be done away with. But for now, and probably for many years to come, taxpayers and the IRS are required to comply with the tax code as it exists—and as it changes every year.

Simplifying the Parts of the Code That Affect Most Taxpayers

Waiting until the whole tax code is simplified to stop the deterioration in the tax system is like thinking you have to boil the whole ocean to get a drink of water. The key to making practical progress *today* is recognizing that *most of the tax code doesn't affect most taxpayers.* For example, 83 percent of the tax code does not apply at all to the 71 percent of taxpayers who get all of their income from wages and investment income. By simplifying a relatively few provisions—those that create the most complications for most taxpayers—we could make much progress. My top three for action are family provisions, savings accounts, and the alternative minimum tax.

The tax code provisions that create the most complexity for the most taxpayers are those that define families and children. Approximately 44 million taxpayers claim children as a dependent exemption; 26 million claim the child credit; 19 million claim the earned-income credit; 6 million claim the child and dependent care credit; 18 million claim the head-of-household filing status; and almost 5 million claim the education tax credit.

If your eyes glazed over just reading that list, think of this—each one of those provisions requires taxpayers to satisfy different eligibility criteria, such as their relationship to dependents, their age and their children's age, and the support they provide for the household. Child-related information in the IRS's basic 1040 tax package and related publications runs to 202 pages. I still remember Treasury Secretary O'Neill's reaction to this information. He about leaped out of his chair. "How can we tell the public the Treasury Department has to define a child six different ways?"

The IRS National Taxpayer Advocate and the Treasury Department have proposed to simplify these family-related provisions by writing a uniform definition of a qualifying child. The definition would be based only on the relationship of the claiming taxpayer to the child, the age of the child, and the principal place where the child lived during the year.[4] This is an eminently sensible proposal that should be acted on.

In the derby for imposing the most confusion on the most taxpayers, the second-place prize goes to the bewildering array of separate provisions Congress has provided to taxpayers for tax-favored savings accounts. Roth IRAs, SIMPLE IRAs, 401(k)s, SIMPLE 401(k)s, 403(b)s, Education IRAs, and state tuition bonds are just some of the tax code provisions designed to encourage taxpayers to save money for worthy purposes such as retirement and children's college education.

The Treasury Department included proposals in the fiscal year 2004 budget to simplify these provisions by reducing them to just two flavors of tax-favored accounts, one for individuals and another for employers.[5] Congress should act on these proposals.

Another highly unusual provision of the tax code will inevitably require attention from Congress—the ominous and obsolete alternative minimum tax. Originally enacted in 1969, after testimony that 155 people in the United States with income over $200,000 paid no income tax in 1966, this provision was intended to make sure that very high income individuals paid some minimum tax, regardless of their deductions. Taxpayers who might be affected must go through a five-step process involving two, three, or four separate forms after completing all the other 1040 forms. If no changes are made in the tax code, thirty-five million taxpayers will be subject to the alternative minimum tax by 2010.[6] But the provision has outlived its original purpose, because very high income taxpayers who wish to shelter income employ techniques, such as tax shelters, that this provision does not address. The alternative minimum tax should be abolished for individual taxpayers.

If Congress simplified just these three areas of the tax code, without succumbing to the ever present temptation to complicate the simplifications, it would be taking a big stride toward reducing the time and money most taxpayers spend to comply with the code and to deal with the IRS.

Outlaw Tax Shelters

The second practical legislative step the Congress must take to turn around the deterioration of the tax system is to outlaw tax shelters.

Outlaw tax shelters? Aren't they already illegal?

Well, not quite.

Most of the complexity in the tax code is driven by rules defining taxable business income, which is the amount left over after expenses are subtracted from revenues each year. The inherent complexity of such calculations is evident from the enormous resources devoted to applying generally accepted accounting principles to the financial statements that businesses use to report their results to shareholders. The Financial Accounting Standards Board, an independent, standard-setting organization, regularly issues elaborate rules defining accounting standards; businesses maintain internal staffs of accountants to apply these rules, and the businesses pay large fees every year to independent accounting firms to certify that they have complied with the standards. The tax code is a parallel set of business accounting principles. It generally covers the same ground as do the generally accepted accounting principles, but with many exceptions and unique definitions set by Congress over many years.[7] This parallel accounting system to calculate taxable business income does not apply to most individual taxpayers, so they have little awareness of it. But it does apply to any taxpayer with business income, which includes almost all very high income individuals and all large corporations.

Supposedly reputable law and accounting firms have taken advantage of this inherent complexity to contrive tax shelters that seem to comply with all the technical requirements of the code while in fact serving simply to reduce the taxes on their clients' legitimate profit-making business activities. The accounting and law firms also earn fat fees for devising the shelters. As described in chapter 13, these tax shelters are usually disguised as enormously complicated investments, ranging from the leasing of city halls in Germany to the trading of stocks and bonds through foreign partnerships.

To challenge this kind of complex tax-shelter transaction, constantly reinvented by clever and highly paid lawyers and accountants, the IRS and the Justice Department must rely on a set of court cases going back to 1932 and setting forth ever changing versions of something called the *economic substance doctrine.* This doctrine is supposed to prevent taxpayers from reducing taxes by conducting transactions that may comply with specific sections of the tax code but that in total have no real business purpose other than reducing taxes. This court-evolved doctrine, which has never been written into the tax code by Congress, is a weak barrier to tax-shelter transactions by large corporations and very high income individuals.

In practice, large corporate and other very high income taxpayers have little economic risk and great potential gains by engaging in tax shelters. Likewise, the promoters stand to earn lucrative fees with little risk by devising new shelters. This combination creates a powerful "heads I win, tails you lose" incentive to continue this activity.

If the taxpayer is not caught, or is caught but wins a partial concession in IRS appeals or in court, he or she keeps a huge tax savings. If a transaction is identified and the taxpayer is eventually forced by the IRS or the courts to pay, the taxpayer has effectively secured a loan from the government. These taxpayers face virtually no risk of paying real penalties if they have a legal opinion that seems to support the transactions, which are deliberately set up to be complex and highly technical.[8] And there is no risk to the lawyers who give the supporting opinions to taxpayers. I am not aware of any lawyer who has ever been disciplined for giving a tax-shelter opinion.[9] This situation will not change as long as the IRS must combat this activity by relying on conflicting court decisions interpreting a vague—and contested—standard.

The economic substance doctrine needs to be enacted into law by Congress and interpreted correctly by treasury regulations. If this doctrine became the law of the land, the ambiguities created by inconsistent court decisions would be resolved. Acceptance of this doctrine would unequivocally inform business taxpayers that an investment that does not provide an acceptable return on a business basis—before considering taxes—cannot be converted to a good investment because of alleged tax savings based on legal technicalities. The prospect of removing the opportunity to use such technicalities to create shelters is why legislation is so vigorously opposed by promoters and tax professionals who stand to make millions by continuing their tax-shelter activity.[10]

Fund the IRS to Do Its Job

One might think that in deciding on the IRS's budget, the president and Congress would see a close connection, or least *some* connection, with the work that the IRS is required to do by the tax law. After all, administering the tax law is not optional. The government needs to collect the revenue that the law is supposed to produce, and the taxpayers need an organization to process their returns, maintain their accounts, and answer their questions. Certainly in any business, one would never plan for getting cash from customers without the means to bill and collect what is owed.

When I talked to business friends about my job at the IRS, they were always surprised when I said that the most intractable part of my job, by far, was dealing with the IRS budget. The reaction was usually "Why should that be a problem? If you need a little money to bring in a lot of money, why wouldn't you be able to get it?"

In an annual federal budget of over $2 trillion, it would not seem hard to allocate the funds, less than 0.5 percent of revenue, needed by the IRS to provide whatever help is needed by taxpayers trying to pay their taxes and to make sure the government collects what it is owed.

But after mandatory retirement and medical benefits, interest on the debt, and national security are taken off the top of the huge federal budget, only about 18 percent of it is left for everything else—from the IRS to an enormous array of activities, including such disparate items as the national parks, education, medical research, veterans hospitals, and the FBI. The fierce annual battle for this 18 percent slice of the federal budget consumes a big part of the political year. Most of the items up for funding in this ongoing political budget fight are more politically appealing than the IRS.

Since the early 1990s, the net result of the interplay in this political market has been to steadily shrink the IRS, despite the increasing size and complexity of the economy and the tax code. In the ten-year period ending in 2001, while Congress was passing dozens of new tax provisions every year and the number of tax returns increased by 16 percent, the IRS staff decreased by 16 percent.[11]

The IRS workload increased not only because it was collecting more money but because it was becoming a big administrator of government

FIGURE 14-1

Trends in Indicators of IRS Workload and Resources

Since 1991, IRS workload, by every measure, has increased substantially, while IRS staff has declined. Returns with over $100,000 of income increased by 342 percent, while IRS field compliance staff—the people who audit such returns—declined by 30 percent.

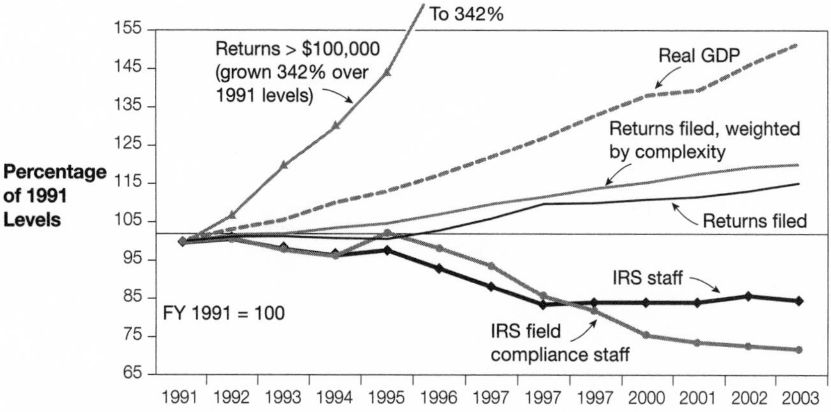

benefits. By the time I left office in 2002, the IRS was even starting to rival the Social Security Administration in the amount of money it *paid out,* because of the rapid increase in the number of credits and incentives in the tax code. In just five years, refunds issued by the IRS to individuals and businesses increased by 61 percent to $250 billion, an amount equal to more than half of what the Social Security Administration distributed for all its benefits. But there was one big difference: The IRS had proportionally only *one-quarter* as much budget available to collect taxes *and* distribute benefits as did the Social Security Administration—a well-managed agency with more modern computer systems—to distribute its benefits.[12]

But why, one might reasonably ask, would anybody outside the IRS care about the size of its budget? The answer is that it is all honest taxpayers, not the IRS, who are stuck with the bill when the IRS budget is cut.

When the agency's budget is inadequate, it means leaving more and more of its essential work undone—at a vast cost to honest taxpayers.

The cumulative effect of the growing economy and tax code and the shrinking IRS over a ten-year period was to create a huge gap between, on the one hand, the number of taxpayers who are not filing, not reporting, or not paying what they owe and, on the other hand, the IRS's capacity to require them to comply.

FIGURE 14-2

Comparison of Social Security Administration and IRS Programs and Costs (FY 2001 data)

Not only was the IRS collecting over $2 trillion, it was paying out $250 billion for benefits in the tax code, half as much as the Social Security Administration distributed. But the IRS budget was only $3.80 per dollar administered, compared with $15.30 for the Social Security Administration. The IRS was forced to leave a lot of its essential compliance work undone, leaving honest taxpayers to pay hundreds of billions of dollars for free riders who failed to pay what they owed and got away with it.

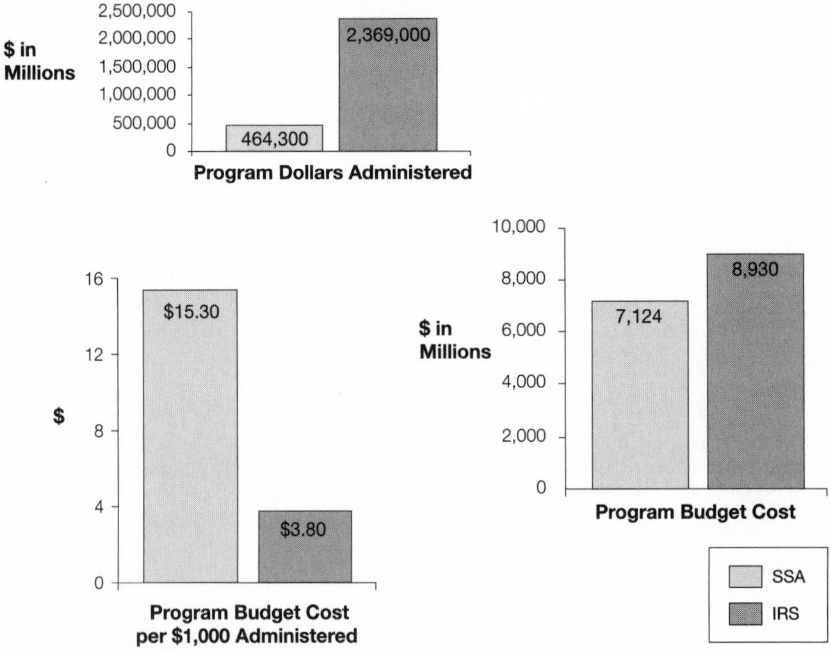

Source: Data from IRS research.

Program budget cost includes appropriated funds plus user fees. Program dollars administered equals gross tax collections plus refunds.

By 2002, the IRS was not even able to follow up on most of the cases in which it *knew* of specific taxpayers who were not paying, even in cases in which taxpayers were seriously abusing the system. Of the taxpayers who the IRS believed with high probability were either not filing returns at all, were using abusive trusts and overseas accounts to hide income, or were underreporting very large amounts of income, more than 70 percent could not be pursued because of the lack of resources.

The IRS is simply outnumbered when it comes to dealing with the millions of individuals and businesses that are not paying what they owe. It is like a lone cop seeing crooks robbing all four banks on the corners of the main intersection in town and having no choice but to just watch three of them drive away.

The enormous amount of taxes left unpaid comes to about $1,800 per year per taxpayer, more than the average annual refund. This free-rider surcharge on honest taxpayers *every year* is three times the amount of the special per-couple refund passed by Congress to stimulate the economy in 2001. By comparison, the savings from the Office of Management and Budget's cuts to the IRS budget request each year typically amounted to about $3.13 per taxpayer.

Never were so many paying so much to save so little, to borrow a formulation from Winston Churchill.

The Main Culprit: The White House

When newspaper editorials or political commentators occasionally criticize Congress for foolishly failing to provide enough money for the IRS to keep the tax system operating fairly and efficiently, members of Congress often react angrily, pointing out that they have "fully funded" the administration's budget requests. If the IRS couldn't do its job, they would say, it wasn't because Congress didn't provide the money requested.

And the numbers bore out this statement. For a few years in the mid-1990s, when Congress and the public were complaining about IRS management failures, Congress did appropriate significantly less than what was requested. But since 1998, Congress cumulatively passed more than 99 percent of the amount requested for the IRS. In 2002, in an almost unprecedented act, Congress actually passed slightly more money for the IRS than the president requested. If Congress was largely passing the IRS budget request, where then was the problem?

In the White House.

For five years, under two very different presidential administrations—one Democratic, the other Republican—I watched the process of deciding on how much IRS funding would be included in the president's budget work in the same, nearly mindless, way.

Every president wants to present a budget that appears fiscally responsible by holding the percentage increase in overall government spending to some politically acceptable number, like 4, 5, or 6 percent. After setting this ceiling, the president and his staff take dollars off the top for mandatory retirement and national defense programs and a few presidential priorities such as education or medical research. Then they give the small leftover slice to the Office of Management and Budget, the White House's budgeting arm, to allocate.

However, most of the other agencies competing for these OMB leftovers have influential supporters inside and outside the government. For these agencies, the OMB-approved budget, as the budget office itself well knows, is just a way station en route to Congress, where the budget is usually increased. But for the IRS, the OMB-approved leftovers are the end of the line. The IRS has no supporters lobbying members of Congress, contributing to political action committees, or knocking on doorbells before elections.

The result is an IRS budget that year after year barely covers mandated costs like pay raises. Its budget typically bears no relation to the responsibilities it is given by the tax code. Nor does the budget take into account the laws with which the public is required to comply, the growing volume of services the IRS is required to provide to citizens, or the tax revenues that these programs provide.

Incredibly, the OMB tries to appear fiscally responsible by neglecting the collection of its revenues and accounts receivable! No ordinary business in America could survive if it did this.

There is an old story about prisoners who have been locked up in jail together for so long that they don't need to tell jokes to each other anymore. All the jokes are numbered, and everybody agrees to laugh when somebody just calls out a number. The OMB budget process reminded me of that jailhouse story in one respect. Everybody in the IRS and OMB knew the jokes, which were OMB's budget evaluations, but everybody was required to repeat the shaggy dog stories every year, even though everybody already knew the punch line—no money.

One of the rituals every fall was a budget "hearing" in which each agency was given an opportunity to explain its budget request to the OMB officials responsible for evaluating the request. In October 2002, I trudged over to the OMB conference room near the White House for my last of these futile meetings. Four or five OMB budget staffers were on one side of the table with their boss, a midlevel political appointee. They looked very much like people who were doing their duty by attending the funeral of a distant relative but without wanting to hear anything much about the deceased. Although the meeting was scheduled for two hours, the OMB boss left after half an hour, and with only a few perfunctory questions, the meeting broke up another half-hour later.

I was shaking hands with one of the OMB analysts on the way out when he said, "I'm glad you will be gone before we have to give the IRS our passback," meaning that at least I wouldn't have to be there this year, when the OMB did what it always did—reject whatever the IRS requested. I replied that it would be better for everybody if the OMB just sent a cover note saying that there was no money available for the IRS budget request and eliminated the typical verbiage attempting to justify why the money was unnecessary. He said, "I understand that, but our bosses want us to write up a rationale for our numbers."

Sadly, I knew what he said was true. The OMB's staff had been reduced to thinking up so-called justifications for a budget that was actually driven by appearances and percentages. Their repertoire of techniques for such justifications was time-worn, proven to conceal what was really going on. One of the favorites was putting in money with attractive labels, such as "fighting tax shelters," while deliberately underestimating obscure things like the cost of legally mandated pay raises. They knew that, once the mandated expenses were paid, no money would remain for the advertised initiatives, but they insisted on including them, anyway.

The OMB staff had become like the finance staff of a large corporation that gave up making the necessary investments for the long-term health of the business, and instead used its skills to make the numbers look good to Wall Street for that year or quarter.

Unlike most of the important problems that the federal government faces, it would not take enormous resources to turn around the dangerous downtrend in the tax system. It would simply take a decision by an incumbent president and his budget staff to put the modest allocations required in the president's budget and to support them as they move through Congress. As detailed in my 2002 report, my recommendations can be boiled down to two key items:

1. *Fund technology investment to increase productivity.* In my report, I estimated that with extremely skillful management and adequate funding of technology, the IRS could potentially sustain a 3 percent per year increase in overall staff productivity. If achieved, this rate of productivity improvement would substantially exceed the average level achieved in the private sector over the previous decade. Over ten years, such productivity gains would produce the equivalent of thirty thousand additional staff-years of work, which would otherwise require around $3 billion per year in budgetary cost. The IRS was already realizing benefits from its technology investments. For example, it was closing paper-processing centers as electronic filing increased and answering more taxpayer inquiries through the Web site. Productivity gains of this kind would fill a major part of the gap in the IRS workload and would produce tens of billions of dollars per year in increased tax revenues.

   It is indeed difficult to manage such large-scale business and technology modernization programs, and some setbacks are likely to occur along the way. But the potential productivity gains are enormous. They cannot be achieved without investment in business systems modernization.

2. *Fund the IRS to rebuild staff each year for the remainder of the decade.* The IRS must receive budgets adequate to gradually rebuild its staff. Because of the continued growth in its

workload—which averages 1.5 to 2.0 percent per year—and the large accumulated deficit in work that should be done but cannot be, productivity growth alone, even at an aggressive level, cannot possibly close the gap. My report estimated that a net increase in staff of about 2 percent per year, together with a 3 percent per year productivity growth, could close the known workload gap by 2010.

If the IRS staff were to grow by 2 percent per year through 2010, the total staff would still be smaller than it was twenty years earlier, in 1990, whereas the economy is projected to be 86 percent larger and the tax system far more complex.

For this approach to work, the budget must provide for a net increase in staffing on a sustained yearly basis. In the past, projected net increases have not materialized, even when called for in the budget, because of OMB's numerous budget tricks, such as failing to pay for pay raises and other increased expenses. In other cases, increases in one year have been reversed by decreases the following year. In the IRS, "absorbing" a pay raise simply means cutting the number of staff-years available to do the work, which in turn means adding to the already large deficit in essential work that is left undone and taxes that are left uncollected.

Some critics argue that the IRS should solve its budget problem by reallocating resources from customer support to enforcement. In the IRS, customer support means answering letters, phone calls, and visits from taxpayers who are trying to pay the taxes they owe. Apart from the justifiable outrage it causes among honest taxpayers, I have never understood why anyone would think it is good business to fail to answer a phone call from someone who owed you money.

I am sometimes asked, "So why wait? Why not provide the money to close the gap now, as was attempted for the SEC?" In reaction to widely reported accounting scandals, the Security and Exchange Commission finally received a budget increase—63 percent in one year.[13] A big onetime increase like this will not work for the IRS. It takes time and careful management to hire, train, and deploy qualified professional staff and to implement complex modernization programs. Consistent but modest annual increases (the very formula recommended by the restructuring commission in 1997) are what is needed.

The taxpaying public in 1997 had a right to insist that the IRS change. The agency has changed. And taxpayers today have a right to expect the IRS to continue to improve its performance on all of its goals: service, compliance, and productivity. But taxpayers also have a right to demand that the president and Congress change the tax code and the budget to provide a tax system that works for all honest taxpayers. It is time for all parts of this problem to be addressed before the cost to honest taxpayers becomes unbearable.

EPILOGUE

What the Story Tells Us

THE LOBBY OF THE IRS BUILDING on Constitution Avenue has always seemed to me like a modern reconstruction of an ancient tomb. The ornate brass fixtures cast the harsh stone surfaces and classic columns in a foreboding light. The two-story atrium only adds to the gloomy feeling.

The tone in the IRS on the day of my swearing-in as commissioner matched the grim architecture where the ceremony took place.

Accusations of mistreatment of taxpayers, failures of management, and demands for firing people were rampant in Congress and the press. The attitudes of groups representing taxpayers and tax practitioners ranged from strained to hostile. Employees felt unfairly attacked for doing what they thought they had been told to do. Everyone had proposals for what the IRS should do, but few expected much to change for the better. Many people wished me well, as they would someone who was going to lead an army that seemed trapped in a hopeless war.

I signed on for the job after Robert Rubin and Larry Summers convinced me that the crisis presented a unique chance to turn around a huge and essential agency. But I soon found that they were a distinct minority in their own administration. The White House and most of the treasury staff viewed the whole thing as a tactical battle of the flak.

They acted as though my job was to edit press releases and fight fires, not to make major changes in the agency—and certainly not to make changes that would cost money or stir controversy.

I plunged in, fighting the fires and trying to rebuild relationships with stakeholders, but determined to do what I really came for—to make the agency perform better for taxpayers. As in any difficult business situation, I knew success would only come from solving pressing immediate problems while also making fundamental changes that could drive major long-term improvements. I wasn't sure I'd survive long enough to make the big, necessary changes. But since that was the reason I took the job, I figured I'd do my best. If it didn't work, at least I'd know it wasn't for lack of trying.

The lobby of the IRS building was also the scene of ceremonies during my last days in office. It looked just as depressing as when I started. (Spending money to fix up a lobby is not a winning move in a government agency.)

During those last days, five years from when I had first entered that lobby, I was still fighting the kind of fires that can, if you let them, consume all the time of any government official. In my last week in office, I was deciding how to cope with Congress's failure to pass an appropriations bill well after the start of the fiscal year. I was also responding to an absurd audit report alleging that the IRS could be liable for $27 billion in damages because of a dispute about a file sent to the Health and Human Services Department. And I was fending off the latest OMB trick to slyly slice the information systems budget.

Big problems remained. IRS performance still left much to be improved. Years of work remained on the modernization of its business systems, and some of the projects were well behind schedule. My own final report to the IRS Oversight Board identified the continuing, serious deterioration of the tax system, as promoters and taxpayers seized the opportunities presented by declining IRS capacity to administer the tax law.

But the whole tone of my last days couldn't have differed more from the tone five years before, the gloomy architecture notwithstanding. At the going-away ceremony, Treasury Secretary Paul O'Neill surprised me with the Alexander Hamilton Medal, for leading the turnaround. It was the highest award he could give me. Colleen Kelley gave me a running suit with the name of the employees' union plastered all over it, which she said was a token of thanks for "listening to employees." Members of Congress from both parties came to speak; others sent notes about the changes they had seen in the IRS.

Representatives of groups I dealt with commented on the difference they saw in the IRS and gave me souvenirs, both funny and serious. An advisory committee of taxpayer and practitioner groups gave me a folder with personal thank-you notes from everyone who had served on the committee during my tenure. One of the IRS operating division teams gave me an authentic stamping machine—the kind that the IRS still uses to hand-stamp document numbers on every tax return it receives—a true symbol of the need for continuing modernization. The IRS criminal investigators gave me special agent credentials (canceled, of course, so I couldn't actually arrest anybody). True as always to their convictions about independence from the rest of the IRS, the lawyers held a delightful, but separate, dinner for me.

I spent most of one morning in a receiving line as employees came in to shake hands. I got many more e-mails and notes from employees around the country, some from people I had met in my trips and visits.

The difference in tone reflected real changes in the IRS. Government agencies don't have profit-and-loss statements, but as the IRS emerged from the first few years of its massive change program, performance had turned around. Anecdotal and quantitative measures showed improvement in nearly all the agency's activities, and these trends continued into 2003 and early 2004.

Most important, public confidence in the IRS had rebounded from the historic lows of the 1990s. The IRS approval rating in the Roper survey continued to trend upward, reaching 49 percent in 2003, still well below many other agencies but far above the low point of 32 percent. Electronic filers, almost sixty million strong in 2004, gave the IRS even higher approval ratings. Congressional offices noted a drastic decline in the number and severity of taxpayer complaints. IRS internal statistics showed continued improvements in the quality of service to taxpayers. New electronic services through the Internet were being rolled out.

The turnaround in the attitudes of taxpayers and their representatives was essential for the IRS to do any part of its job effectively. When honest taxpayers view the IRS as an adversary or an incompetent bureaucracy, these attitudes dominate their views and those of their representatives in Congress. Under these circumstances, it is impossible to make the case that it is in the best interests of honest taxpayers for the IRS to have the authority and resources needed to collect taxes from those who don't pay what they owe. Even city police forces, whose job is to deal mainly with lawbreakers, cannot operate effectively without the support of the general citizenry. And the IRS deals not only with lawbreakers, but routinely with nearly every individual and business in America.

Although it was not widely understood when I took office, the IRS needed to improve the way it conducted its compliance activities as much as it needed to improve its service to taxpayers. With all three treasury secretaries during my term in office, I argued that the changes we were proposing in organization, management, and technology would eventually produce much higher levels of IRS effectiveness.

The turnaround in compliance activities took a little longer than the turnaround in the service activities because of the shock from the micromandates in the IRS Reform and Restructuring Act and the continued decline in IRS resources. But by the end of my term, and into 2003 and 2004, the uptrend was evident. Traditional enforcement statistics improved, despite static resources. What was more important, the new IRS operating units were focusing much more specifically on the key compliance problems in each part of the taxpayer base, going after promoters, tax shelters, and a wide range of other schemes. The available resources, though far too limited to do a minimally acceptable job, were at least being reallocated so that the agency could focus on higher-income taxpayers and the enormous but largely neglected flow-through entities. IRS criminal investigators were focusing much more on tax cases. Increased congressional confidence in the IRS allowed the agency to conduct its first program to measure compliance since 1988.

Gradually, layers of obsolete practices that had impeded enforcement were being stripped away. With strong leadership from my successor, Commissioner Mark Everson, the ridiculously slow process for auditing large corporations was being sped up by the newly empowered IRS division in charge of corporate audits. A key tool for auditing the tax returns of large corporations, the schedule that reconciles income reported to shareholders with that reported to the IRS, was revised for the first time in forty years. The division responsible for tax-exempt entities was focusing new energy on abuses in that huge and unique sector.

While the improvements in performance achieved so far are important, they are only the beginning of what can be done. With a sound management foundation in place and with continued investment in modernization, major gains in productivity and quality are possible. It is much harder to measure productivity in a government agency than in a business with competitively determined revenue and profit results. But through the creative efforts of the financial staff led by Todd Grams, the IRS has developed useful and meaningful numbers to measure the productivity increases. The last annual budget and performance plan prepared in my term incorporated an overall productivity increase of about 3 percent, well above the historical average in the private financial sector.[1]

As I left the government and returned to private business, I heard questions such as "Was it worth it?" and "Did you enjoy it?" I didn't enjoy my time at the IRS like a day at the beach. But my time in government was worth it because I believe that, to a measurable degree, I accomplished what I came to do, namely, to set the IRS on a course to perform better for taxpayers.

Big and Old Does Not Always Mean Impossible

So what does this story tell us? What lessons are to be learned?

The most important conclusion I can draw from my experience is that it is wrong to assume that a big, entrenched institution that gets into deep trouble cannot be changed for the better. The crisis can be turned into an opportunity. If it is important enough to do, it can be done.

It is a cliché that big, bureaucratic organizations are hard to change. When the troubles of an important organization get really serious, observers often argue that changing the way the organization works is hopeless and that a solution must be sought in some radically different approach.

When IBM was in real trouble in the early 1990s, many in the industry said that the company was too big and ossified to be fixed—the only solution was to sell it off in pieces. At the peak of the IRS storm in 1997, some observers were making similar arguments that fixing the IRS was hopeless. Finding an alternative to the IRS was harder than for a company, but some did propose such options as turning the job over to the fifty states or breaking the IRS up into pieces and assigning them to different parts of the Treasury Department. Others just said that nothing significant could be done with the IRS. In effect, they were saying that taxpayers would just learn to live with the institution the way it was no matter how badly it served them. Tough luck.

IBM's turnaround disproved the "it's hopeless" theory. So, I believe, did the IRS's.

Of course, sometimes the naysayers turn out to be right. AT&T and Polaroid, once two of the most successful companies in America, failed to adapt, at great cost to their shareholders and employees. Those companies made many changes but unfortunately the changes were not successful. Change itself is not hard. It is easy to destroy what exists. What is hard is building on what exists and changing it for the better. The risk of failure always accompanies the attempt to change.

This debate about what can be changed, and how to do it, goes on today as the pubic and the government try to decide how to reshape many public agencies to respond to the new challenges of terrorism and homeland security.

What makes the difference between success and failure in these high-stakes situations?

I've never been a believer in recipes and formulas for success in management. The facts of each situation are too diverse and the application of the principles is often not easy to discern. Frequently, valid principles conflict with each other and there is no really good solution, just a practical choice.

But after twenty-eight years of running AMS and consulting with dozens of clients, I brought with me to the IRS some basic beliefs about what works in leading an organization during a period of change. Five years of leading a difficult turnaround at the IRS sharpened my views. I can summarize them in nine principles.

Successful Change Means Improving the Way an Organization Performs Its Mission on Behalf of All Its Stakeholders and Rejecting an Either/Or Model of Performance. In the IRS, we had to improve our service and treatment of taxpayers and our effectiveness in enforcing compliance with the law. To accomplish this, we also had to meet the legitimate interests of our employees by providing them the tools, training, and supervision they needed.

One of the hardest parts of raising the performance of any organization, including the IRS, is getting people inside and outside the organization to buy into the crucial idea that top-performing organizations don't accept the obsolete and fatally flawed either-or model of doing business, like the notion that a company must choose between serving its customers well or making a profit. Insisting on the bedrock principle of raising performance across the board was the most fundamental part of what I tried to do at the IRS. It is the essence of successful change.

Part of the reason for the tendency of people to assume an either-or idea of organizational performance, known as the *swinging pendulum* at the IRS, may be related to the long-held and self-fulfilling belief that tax collectors are adversaries of the citizens. But I think this propensity is deeper than that. In my first week at Harvard Business School, after the class read a case study of a business, a professor asked the class what the purpose of the business was. Many classmates said the business had only one purpose—to maximize profits for shareholders. The professor challenged the class. Of course the company wanted to maximize profits—but so did every other company. What is it about this particular company that would allow it to succeed? That class was in 1962, and the shallow views of the students reflected the widespread beliefs of the times. Today, most successful businesspeople know well that they can only meet the needs of their shareholders by constantly improving the way they meet the needs of their customers.

It takes longer for such basic understandings in the way organizations succeed to penetrate the thinking of those who oversee government agencies, but the principle is as fundamental in government as it is in business.

Successful Change Means Getting the Right People in the Right Jobs. Setting direction is critical, but making it real to people is even harder.

In my first serious conversation with Treasury Deputy Secretary Larry Summers about the IRS job, I asked if I would be able to select my own senior management team, in which I wanted to include some senior executives from the private sector. I got this authority, and many people incorrectly assumed that I planned wholesale firings of the career IRS executives. I knew from my experience that most of the change would be led by inside people who both wanted to be part of making change happen and knew better than anyone else what should be changed. I had to find these internal leaders and get them in the right jobs. But they also needed help from a few senior executives who had real-life experience in places where things actually worked differently.

Successful change in long-established organizations often follows this pattern of finding leaders among both inside and outside people. This is the key way to build on what made the organization successful in the past while changing what needs to be changed for the future.

Successful Change Requires the Right Measurements and Incentives. The press has been filled with stories of how big bonuses and stock options distorted incentives of some business executives to the point of violating ethical standards and seriously damaging their organizations. Although the point is less obvious, internal performance measurements and incentives are extraordinarily powerful influences even in organizations in which the financial incentives are modest. No matter what the financial incentives, people in any organization pay attention first and foremost to how they are doing relative to other people in their own organization.

For decades, one of the most powerful influences on the behavior of the IRS was its practice of judging people's performance by using narrow, unbalanced, and frequently perverse—but easily gathered—statistics that focused almost entirely on revenue coming from audit assessments and property seizures. I believed that developing a more balanced set of measurements, one that included feedback from taxpayers and employees, as well as measures of business results that were meaningful, not just easy to count, was a critical step in changing attitudes. Adopting measurements that are roughly right rather than precisely wrong was a difficult but essential part of changing the IRS, and is usually a crucial element in changing any substantial organization.

(As I left office, the OMB sent over instructions saying that it would judge IRS performance in the coming budget year by how much enforcement revenue the agency brought in. It reminded me of the person who woke up in the Woody Allen movie after being asleep for thirty years, apparently alive but knowing nothing that was learned in the previous three decades.)

Successful Change Depends on Moving to an Organizational Structure, Business Practices, and Technology That Are Up-to-Date and Aligned with the Needs of Customers. One of the main reasons I was recruited for the IRS job was my background in technology. But in any information-intensive enterprise, technology simply codifies its organization, practices, and strategies. A critical decision in any change program is assessing how these basic structural elements need to change to reflect current business objectives, best practices in other similar organizations, and especially the current needs and characteristics of its customers. At the IRS, all these structural elements, not just the technology, were seriously out-of-date. Hence a long-term and comprehensive program to modernize all of them was essential. I concluded that any attempt to change technology in isolation would be bound to fail, as would a program only of quick fixes.

Successful Change Requires Knowing What Is Really Going on Where It Counts—At the Front Line. Reports, studies, and briefings are essential tools for a leader trying to assess problems and progress in an organization. But I have never found them sufficient to understand what is going on where it counts: real employees dealing with real customers. As I had done for decades in my prior work, I spent a lot of time every year at the IRS traveling and talking to people at all levels inside and outside the organization, including frontline employees, taxpayers, vendors, and innumerable other groups who deal with the IRS. Occasionally I would make it a point to dive deep into a specific case or problem that I thought was particularly important or stalled. I have no idea how I could have gained even a slightly accurate understanding of how the IRS was actually working without doing this, although many people in the agency considered it slightly eccentric behavior for a commissioner.

Successful Change Requires Open and Honest Communication Inside and Outside the Organization. Knowing that the road ahead was sure to be a long, uncertain, and rocky one, I made only one commitment at my confirmation hearing: to promise open and honest communication inside and outside the IRS. I did not mean that we would issue more one-way broadcasts about how well we were doing. From all my personal experience and beliefs, I thought that our only chance of regaining confidence was to level with people on the bad news as well as the good every step of the way, to try to build relationships of trust, and to get people, even severe critics, involved in solving our problems rather than just throwing darts.

People will often forgive mistakes and will accept not getting everything they want, if they feel that leaders are making principled decisions based on knowledge of the facts. Also, all these people know a lot that can help to produce better solutions, if their knowledge is tapped early enough. On the other hand, people often react harshly to perceived cover-ups or to incomprehensible decisions not based on an accurate understanding of reality. Throughout the change program, I established a policy of "engage, and then decide" rather than "decide, and then explain" with stakeholders, including dozens of groups representing taxpayers and employees, congressional committees, and oversight bodies. Although this policy had its costs and risks, most of the time it worked.

Successful Change Requires Change, Not Just Communication About Change. The most profound irony I encountered immediately after accepting the IRS job was that the White House and most of the treasury staff were trying desperately to communicate that they were responding to the public's demand for changes in the IRS. They were trying to do this by issuing announcements, but they had no real plan to change anything fundamental—and sometimes even neglected to tell the IRS what was being announced. This propensity to respond to crises by manufacturing press releases is not uncommon in government—or even in business. Ironically, it is a strategy bound to fail. It is another version of managing by cover-up. Yet, just as people never seem to learn that the cover-up is worse than the crime, the practice of seeming to change without actually changing is powerfully attractive, even though it is ultimately ineffective. By contrast, I gained a great deal of credibility with Congress and other stakeholders by flatly stating that we could not immediately do everything that needed to be done.

Successful Change Depends More on Having the Right Governance, Leadership, Direction, and Authority Than on Rules and Mandates. The IRS situation was a laboratory for testing the old debate over whether change in entrenched organizations is best achieved by imposing new rules or by establishing new direction and new management with the right authority and proper governance. In the massive IRS reform bill passed by Congress in July 1998, both approaches were included. After five years, the verdict was clear: The rules and mandates, although well intentioned, generally imposed unnecessary costs, unintended side effects, and distractions from real progress. They were a key reason that some essential enforcement activities dropped. On the other hand, the provisions of the bill setting new direction for the IRS, and providing authority for management to reorganize and modernize the agency, were essential to progress.

One of the biggest unintended consequences of the new law, strangely enough, involved governance and oversight.

Long before the Sarbanes-Oxley Act focused attention on inadequate governance as a source of problems in corporate America, the Kerrey-Portman Commission identified this same weakness as a source of problems in the IRS. The reform bill created an IRS Oversight Board, a Treasury Inspector General for Tax Administration, and an annual joint hearing in Congress. However, as the bill emerged after many political compromises, all these new oversight activities were simply added to the many that already existed, without any required coordination. Regrettably, and despite the sincere efforts of many individuals in these groups, what happened was a triumph of quantity over quality.

By the end of my term in office, the IRS was answering about 250 regular audits per year from the treasury inspector general and the GAO, nearly one every business day. Beyond these formal audits, requests for information from the treasury staff, the IRS Oversight Board, the OMB, and the six congressional committees with jurisdiction over the IRS were frequent. No management can respond seriously to that many reports. They simply divert attention from the scarcest resource in the IRS or any large organization, which is top management attention to improving quality and productivity. It is as though the board of directors of an automobile manufacturer tried to improve quality by adding more and more inspectors at the end of the assembly line, while taking away workers from the factories actually making the cars.

In the IRS, as in corporate America, effective governance can only be achieved by a relatively few well-informed, competent, and diligent people paying serious and sustained attention to the health of the organization, not by the quantity of audits and procedures.

Successful Change in Any Organization Has Its Limits—Set by the Broader Constraints of the Context Within Which It Operates. The real goal of the IRS is to assist in maintaining a healthy tax system. Its own operations are only a part of what is needed to achieve this broader goal.

Years ago, I heard a story about a television interview with the famous hotel owner Conrad Hilton. The journalist ended the interview by asking, "Mr. Hilton, in your decades building one of the world's biggest hotel businesses, you must have learned many things. For our viewers out there who would like to learn from your experience, what advice would you give them?"

Hilton answered, "Remember, the shower curtain goes *inside* the tub."

I always liked this story, whether true or apocryphal, because it makes the point that business is an intensely practical activity. No matter how brilliantly conceived someone's theory may be, if it doesn't work out in the practical, everyday world of customers and employees, profits and losses, then the business will not succeed, at least not for long.

The tax system has many of the same practical characteristics that a business has: Real work has to get done and be paid for. Returns have to be processed, phones have to be answered, tax money has to be accounted for, taxpayers who don't pay what they owe have to be dealt with appropriately. If this work is not done, bad things will eventually happen.

This practical businesslike character is one reason I accepted the IRS commissioner job. It was something that had to get done. And during my term, I focused on the practical improvements I could make.

But the IRS is only one part of the broader tax system, which comprises the tax code and the budget. And in one fundamental respect the tax system, being a government program, is different from a business. Because they are not quickly obvious, the practical consequences of making expedient but profoundly irresponsible decisions about this broader system can be ignored for much longer than such unsound decisions could be ignored in a business. It is like the story of throwing a frog into a vat of hot water; if you throw him in when the water is already boiling he may jump out and survive, but if you turn up the heat gradually he may die before he notices the rising temperature.

Because of the immense size and complexity of the tax system and the difficulty of measuring how effectively it is operating, its deterioration will not become totally evident until things get so bad that the cost of recovery will be immense.

It is now time to fix the whole tax system, not just the IRS, which is why I broke my own guidelines to address this broader problem in my final report to the oversight board. This problem will never be solved until honest taxpayers rise up and *demand* that the president and Congress solve it. And then, believe me, it will be solved.

Deeper Reasons for Success

I'm sure the beliefs and principles I applied at the IRS enabled me to help the IRS change for the better. But I've often reflected also on what, at a deeper level, made the program work tolerably well. I could have tried the same things at a different time or in a different organization and had less success or even outright failure.

At this more fundamental level, what made it work was that there were enough people inside and outside the IRS who knew the IRS had to change and who had the courage, skill, and dedication to the public good to commit themselves to making the change happen:

- The three treasury secretaries who invested real political capital in supporting the program
- Senator Kerrey and Congressman Portman, who took on the first serious study of the IRS in fifty years and pushed reform legislation through Congress
- Bob Wenzel, the quintessential public servant who knew better than anyone else what was good and what needed to change in the IRS
- The several dozen senior business executives who, to their own surprise, agreed to come to the IRS for several years to help lead the turnaround
- The several thousand IRS employees at all levels who volunteered at personal sacrifice to lead the change internally
- Numerous other individuals—even outspoken critics of the agency—who were willing to suspend disbelief long enough to give the program a chance

These people were the real reason for whatever success we achieved. I owe them a debt of gratitude, as do the American taxpayers they served so skillfully and energetically.

APPENDIX

IRS Budget and Productivity

How the IRS Uses Its Budget

CONFUSION IS RAMPANT, even within the government, over how the IRS uses its budget. Because TV programs like to show pictures of trucks unloading paper returns on April 15, many people think that most of the IRS budget is used for processing returns. Others think that most of the money previously used for enforcement was reallocated to customer service because of criticism from Congress over poor service. Still others think that most of the money is chewed up by headquarters in Washington.

None of these misperceptions is even close to true.

As the pie charts in A-1 and A-2 show, 83 percent of the IRS staff and 63 percent of the budget is used for tax administration operations, which include processing returns, assisting taxpayers, and performing compliance activities. Most of the rest of the budget is used for shared services, such as facilities, procurement, and personnel administration, and for operating the IRS's huge network of information systems. These activities enable the employees in the tax administration operations functions to do their job by providing them essentials such as space to work in and computer systems to work with. All of the nonsalary costs for rent and computers is included in the budgets of the information

FIGURE A-1

Distribution of IRS Staff and Budget

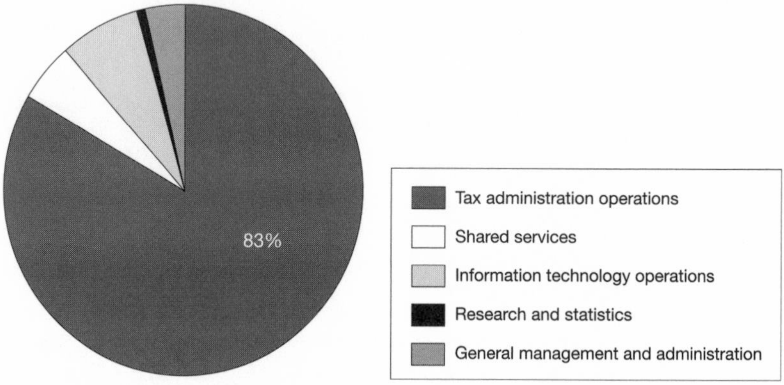

technology and shared services units, which is why they have a much larger percentage of the budget than they have of the staff.

About 3.5 percent of the employees and 6.5 percent of the budget is used by the IRS for management and administrative functions. This portion of the staff includes personnel engaged in management and administration activities, from Washington down to the field unit level.

In recent years, about 4.5 percent of the budget has been allocated for modernization investments.

The pie chart of tax administration operations shows a further breakdown of the IRS budget. It shows that only 12 percent of the tax administration operations budget is used for the "back office" returns processing centers so often featured on television. The biggest part of the budget, 62 percent, is used for compliance activities—investigating, auditing, and collecting from taxpayers who don't file, don't report, or don't pay what they owe. Answering taxpayer phone calls, letters, and visits and maintaining their tax accounts (officially called taxpayer filing and accounts services and colloquially called customer service) uses 15.5 percent of the tax administration operations budget. The remaining 10.5 percent is used for taxpayer prefiling services, which include printing and distributing forms and publications, making legal interpretations of the tax law, and performing taxpayer education programs.

FIGURE A-2

Tax Administration Operations Budget Distribution

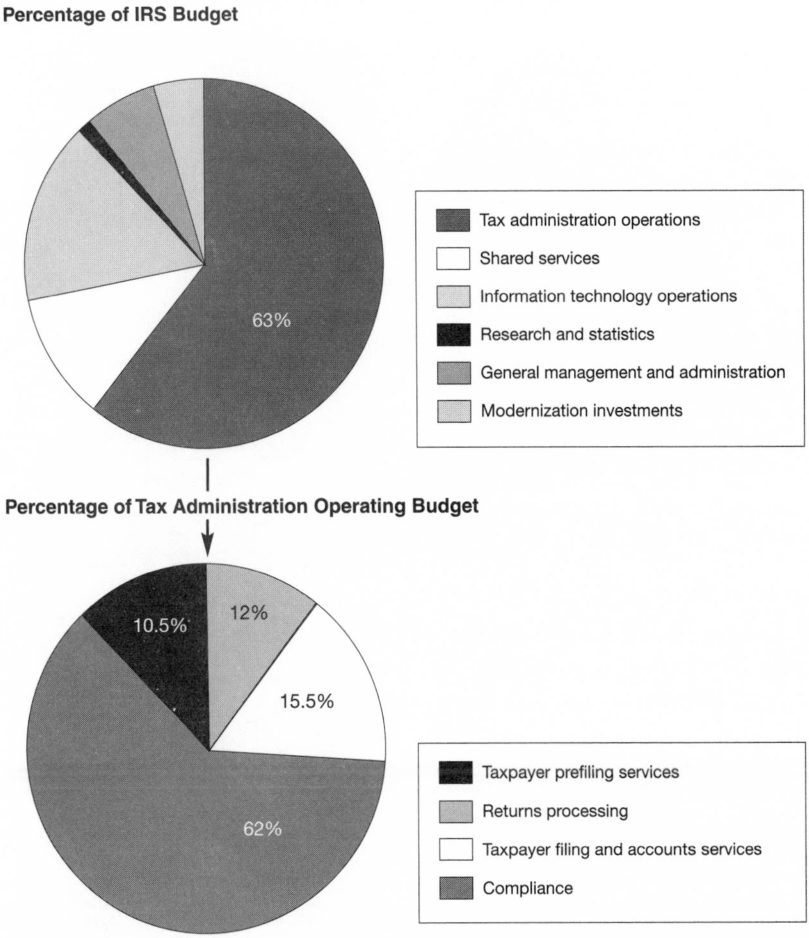

IRS Productivity Growth

As the IRS's new organization and new financial management approach came into being in 2001 and 2002, the IRS began to drive the realloca- tions of resources specifically to improve productivity. Most of the real- locations were made possible by successful investments in technology. In the last budget submission of my term, which was for fiscal year 2004,

TABLE A-1

Calculation of IRS Productivity Growth in FY 2004 Budget

	FTE FY 2003	FTE FY 2004 reallocations	Increase in FTE	Increase in output	Weighting	Weighted output growth
Key tax administration programs with gap	34,619	3,261	9.4%	9.4%	35.1%	3.3%
All other programs	63,917	(1,261)	(2.0%)	1.8%	64.9%	1.2%
Total	98,536	2,000	2.0%			4.5%

Output growth	4.5%
Overall FTE growth	2.0%
Productivity growth solely from FTE savings and reallocations	2.4%

FTE means full-time-equivalent employee. Output growth in key tax administration programs is assumed to be equal to FTE growth. This does not take into account additional output growth from internal productivity enhancements within these programs. Output growth from other programs is equal to overall IRS workload growth of 1.8 percent per year.

the IRS proposed reallocations and savings of staff sufficient to provide productivity growth equal to 2.4 percent.

The basis of this calculation is shown in the table. As a result of budget decisions by the IRS senior management team, the equivalent of 3,261 full-time employees (referred to as full-time-equivalents, or FTE, in IRS jargon) would be added to the key tax administration programs—those that had a gap in the amount of work they were doing as compared to what was needed. For example, more auditors were needed to work the high-priority cases of taxpayers hiding income offshore or not paying known tax bills. These additional staff years represented a 9.4 percent increase in staff in these high-priority programs.

All other programs were considered to be in balance. That is, they just needed to keep up with the increased workload from receiving more tax returns and dealing with more taxpayers, which amounts to about 1.8 percent per year. Through productivity-enhancing projects, these programs actually were allocated 1,261 fewer staff while being expected to keep up with the increased workload.

Computing a weighted average of the change in the two categories of programs yields a weighted average of 2.4 percent increase in output per staff year.

Beyond this 2.4 percent productivity gain from savings and reallocations of staff, additional productivity gains were expected by the setting of goals for more output per staff year within the high-priority programs. For example, a division might do more audits with the same staff by steamlining the audit process. These gains are harder to aggregate into a single number, but they were significant enough to bring the estimate for the overall productivity target for the year to about 3 percent.

Notes

Prologue

1. Michael Hirsch, "Infernal Revenue Disservice," *Newsweek,* 13 October 1997, 33.

2. All statistics about the IRS are from the author's notes, which are based on IRS research and data during his term.

3. "More Consumers Give Government Services Thumbs-Up," *USA Today,* 17 December 2001.

Chapter 1

1. Bob Schieffer, *Face the Nation* (Washington, DC: CBS-TV, 28 September 1997).

2. Senate Committee on Finance, *Hearings on the Practices and Procedures of the Internal Revenue Service,* 105th Cong., S. Hrg. 105-190, 23–25 September 1997, 1.

3. Ibid., 75–82.

4. Ibid., 95.

5. Ibid., 82–85.

6. Ibid., 86.

7. Ibid., 120.

8. Ibid.

9. Peter Jennings, *ABC World News Tonight* (New York: ABC-TV, 24 September 1997).

10. Senate Committee on Finance, *Hearings on the Practices and Procedures,* 198.

11. All statistics about the IRS are from the author's notes, which are based on IRS research and data gathered during his term.

12. Internal IRS management reports on telephone traffic.

13. Senate Committee on Finance, *Hearings on the Practices and Procedures,* 69.

14. Ibid., 8.

15. Albert B. Crenshaw, "A Struggling IRS Collects Its Fair Share of Problems," *Washington Post,* 14 April 1997.

16. "IRS Fails Financial Audit for Fourth Consecutive Year," *Fort Worth Star Telegram,* 7 June 1996.

17. Albert B. Crenshaw, "Computer Problems Taxing IRS," *Washington Post,* 15 March 1996.

18. Ralph Vartabedian, "IRS Pulls Plug on Its Electronic Tax-Filing System," *Los Angeles Times,* 11 September 1996.

19. Ibid.

20. Rob Portman, press release, 31 January 1997.

21. National Commission on Restructuring the Internal Revenue Service, *A Vision for a New IRS* (Washington, DC, 25 June 1997), 63.

22. Albert B. Crenshaw, "IRS Oversight Plan Draws White House Fire," *Washington Post,* 30 September 1997.

23. Ibid.

24. National Commission on Restructuring the Internal Revenue Service, *A Vision for a New IRS,* v.

25. Ralph Vartabedian, "To an IRS Mired in the '60s, '90s Answers Prove Elusive," *Los Angeles Times,* 9 December 1996.

26. RoperASW Survey (New York, 1997).

27. Mitch McConnell, National Republican Senatorial Committee, fund-raising letter, July, 1997.

28. Michael Hirsch, "Behind the IRS Curtain," *Newsweek,* 6 October 1997, 28.

29. Michael Hirsch, "Infernal Revenue Disservice," *Newsweek,* 13 October 1997, 33.

30. Ibid.

31. Ibid.

32. "Business Owners Tell of IRS Raids," *Newsday,* 30 April 1998.

Chapter 2

1. Charles C. Rossotti, letter to author, July 1965.

2. AMS, "AMS Announces Year to Year First Quarter Revenue Growth," Washington, DC, AMS, Inc., 19 April 2001.

Chapter 3

1. Tom Herman, "Tax Report," *Wall Street Journal,* 14 May 1997.

2. Senate Committee on Finance, *Nomination Hearing of Charles O. Rossotti, to Be Commissioner of the Internal Revenue Service,* 105th Congress, 23 October 1997, (Washington, DC: Moffitt Reporting Associates, 1997) 2–4.

3. Ibid., 54.
4. Ibid., 76.
5. Ibid., 13–14.

Chapter 4

1. Killefer remained a vital force for change at the IRS even after she left the Treasury Department. She was appointed to the IRS Oversight Board and later became its chairperson.

2. Bob Tobias became an active member of several senior steering committees that addressed the many changes under way at the IRS. Upon retiring as president of the National Treasury Employees Union, he continued to provide important insights and leadership as a member of the IRS Oversight Board.

3. Rob Wells, "IRS Tries to Reform Itself as Congress Debates," Associated Press, 31 January 1998.

4. Ibid.

Chapter 5

1. Albert B. Crenshaw, "Panel to Recommend New IRS Management," *Washington Post,* 6 June 1997.

2. "Naming of Oversight Board for IRS Is Recommended," *New York Times,* 26 June 1997. The restructuring commission's report itself went into more detail about its reasons for proposing a new board to govern the IRS: "The current IRS governance structure is often reactive rather than strategic. The IRS reacts to pressures applied by the Congress through seven different oversight committees, often focusing issue by issue, rather than on an integrated and consistent strategic direction. Treasury reacts to problems at the IRS, typically after the IRS has been unable to resolve them. . . . [T]he traditional congressional role has been to respond to specific complaints or problems with particular programs or initiatives. The result is inconsistent and inadequate attention to the core issues facing the IRS, and scattered attention to a host of non-strategic issues. Moreover, the result is an IRS and Treasury that cannot be held accountable for achieving the IRS mission." National Commission on Restructuring the Internal Revenue Service, *A Vision for a New IRS* (Washington, DC, 25 June 1997), 2.

3. Albert B. Crenshaw, "White House Ends Resistance to Hill Plan for IRS Overhaul," *Washington Post,* 22 October 1997.

4. As part of its recommended overhaul of IRS governance, the Kerrey-Portman commission proposed not only a new oversight board but also that the IRS commissioner be appointed for a five-year term. As political appointees of the president, all previous commissioners had no fixed term and therefore ended their service automatically at the end of the president's term. This proposal for a fixed term, although unusual for politically appointed positions in the executive branch, was far less controversial than the

proposed oversight board and was included by Congress in the July 1998 reform law. Although I was the incumbent commissioner, this provision applied retroactively to me. I therefore served exactly five years, including approximately three in the Clinton administration and two in the Bush administration.

5. Tom Herman, "Tax Report," *Wall Street Journal,* 25 November 1998.

6. Congressman Archer later became one of my most powerful supporters. On one occasion, he invited me to lunch with the Republican members of his committee and advised them to help me any way they could. He said it was the best thing they could do to fix the IRS. He also assigned Representative Amo Houghton the job of overseeing the IRS on behalf of the whole Ways and Means committee. A former CEO of Corning Glass Works, Houghton understood the challenges of changing a big organization and regularly offered me helpful advice and counsel during informal meetings in his office.

7. Richard W. Stevenson, "GOP Chief Aims to Shift Burden in IRS Disputes," *New York Times,* 20 October 1997.

8. Senate Committee on Finance, *Nomination Hearing of Charles O. Rossotti, to Be Commissioner of the Internal Revenue Service,* 105th Cong., 23 October 1997 (Washington, DC: Moffitt Reporting Associates, 1997), 101.

9. Richard W. Stevenson, "Legislation Reining In the IRS Clears House on Vote of 426 to 4," *New York Times,* 6 November 1997.

10. Rob Wells, "House Passes Broad Bill Overhauling IRS," *Chicago Sun-Times,* 26 June 1998.

Chapter 6

1. SURVEY1997, IRS employee survey administered by International Computers and Telecommunications Inc., Ventura, CA, 8–22 August 1997.

2. Ibid.

3. Ted Bunker, "Mac Fans Brushed Back by an IRS Purpose Pitch," *Boston Herald,* 14 September 1998.

4. David L. Greene, "Baseball: McGwire Passes Maris," *Baltimore Sun,* 9 September 1998.

5. "IRS: No Taxes Would Have Been Due on Home Run Ball Returned by Fan," Associated Press, 9 September 1998.

6. A couple of days later, Don Lubick, the assistant secretary for tax policy at the Treasury Department, sent me a law review article analyzing baseball's infield fly rule as an example of an antiabuse rule, a concept often used in tax regulations. Apparently, I was not the first one to compare baseball rules to tax rules.

Chapter 7

1. Matthew 9: 9–13 (New International Version).

2. David R. Francis, "IRS Swings Back into Old Role: Enforcer," *Christian Science Monitor,* 16 September 2002.

3. IRS Oversight Board, Annual Report 2001, January 2002, 2.

4. Senate Committee on Finance, *Hearings on IRS Restructuring, Testimony of Charles O. Rossotti,* 105th Cong., S. Hrg. 105-529, 28 January 1998, 20.

5. As a further elaboration of the mission, we also established three strategic goals: for service, compliance, and productivity. The service and compliance goals reflect the two major dimensions of the IRS mission. The productivity goal reflects the agency's obligation to improve continuously the efficiency by which it carries out the mission.

6. Tom Herman, "Tax Notes," *Wall Street Journal,* 30 September 1998.

7. Charles O. Rossotti, *Modernizing America's Tax Agency* (Washington, DC: IRS, 1999), 58.

8. Ibid.

9. Ibid., 59.

10. Ibid., 56.

11. Senate Committee on Finance, *Hearings on the Practices and Procedures of the Internal Revenue Service,* 105th Cong., S. Hrg. 105-190, 23–25 September 1997, 3.

12. Senate Committee on Finance, *Nomination Hearing of Charles O. Rossotti, to Be Commissioner of the Internal Revenue Service* (Washington, DC: Moffitt Reporting Associates, 1997), 89.

13. IRS Customer Service Task Force, *Reinventing Service at the IRS* (Washington, DC: GPO, 1998), 75.

14. *Internal Revenue Service Restructuring and Reform Act of 1998,* Public Law 105-206, 105th Cong., 112 Stat 685, Section 1204.

15. Rossotti, *Modernizing America's Tax Agency,* 60.

16. Senate Committee on Finance, *Hearings on the Practices and Procedures of the Internal Revenue Service,* 124.

17. David R. Francis, "Incredible Shrinking Tax Collector," *Christian Science Monitor,* 23 February 2000.

18. Charles O. Rossotti, "Customer Service Measure," speech to IRS midyear business meeting, New Carrollton, MD, 11 May 1999.

19. Amy Feldman, "Please, IRS: Stop Playing Nice Guy," *USA Today,* 16 April 2001.

20. Ibid.

21. *Boyd Gaming Corporation v. Commissioner of Internal Revenue,* no. 98-70123, 177 F. 3d 1096 (9th Cir. 1999).

22. RoperASW Survey (New York, 1999).

Chapter 8

1. Rob Portman and Ben Cardin, "Reforming a Taxing System," *Washington Post,* 29 September 1997.

2. IRS Customer Service Task Force, *Reinventing Service at the IRS* (Washington, DC: GPO, 1998), 83.

3. Tom Herman, "Tax Report," *Wall Street Journal,* 20 May 1998.

4. IRS Customer Surveys.

5. U.S. General Accounting Office, *2002 Tax Filing Season:* Returns and Refunds Processed Smoothly; Quality of Assistance Improved, GAO-03-314 (Washington, DC, December 2002), 21.

6. Kerry Hannon, "Cranky Consumer: Seeking Fast Answers on Taxes," *Wall Street Journal,* 8 April 2003.

7. *Internal Revenue Service Restructuring and Reform Act of 1998,* Public Law 105-206, 105th Cong., 112 Stat 685, Section 1102.

8. Senate Committee on Finance, *Hearings on the Practices and Procedures of the Internal Revenue Service,* 105th Cong., S. Hrg. 105-190, 23–25 September 1997, 229.

9. Anonymous, letter to author from taxpayer, November 2002. The taxpayer's name is not provided to protect the taxpayer's privacy.

10. Curt Anderson, "IRS: Taxpayers Increasingly Turning to Computers," Associated Press, 26 April 2001.

11. Amy Hamilton, "IRS Surges Past Britney Spears in the Zeitgeist," *Tax Analysts' Tax Notes,* 17 April 2002.

12. Charles O. Rossotti, "Concerns About Proposed Guidance on Accrual Accounting for Small Business," Memorandum for Acting Assistant Secretary (Tax Policy), 10 November 1999.

13. *Osteopathic Medical Oncology and Hematology P.C. v. Commissioner of Internal Revenue,* No. 11551-98, 113 T.C. 376 (Tax Court, 1999).

Chapter 9

1. Senate Committee on Finance, *Hearings on IRS Oversight,* 105th Cong., S. Hrg. 105-598, 28 April–1 May 1998, 212–226.

2. William J. Clinton, *Radio Address of the President to the Nation,* 2 May 1998 (The White House, Office of the Press Secretary, Palo Alto, CA).

3. Senate Committee on Finance, *Hearings on IRS Oversight,* 219.

4. David Ivanovich, "IRS Offices Used Quotas, Audit Shows," *Houston Chronicle,* 14 January 1998.

5. Senate Committee on Finance, *Hearings on IRS Oversight,* 198.

6. Charles O. Rossotti, Comments to IRS Executive Committee Meeting, 23 September 1998.

7. Anonymous, e-mail message from IRS employee to author, 22 May 2001. The employee's name is not provided to protect the employee's privacy.

8. Ibid.

9. IRS Customer Service Task Force, *Reinventing Service at the IRS* (Washington, DC: GPO, 1998), 77.

Chapter 10

1. Internal Revenue Service, *Commissioner's Annual Report,* Washington, DC, 1952.

2. Senate Committee on Finance, *Hearings on IRS Restructuring, Testimony of Charles O. Rossotti,* 105th Cong., S. Hrg. 105-529, 28 January 1998, 20.

3. National Commission on Restructuring the Internal Revenue Service, *A Vision for a New IRS* (Washington, DC, 25 June 1997), 12.

4. Senate Committee on Finance, *Hearings on IRS Restructuring,* 20.

5. Albert B. Crenshaw, "Rossotti Promises Reorganized IRS," *Washington Post,* 29 January 1998.

6. With the appointment of this new top management team, we also reinstituted the practice of holding official swearing-in ceremonies for major appointments in the IRS. The ceremonies, held in an auditorium with employees and family members present, usually included a color guard bringing in the flags, an employee singing the national anthem, a short speech by me and by a colleague of each of the appointees, and then the administration of the oath of office to the appointee on the stage with his or her family. Afterward, we held a punch-and-cookies reception. Throughout the ceremony, a photographer took pictures, which we later gave to the appointees. We also held such ceremonies when giving out awards. These rituals were a powerful way of communicating to appointees that they were taking on an important public trust, and of providing them recognition for their commitment.

7. Anonymous, e-mail message from IRS employee to author, 15 September 1999. Name withheld to protect the privacy of the employee.

8. Louis Gerstner, *Who Says Elephants Can't Dance: Inside IBM's Historic Turnaround* (New York: HarperCollins, 2002), 187.

9. The author of this poem, an IRS employee, mailed this poem directly to me. The text of the poem is slightly changed to avoid identifying any individuals.

10. SES'ers refers to IRS executives, who are members of the federal government's Senior Executive Service, or SES.

11. Although based on archaic systems that did not meet modern accounting standards, the IRS did maintain meticulous and honest stewardship of taxpayer money. By fiscal 2000, the IRS improved the accounting process sufficiently to receive clean General Accounting Office opinions of IRS financial statements. By fiscal 2002, the audited statements were out within six weeks of the end of the fiscal year.

12. Charles O. Rossotti, Comments at American Tax Policy Institute IRS Modernization Conference, Washington, DC, 13 January 2000.

13. SURVEY2003, IRS employee survey conducted by the Gallup Organization, 2 April–3 May 2003.

14. B. John Williams, "The Office of Chief Counsel: A Renewed Commitment to Guidance," *Tax Executive,* March–April 2002.

Chapter 11

1. "After Eleven Years, $4 Billion, IRS Computers Don't Work," *USA Today,* 4 February 1997.

2. The Social Security Administration also keeps records on almost all Americans, but generally does not conduct financial transactions with them until they begin to collect benefits.

3. Charles O. Rossotti, "But What Is a Business System Anyway?" (white paper, 9 April 1998).

4. In the fall of 2000, Levitan was elected chair of the IRS Oversight Board.

Chapter 12

1. Senate Committee on Finance, *Hearings on the Practices and Procedures of the Internal Revenue Service,* 105th Cong., S. Hrg. 105-190, 23–25 September 1997, 143.

2. Michael Hirsch, "Infernal Revenue Disservice," *Newsweek,* 13 October 1997.

3. Charles O. Rossotti, first voice mail and e-mail to IRS employees, 8 November 1997.

4. Curt Anderson, "IRS to Rewrite Its Letter Warning of Audit Contacts," Associated Press, 3 March 1999.

5. Ibid.

6. Michael Mansur, "Suspicious Letter Is Found at IRS Center in KC," *Kansas City Star,* 24 October 2001.

7. Ramona Smith, "IRS Worker Cleared in Anthrax Test," *Philadelphia Inquirer,* 30 October 2001.

Chapter 13

1. Transcribed from author's notes of my visit on *The Diane Rehm Show* (Washington, DC: WAMU Radio, 12 February 1998).

2. Lisa Myers, *NBC Nightly News* (Washington, DC: NBC News, 24 September 1997).

3. William Glaberson, "Helmsley Gets Four-Year Term for Tax Fraud," *New York Times,* 13 December 1989.

4. Roger Lowenstein, *When Genius Failed* (New York: Random House, 2000), 35.

5. Corporations of this type are commonly referred to as *S corporations,* for the part of the tax code that allows their formation.

6. Internal Revenue Service, "IRS Issues Tips on Completing Schedules K-1," Press Release IR-2003-27, 10 March 2003.

7. David Cay Johnston, "Job Fears Push IRS Workers to Relax Effort," *New York Times,* 18 May 1999.

8. Treasury Inspector General for Tax Administration, *Trends in Compliance Activities Through Fiscal Year 2002,* 2003-30-078 (Washington, DC: March 2003), 2.

9. *Boca Investerings Partnership and American Home Products Corporation v. United States of America,* No. 01-5429, 314 F. 3d 625 (DC Cir., 2003).

10. Internal Revenue Service "Agreement with PricewaterhouseCoopers LLP," Press Releases IR-2002-82, 27 June 2002, and "Announcing a Closing Agreement with Ernst & Young," IR-2003-84, 2 July 2003.

11. Ben White, "Long-Term Capital Case Puts Tax Shelters on Trial," *Washington Post,* 23 July 2003.

12. Curt Anderson, "Justice, IRS Seeking VISA Records as Probe into Offshore Bank Accounts Expands," Associated Press, 25 March 2002.

13. Equity Development Group, "Our Complete Offshore Package," available at <http://www.equitydevelopers.com> (accessed 15 October 2003).

14. Ernesto Hernandez and Karen Gaughan, "Unscrupulous Trust Promoters Target Medical Profession," *American Academy of Otolaryngology—Head and Neck Surgery Bulletin,* February 2002.

15. David Cay Johnston, "IRS Audits of Working Poor Increase," *New York Times,* 1 March 2002.

Chapter 14

1. The amount of taxes that should be paid and are not paid is known as the *tax gap.* The numbers cited are estimates based on extrapolating the last research studies done by the IRS. Although subject to considerable uncertainty because of the age of the underlying research, there is more reason to believe the tax gap numbers are too low than that they are too high. The numbers cited as "per taxpayer" count joint returns as one "taxpayer."

2. IRS Oversight Board, Annual Report 2001, January 2002, 13.

3. In his acceptance speech at the Republican Convention on September 2, 2004, President Bush said that he would commission a study of tax simplification.

4. Simplifying changes in family provisions and several other onerous sections of the tax code are included in the IRS Taxpayer Advocate's reports (on <www.irs.gov> under Taxpayer Advocate).

5. Objections concerning the amount and distribution of tax revenue lost could be addressed if there were a uniform set of limits imposed on the amount a taxpayer could set aside in these accounts.

6. IRS National Taxpayer Advocate, *2001 National Taxpayer Advocate's Annual Report to Congress* (Washington, DC: IRS, 2001), 166.

7. An obvious way to simplify this major part of the tax code would be to make taxable income, for businesses over a certain size, the same as income reported according to generally accepted accounting principles. Such a change not only would simplify the code and increase compliance, but could also significantly reduce corporate tax rates without reducing tax revenue. Nevertheless, the idea is politically a total nonstarter. Such a change would increase taxes for the politically best connected corporations while

reducing them for the less powerful—especially medium-sized businesses. The change would also reduce the political power of the members of the tax-writing committees.

8. In the five-year period from 1996 to 2000, out of more than $16 billion in all types of penalties paid by all taxpayers, the amount of penalties paid by large corporations for negligence or substantial understatement of tax (the penalty that would apply to the use of tax shelters) was *zero.*

9. Although the IRS has taken enforcement action against tax-shelter promoters, and in some cases promoters have paid fines as part of a settlement, these actions dealt with failures of disclosure, not the substance of the tax shelters themselves or the legal opinions that supported them.

10. If it is passed into law, an amendment passed by the Senate in 2003 and again in 2004 to codify the economic substance doctrine would provide a sound foundation to address this tax-shelter problem. Although passage of the amendment is an essential step, the amendment would only be effective if the Treasury Department follows up with regulations making it clear that technical legal opinions will not protect large taxpayers from penalties if they engage in "investments" that no reasonable businessperson would make if there were no taxes at all on the investment, that is, if no tax benefits were generated to shelter business income unrelated to the so-called investment. In October 2004, Congress passed a major corporate tax bill that included some anti-tax-shelter provisions. However, the Senate provision that would have codified the substantive definition of a tax shelter—by far the most effective anti-shelter proposal—was rejected.

11. Tax returns weighted for complexity, a measure of IRS workload.

12. Please see the appendix for an explanation of how the IRS spends its budget.

13. Bloomberg News, "SEC Running Behind on Spending Its Budget," *Los Angeles Times,* 24 July 2003.

Epilogue

1. See the appendix for an explanation of how this calculation was made.

Bibliography

"After Eleven Years, $4 Billion, IRS Computers Don't Work." *USA Today.* 4 February 1997.

Alexander, Delroy. "IRS Eases Rules on Accounting Methods for Small Firms." *Chicago Tribune.* 20 December 2001.

Alvarez, Lizette. "Senate Hearings Open with Talk of a Sweeping IRS Shake-Up." *New York Times.* 29 January 1998.

Anderson, Curt. "Computer Sciences Team Gets Contract to Modernize IRS Systems." Associated Press. 10 December 1998.

———. "Despite Crackdown, Government Struggles to Keep Pace with Growing Tax Evasion Problem." Associated Press. 12 April 2002.

———. "Dozens of Changes Confront Taxpayers After Enactment of Sweeping Tax Law; Filing Errors Abound." Associated Press. 22 February 2002.

———. "IRS Audit Rate No Longer Dropping, but an Individual's Chance of Exam Remains Low." Associated Press. 1 March 2002.

———. "IRS Chief Lobbies for Budget Increase as Congress Tackles Busy Tax Week." Associated Press. 10 April 2000.

———. "IRS Chief Predicts Increase in Audits." Associated Press. 12 April 2001.

———. "IRS Chief Says High Audit Rate Unnecessary with Technology." Associated Press. 28 March 2001.

———. "IRS Collections Actions Drop $1.3 Billion amid Reform Struggles." Associated Press. 10 December 1999.

———. "IRS Cracking Down on Fraudulent Trusts." Associated Press. 11 December 2000.

———. "IRS Cuts Down on Using 'Threat' Audit Letters." Associated Press. 24 March 1999.

———. "IRS Focusing Audits on High-Income Taxpayers, Evasion Schemes." Associated Press. 12 September 2002.

———. "IRS Seeks More Offshore Credit Card Records in Tax Evasion Probe." Associated Press. 15 August 2002.

———. "IRS: Taxpayers Increasingly Turning to Computers." Associated Press. 26 April 2001.

———. "IRS to Rewrite Its Letter Warning of Audit Contacts." Associated Press. 3 March 1999.

———. "IRS Will Waive Penalties and Interest for Legitimate Y2K Tax Problems." Associated Press. 23 December 1999.

———. "Judge Approves IRS Summons for Visa Card Records from Banks in Thirty Tax-Haven Countries." Associated Press. 28 March 2002.

———. "Justice, IRS Seeking Visa Records As Probe into Offshore Bank Accounts Expands." Associated Press. 25 March 2002.

———. "Save Those Records: IRS to Examine 50,000 Tax Returns at Random." Associated Press. 17 January 2002.

———. "Taxes: Y2K, with Optimism." Associated Press. 5 January 1999.

———. "Tax Cheats Get Sophisticated." Associated Press. 24 September 2002.

———. "Tax Evasion Investigation Expands into Offshore Bank Card Accounts." Associated Press. 25 March 2002.

———. "Taxes: Dozens of Changes." Associated Press. 7 January 2002.

———. "Taxpayers Embrace Electronic Filing." Associated Press. 17 April 2000.

Associated Press. "Business Owners Tell of IRS Raids." *Newsday.* 30 April 1998.

———. "Help by Phone Is Slower and Often Wrong, Study Finds." 31 December 2001.

———. "IRS Fails Finance Audit for Fourth Consecutive Year." *Fort Worth Star Telegram.* 7 June 1996.

———. "IRS: No Taxes Would Have Been Due on Home Run Ball Returned by Fan." 9 September 1998.

———. "IRS Plans Random Audits, but It Promises to Be Gentle." *New York Times.* 17 January 2002.

———. "Maid Testifies Helmsley Denied Paying Taxes." *New York Times.* 12 July 1989.

———. "Merrill Lynch Settles Tax Case." *New York Times.* 30 August 2001.

Aversa, Jeannine. "Again in 2000, IRS Audits Fewer Taxpayers." Associated Press. 16 February 2001.

Barr, Stephen. "In Tax Offices, Performance Goals Sounded Like Quotas." *Washington Post.* 26 September 1997.

Bloomberg News. "IRS Sues for Disclosure of Offshore Accounts." *New York Times.* 30 August 2002.

———. "SEC Running Behind on Spending Its Budget." *Los Angeles Times.* 24 July 2003.

Boca Investerings Partnership and American Home Products Corporation v. United States of America. 314 F.3d 625 (DC Circuit 2003).

Boyd Gaming Corporation v. Commissioner of Internal Revenue. 177 F. 3d 1096 (9th Cir. 1999).

Boyd Gaming Corporation v. Commissioner of Internal Revenue. 106 T.C. 343 (Tax Court 1996).

Bunker, Ted. "Mac Fans Brushed Back by an IRS Purpose Pitch." *Boston Herald.* 14 September 1998.

"Casino Workers Who Dine In-House Face New Tax." *Las Vegas Sun*. 26 January 1998.

Compaq Computer Corporation and Subsidiaries v. Commissioner of Internal Revenue. 277 F.3d 778 (5th Circuit 2001).

Crenshaw, Albert B. "Computer Problems Taxing IRS; Multibillion-Dollar Upgrade 'Off Track,' Treasury Official Says." *Washington Post.* 15 March 1996.

———. "House Panel Approves IRS Reform Bill." *Washington Post.* 15 March 1996.

———. "IRS Lets Some Larger Businesses Switch to Cash Accounting." *Washington Post.* 17 December 2001.

———. "IRS Oversight Plan Draws White House Fire; Sperling, Rubin Oppose Creation of Independent Board, Prompting Rebuke from Republicans." *Washington Post.* 30 September 1997.

———. "IRS Shelves Its Plans for 'Audits from Hell.'" *Washington Post.* 24 October 1995.

———. "Panel to Recommend New IRS Management; Independent Board Would Handle Operations." *Washington Post.* 6 June 1997.

———. "Reform Could Prove Overtaxing for IRS." *Washington Post.* 28 February 1999.

———. "Rossotti Promises Reorganized IRS; Commissioner Faces Skepticism at Senate Committee Hearing." *Washington Post.* 29 January 1998.

———. "A Struggling IRS Collects Its Fair Share of Problems." *Washington Post.* 14 April 1997.

———. "The Tax Protesters' Refrain Works for Once." *Washington Post.* 17 August 2003.

———. "U.S. Sues California Tax Preparer; Refunds Too Big, Audits Indicate." *Washington Post.* 12 March 2003.

———. "White House Ends Resistance to Hill Plan for IRS Overhaul." *Washington Post.* 22 October 1997.

Dedman, Bill. "Fan Snaring No. 62 Faces Big Tax Bite." *New York Times.* 7 September 1998.

Delafuente, Charles. "Your Taxes; Shelters Can Turn Perilous." *New York Times.* 16 February 2003.

Dineen, J. K. "IRS Assistance Gets a Fat 'F.'" *Daily News.* 4 April 2001.

Edward G. Smith and Jan Smith v. Commissioner of Internal Revenue. T.C. Memo 2000-353 (Tax Court 2000).

Farrell, Greg. "IRS Sues BDO Seidman, KPMG in Tax Shelter Cases." *USA Today.* 10 July 2002.

Feldman, Amy. "Please, IRS: Stop Playing Nice Guy." *USA Today.* 16 April 2001.

Francis, David R. "Incredible Shrinking Tax Collector." *Christian Science Monitor.* 23 February 2000.

———. "IRS Swings Back into Old Role: Enforcer." *Christian Science Monitor.* 16 September 2002.

Gerstner, Louis. *Who Says Elephants Can't Dance: Inside IBM's Historic Turnaround.* New York: HarperCollins, 2002.

Gerth, Joseph. "Lab Tests Detect No Danger Inside Letter to IRS." *Louisville (KY) Courier-Journal.* 10 October 2001.

Gibeaut, John. "Shelter Game: The IRS Is Counting on New Powers to Hunt Tax Cheats, but Some Worry That Legislation May Make Bendable Laws Too Rigid." *ABA Journal.* August 2003.

"Gimme No Tax Shelter." *Washington Post.* 18 February 2003.

Glaberson, William. "Helmsley Gets Four-Year Term for Tax Fraud." *New York Times.* 13 December 1989.

Glater, Jonathan D. "Court Orders Accountant to Name Shelter Investors." *New York Times.* 24 July 2003.

Goodrich, Lawrence J. "$4 Billion Later, Why IRS Awaits Computer Era." *Christian Science Monitor.* 6 January 1997.

Greene, David L. "Ball Tax Foes Deduct IRS' Plan for '62' Fan; McGwire Passes Maris" *Baltimore Sun.* 9 September 1998.

Guthrie, Julian. "Oops! IRS Goofs on Rebates." *San Francisco Chronicle.* 17 July 2001.

Hamilton, Amy. "IRS Surges Past Britney Spears in the Zeitgeist." *Tax Analysts' Tax Notes.* 17 April 2002.

Hannon, Kerry. "Cranky Consumer: Seeking Fast Answers on Taxes." *Wall Street Journal.* 8 April 2003.

Herbeck, Dan. "Accountant Pleads Guilty in False Tax Returns." *Buffalo News.* 21 March 2002.

Herman, Tom. "A Special Summary and Forecast of Federal and State Tax Developments." *Wall Street Journal.* 20 May 1998.

———. "A Special Summary and Forecast of Federal and State Tax Developments." *Wall Street Journal.* 30 September 1998.

———. "Tax Report." *Wall Street Journal.* 14 May 1997.

———. "Tax Report." *Wall Street Journal.* 20 May 1998.

———. "Tax Report." *Wall Street Journal.* 30 September 1998.

———. "Tax Report." *Wall Street Journal.* 25 November 1998.

Hernandez, Ernesto, and Karen Gaughan. "Unscrupulous Trust Promoters Target Medical Profession." *AAO-HNS Bulletin.* February 2002.

Hershey, Robert D. "Coming Soon: Face-to-Face Help from the IRS." *New York Times.* 2 November 1997.

———. "IRS Does Problem-Solving Day on a Saturday." *New York Times.* 16 November 1997.

———. "IRS Admits Taxpayers' Rights Are Abused by Improper Tactics." *New York Times.* 13 December 1997.

Hirsh, Michael. "Behind the IRS Curtain." *Newsweek.* 6 October 1997.

———. "Infernal Revenue Disservice." *Newsweek.* 13 October 1997.

Internal Revenue Service. *Commissioner's Annual Report,* Washington, DC, 1952.

———. "Changes in Accounting Periods and in Methods of Accounting." *Revenue Procedure 2000-22.* 28 April 2000.

———. "Commissioner Orders Review of Criminal Investigation Division." IRS Press Release IR-1998-35. 28 April 1998.

———. "Internal Audit Review of Seizure Activity in the IRS Collection Field Function and the Examination Division's Use of Measures and Statistics." IRS Fact Sheet FS-98-15. July 1998.

———. "IRS Appoints Discipline Review Project Director." IRS Press Release IR-1998-58. 11 September 1998.

———. "IRS Cuts Number of Third-Party Notices to Taxpayers." IRS Press Release IR-1999-28. 24 March 1999.

———. "IRS Establishes Office of Professional Responsibility." IRS Press Release IR-2003-03. 8 January 2003.

———. "IRS Issues Tips on Completing Schedules K-1; Matching Program Resumes with Improvements." IRS Press Release IR-2003-27. 10 March 2003.

———. "IRS Lets More Small Businesses Use Cash Method of Accounting." IRS Press Release IR-2001-114. 10 December 2001.

———. "IRS Moves To Clarify Third-Party Notices to Reflect New Taxpayer Rights." IRS Press Release IR-1999-19. 2 March 1999.

———. "Agreement with PricewaterhouseCoopers LLP." IRS Press Release IR-2002-82. 27 June 2002.

———. "Announcing a Closing Agreement with Ernst & Young." IRS Press Release IR-2003-84. 2 July 2003.

———. "IRS Takes Further Actions in Response to Internal Audit Review of the Use of Enforcement Statistics in the Collection Field Function." IRS Fact Sheet FS-98-4. January 1998.

———. "IRS Unveils Offshore Voluntary Compliance Initiative." IRS Press Release IR-2003-05. 14 January 2003.

———. "IRS Updates the 'Dirty Dozen' for 2003: Agency Warns of Twelve Common Scams." IRS Press Release IR-2003-18. 19 February 2003.

———. "New Post Created to Assist Crackdown on Abusive Transactions." IRS Press Release IR-2003-16. 12 February 2003.

———. "New Tax Scam Targets Potential Recipients of Advance Child Tax Credit." IRS Press Release IR-2003-79. 18 June 2003.

———. "New Tax Scams Surface." IRS Press Release IR-2003-63. 8 May 2003.

———. "Proposed Revenue Procedure Regarding the Cash Method." IRS Notice 2001-76. 26 December 2001.

———. "Reparation Scams Carry a Price." IRS Press Release FS-2002-08. January 2002.

———. "Seven-Point Plan to Improve the IRS Criminal Investigation Division." IRS Press Release IR-98-34. 27 April 1998.

———. "Slavery Reparation Scams Surge, IRS Urges Taxpayers Not to File False Claims." IRS Press Release IR-2002-08. 24 January 2002.

———. "States Back Offshore Compliance Effort." IRS Press Release IR-2003-46. 7 April 2003.

Internal Revenue Service, Customer Service Task Force. *Reinventing Service at the IRS.* Washington, DC: GPO. 1998.

Internal Revenue Service, National Taxpayer Advocate. *2001 National Taxpayer Advocate's Annual Report to Congress.* Washington, DC: IRS. 2001.

Internal Revenue Service, Office of Chief Counsel. "Change in Litigating Position." Chief Counsel Notice CC-2001-010. 9 February 2001.

Internal Revenue Service Restructuring and Reform Act of 1998. Public Law 105-206, 112 Stat 685. 22 July 1998.

"IRS Harasses Taxpayers with Its 'Special' Audits." *USA Today.* 25 July 1995.

"IRS Meals Tax Rules Held Up." *Las Vegas Sun.* 30 October 1998.

Ivanovich, David. "IRS Offices Used Quotas, Audit Shows." *Houston Chronicle.* 14 January 1998.

Jim Turin & Sons, Inc. v. Commissioner of Internal Revenue. 219 F.3d (9th Circuit 2000).

Johnston, David Cay. "A Smaller I.R.S. Gives Up on Billions in Back Taxes." *New York Times.* 13 April 2001.

———. "Affluent Avoid Scrutiny on Taxes As IRS Warns of Cheating." *New York Times.* 7 April 2002.

———. "Chief Admits IRS Is Lax on Tax Fraud." *New York Times.* 6 April 2001.

———. "Ernst & Young to Pay U.S. $15 Million in Tax Case." *New York Times.* 3 July 2003.

———. "Hunting Tax Cheats, I.R.S. Vows to Focus More Effort on the Rich." *New York Times.* 13 April 2002.

———. "I.R.S. Anticipates Year 2000 Well Ahead, Early in 1999." *New York Times.* 5 January 1999.

———. "IRS Audits of Working Poor Increase." *New York Times.* 1 March 2002.

———. "IRS Closes Loopholes That Let Rich Hide Income." *New York Times.* 26 September 2002.

———. "IRS Is Allowing More Delinquents to Avoid Tax Bills." *New York Times.* 10 October 1999.

———. "IRS More Likely to Audit the Poor and Not the Rich." *New York Times.* 16 April 2000.

———. "IRS Paid Millions in False Claims for Slavery Credit." *New York Times.* 14 April 2002.

———. "IRS Says Offshore Tax Evasion Is Widespread." *New York Times.* 26 March 2002.

———. "Job Fears Push IRS Workers to Relax Effort." *New York Times.* 18 May 1999.

———. "Rate of All I.R.S. Audits Falls; Poor Face Particular Scrutiny." *New York Times.* 16 February 2001.

———. "Reducing Audits of the Wealthy, IRS Turns Eye on Working Poor." *New York Times.* 15 December 1999.

———. "The Cost of Ignoring Tax Evasion." *New York Times.* 16 April 2001.

———. "U.S. Accuses Two Audit Firms of Assisting Tax Violations." *New York Times.* 10 July 2002.

———. "U.S. Takes Aim at Tax Shelters for Companies." *New York Times.* 29 February 2000.

Johnston, David Cay, and Jonathan D. Glater. "Tax Shelter Is Worrying Sprint's Chief." *New York Times.* 6 February 2003.

Kaplan, Robert S., and David P. Norton. "The Balanced Scorecard: Measures That Drive Performance." *Harvard Business Review.* January–February 1992.

Kessler, Glenn. "Treasury Aims to Shut Tax Shelters; Corporations' Use of Schemes Rising." *Washington Post.* 29 February 2000.

Kristof, Kathy M. "Suit Names O.C. Firm in Tax Scam." *Los Angeles Times.* 12 March 2003.

Lochhead, Carolyn. "GAO Paints a Picture of Flabby Government." *San Francisco Chronicle.* 14 March 1995.

Lowe, Roger K. "Small Business Group Seeking to Abolish Tax System." *Columbus Dispatch.* 10 September 1997.

Lowenstein, Roger. *When Genius Failed.* New York: Random House, 2000.

Mansur, Michael. "Suspicious Letter Is Found at IRS Center in KC." *Kansas City Star.* 24 October 2001.

McConnell, Mitch. National Republican Senatorial Committee. Fund-raising letter. July, 1997.

Myers, Lisa. "IRS Employees Testify Before Senate That IRS Does Use Bullying Tactics on Public." *NBC Nightly News.* 24 September 1997.

"Naming of Oversight Board for IRS Is Recommended." *New York Times.* 26 June 1997.

National Commission on Restructuring the Internal Revenue Service. *A Vision for a New IRS.* Washington, DC. 25 June 1997.

"No Tears for 'Audits from Hell.'" *Los Angeles Times.* 25 October 1995.

Norris, Floyd. "He Made $169 Million, but May Lose It All." *New York Times.* 7 February 2003.

Office of Management and Budget. *Analytical Perspectives, Budget of the United States Government, FY2001.* Washington, DC: GPO. 2001.

Osteopathic Medical Oncology and Hematology P.C. v. Commissioner of Internal Revenue. 113 T.C. 376 (Tax Court 1999).

Portman, Rob, and Ben Cardin. "Reforming a Taxing System." *Washington Post.* 29 September 1997.

"Proposed Meal Tax Is Dead, Ensign Says." *Las Vegas Sun.* 22 June 1998.

RACMP Enterprises v. Commissioner of Internal Revenue. 114 T.C. 211 (Tax Court 2000).

Roper ASW. *Survey 1997, Survey 1999,* and *Survey 2003.* New York.

Rosenbaum, David R. "Internal Audit Confirms Abusive IRS Practices." *New York Times.* 14 January 1998.

Rossotti, Charles O. *Modernizing America's Tax Agency.* (Washington, DC: IRS, 1999), 58.

Rossotti, Charles O., and Fred Forman. "The Executive Steering Committee: Its Role in Successful Strategic Projects." *AMS Best Practices* 2, no 1 1995, pp 1–16.

Sachdev, Ameet. "Ernst & Young to Pay IRS Over Tax Shelters." *Chicago Tribune.* 3 July 2003.

Schieffer, Bob. "Jennifer Long, IRS Agent, Discusses Her Testimony Before the Senate Investigating the Internal Revenue Service." *CBS News: Face The Nation.* 28 September 1997.

Schlesinger, Jacob M. "Administration Seeks to Soften IRS Legislation." *Wall Street Journal.* 17 April 1998.

———. "Clinton Officials Reverse Course on IRS." *Wall Street Journal.* 22 October 1997.

Seals, Brian. "Gaming Industry Gets New Meal-Tax Guidelines." *Las Vegas Sun.* 5 August 1998.

———. "Hotel Workers Launch Postcard Drive Over Meal Taxes." *Las Vegas Sun.* 20 May 1998.

Serafin, Barry, and Peter Jennings. "Stunning Testimony Against IRS." *ABC World News Tonight with Peter Jennings.* 24 September 1997.

Shenon, Philip. "Some Letters from IRS Err on Size of Rebate." *New York Times.* 20 July 2001.

Singletary, Michelle. "IRS Displays Good Form." *Washington Post.* 18 February 2001.

Skidmore, Dave. "Congressional Audit Finds IRS Can't Balance Its Books." *Chicago Sun-Times.* 7 June 1996.

Smith, Ramona. "IRS Worker Cleared in Anthrax Test." *Philadelphia Inquirer.* 30 October 2001.

Stevenson, Richard W. "GOP Chief Aims to Shift Burden in IRS Disputes." *New York Times.* 20 October 1997.

———. "Legislation Reining In the IRS Clears House on Vote of 426 to 4." *New York Times.* 6 November 1997.

———. "Unhappy Returns: Pity the IRS, the Tax Code's Whipping Boy." *New York Times.* 26 October 1997.

Stout, David. "As the Filing Deadline Nears, the Top Tax Man Reflects." *New York Times.* 16 April 2001.

SURVEY1997. IRS employee survey administered by International Computers and Telecommunications Inc. 8–22 August 1997.

SURVEY2003. IRS employee survey administered by the Gallup Organization. 2 April to 3 May 2003.

"A Talk with Robert Rubin." *USA Today.* 24 March 1998.

"A Toothless IRS." *New York Times.* 16 December 1999.

Treasury Inspector General for Tax Administration. *Additional Validation and Increased Oversight Are Needed to Effectively Implement the Internal Revenue Service Restructuring and Reform Act of 1998* (Reference No. 2000-40-070). May 2000.

———. *Compliance with Certain Taxpayer Rights Provisions Contained in the Internal Revenue Service Restructuring and Reform Act of 1998 Could Be Improved* (Reference No. 20001-10-147). 13 September 2001.

———. *Computer Programming Can Be Used to More Effectively Stop Refunds on Illegal Claims for Reparations Credits* (Reference No. 2002-30-071). March 2002.

———. *Final Audit Report: Trends in Compliance Activities Through Fiscal Year 2002* (Audit No. 2003-30-006). 31 March 2003.

———. *Further Improvements Are Needed in Processes That Control and Report Misuse of Enforcement Statistics* (Reference No. 2000-10-118). September 2000.

———. *Improvements to the Office of Chief Counsel's Published Guidance Process Would Enhance Guidance Provided to Taxpayers and the Internal Revenue Service* (Reference No. 2003-10-081). March 2003.

———. *Improvements Should Be Made to Better Control and Report Internal Revenue Service Restructuring and Reform Act of 1998 Section 1203 Information* (Reference No. 2001-10-188). September 2001.

———. *Increased Attention Is Needed to Ensure Timely, Accurate Determinations on Innocent Spouse Claims for Relief* (Reference No. 2000-40-063). May 2000.

———. *Internal Revenue Service Should Enhance Processes and Controls to Protect Taxpayers' Rights When Issuing Third Party Summonses and Making Third Party Contacts* (Reference No. 2000-40-064). April 2000.

———. *Internal Revenue Service Could Enhance the Process for Implementing New Tax Legislation* (Reference No. 2000-40-029). March 2000.

———. *Internal Revenue Service Responded to the Needs of Surviving Individual Taxpayers Following the September 11, 2001 Terrorist Attacks* (Reference No. 2002-10-140). August 2002.

———. *Internal Revenue Service Should Continue Its Efforts to Achieve Full Compliance with Restrictions on the Use of Enforcement Statistics* (Reference No. 1999-10-073). September 1999.

———. *Internal Revenue Service Worked Quickly to Assist Business Taxpayers Needing Disaster Relief After September 11, 2001* (Reference No. 2002-30-139). August 2002.

———. *More Taxpayers Can Benefit from the New Offer in Compromise Provisions* (Reference No. 2000-40-093). June 2000.

———. *Opportunities Exist to Improve Large Corporate Examination Results* (Reference No. 2000-30-131). September 2000.

———. *Opportunities Exist to Improve the Administration of the Earned Income Tax Credit* (Reference No. 2003-40-139). June 2003.

———. *Performance of the Customer Service Toll-Free Program Needs Improvement to Better Handle Millions of Taxpayer Calls* (Reference No. 2001-40-079). May 2001.

———. *Significant Efforts Have Been Made to Combat Abusive Trusts, but Additional Improvements Are Needed to Ensure Fairness and Compliance Objectives Are Achieved* (Reference No. 2002-30-050). February 2002.

———. *Trends in Compliance Activities Through Fiscal Year 2002,* 2003-30-078. (Washington, DC: March 2003), 2.

Ullman, Owen. "Treasury to Target Corporate Tax Abuses." *USA Today.* 29 February 2000.

U.S. General Accounting Office. *2001 Tax Filing Season, Systems Modernization, and Security of Electronic Filing* (GAO-01-595T). Washington, DC: GAO. 3 April 2001.

———. *2002 Tax Filing Season: Returns and Refunds Processed Smoothly; Quality of Assistance Improved* (GAO-03-314). Washington, DC: GAO. 20 December 2002.

———. *Alternatives for Improving Innocent Spouse Relief* (T-GGD-98-72). Washington, DC: GAO. 24 February 1998.

———. *Assessment of Budget Request for Fiscal Year 2003 and Interim Results of 2002 Tax Filing Season* (GAO-02-580T). Washington, DC: GAO. April 9, 2002.

———. *Assessment of Fiscal Year 2004 Budget Request and 2003 Filing Season Performance to Date* (GAO-03-641T). Washington, DC: GAO. 8 April 2003.

———. *Budget Justification: Options for Structure and Content* (GAO-02-711R). Washington, DC: GAO: 8 July 2002.

———. *Business and Systems Modernization Pose Challenges* (T-GGD/AIMD-99-138). Washington, DC: GAO. 15 April 1999.

———. *Business Practice, Performance Management, and Information Technology Challenges* (T-GGD/AIMD-00-144). Washington, DC: GAO. 10 April 2000.

———. *Challenges Facing the National Taxpayer Advocate* (T-GGD-98-28). Washington, DC: GAO. 10 February 1999.

———. *Custodial Financial Management Weaknesses* (AIMD-99-193). Washington, DC: GAO. 4 August 1999.

———. *Cyberfile Security Weaknesses* (AIMD-96-85R). Washington, DC: GAO. 9 May 1996.

———. *Cyberfile Was Poorly Planned and Managed* (AIMD-96-140). Washington, DC: GAO. 26 August 1996.

———. *Earned Income Credit: Opportunities to Make Recertification Program Less Confusing and More Consistent* (GAO-02-449). Washington, DC: GAO. 25 2002.

———. *Financial Audit: Examination of IRS' Fiscal Year 1994 Financial Statements* (AIMD-95-141). Washington, DC: GAO. 4 August 1995.

———. *Financial Audit: Examination of IRS' Fiscal Year 1997 Custodial Financial Statements* (AIMD-98-77). Washington, DC: GAO. 26 February 1998.

———. *Financial Audit: IRS' Fiscal Year 1998 Financial Statements* (AIMD-99-75). Washington, DC: GAO. 1 March 1999.

———. *Follow-up to the May 8, 2001, Hearing Regarding the IRS Restructuring Act's Goals and IRS Funding* (GAO-01-903R). Washington, DC: GAO. 29 June 2001.

———. *Formidable Challenges Confront IRS As It Attempts to Modernize* (T-GGD/AIMD-99-255). Washington, DC: GAO. 22 July 1999.

———. *Identifying Options for Organizational and Business Changes at IRS* (T-GGD-91-54). Washington, DC: GAO. 9 July 1991.

———. *Immediate and Long-Term Actions Needed to Improve Financial Management* (AIMD-99-16). Washington, DC: GAO. 30 October 1998.

———. *Information Related to the Scope and Complexity of the Federal Tax System* (GAO-01-301R). Washington, DC: GAO. 6 April 2001.

———. *IRS Faces Challenges As It Restructures the Office of the Taxpayer Advocate* (GGD-99-124). Washington, DC: GAO. 15 July 1999.

———. *IRS Needs to Continue Improving Operations and Service* (T-GGD/AIMD-96-170). Washington, DC: GAO. 29 July 1996.

———. *IRS Personnel Flexibilities: An Opportunity to Test New Approaches* (T-GGD-98-78). Washington, DC: GAO. 12 March 1998.

———. *IRS Restructuring Act: Implementation Under Way but Agency Modernization Important to Success* (T-GGD-00-53). Washington, DC: GAO. 2 February 2000.

———. *Long-Term Effort Under Way, but Significant Challenges Remain* (T-GGD/AIMD-00-154). Washington, DC: GAO. 3 May 2000.

———. *Physical Security over Taxpayer Receipts and Data Needs Improvement* (AIMD-99-15). Washington, DC: GAO. 30 November 1998.

———. *Progress Continues but Serious Management Challenges Remain* (GAO-01-562T). Washington, DC: GAO. 2 April 2001.

———. *Progress in Meeting the Challenge of Modernization IRS Tax Processing System* (T-IMTEC-90-5). Washington, DC: GAO. 22 March 1990.

———. *Restructuring Act Implementation* (GGD-00-71R). Washington, DC: GAO. 28 February 2000.

———. *Results of Review of IRS' Customer Account Data Engine Project* (GAO-01-717). Washington, DC: GAO. 12 June 2001.

———. *Review of the Estimates for the Impact of the September 11, 2001, Terrorist Attacks on New York Tax Revenues* (GAO-02-882R). Washington, DC: GAO. 26 July 2002.

———. *Section 1203* (GAO-03-394). Washington, DC: GAO. 14 February 2003.

———. *Small Business: Taxpayers Face Many Layers of Requirements* (T-GGD-99-76). Washington, DC: GAO. 12 April 1999.

———. *Statement of Rona Stillman Before the Subcommittee on Treasury and General Government, Committee on Appropriations, United States Senate.* Washington, DC: GAO. 15 April 1997.

———. *Systems Security: Tax Processing Operations and Data Still at Risk Due to Serious Weaknesses* (AIMD-97-49). Washington, DC: GAO. 8 April 1997.

———. *Tax Administration: Advance Tax Refund Program Was a Major Accomplishment, but Not Problem Free* (GAO-02-827). Washington, DC: GAO. 2 August 2002.

———. *Tax Administration: Electronic Filing Falling Short of Expectations* (GGD-96-12). Washington, DC: GAO. 31 October 1995.

———. *Tax Administration: Electronic Filing's Past and Future Impact on Processing Costs Dependent on Several Factors* (GAO-02-205). Washington, DC: GAO. 10 January 2002.

———. *Tax Administration: Fiscal Year 1997 Spending, 1997 Filing Season, and Fiscal Year 1998 Budget Request* (T-GGD/AIMD-97-66). Washington, DC: GAO. 18 March 1997.

———. *Tax Administration: Fiscal Year 1998 Budget Request* (T-GGD/AIMD-97-130). Washington DC: GAO. 19 June 1997.

———. *Tax Administration: Fiscal Year 1999 Budget Request and Fiscal Year 1998 Filing Season* (T-GGD/AIMD-98-114). Washington, DC: GAO. 31 March 1998.

———. *Tax Administration: Fiscal Year 2000 Budget Request and 1999 Tax Filing Season* (T-GGD/AIMD-99-140). Washington, DC: GAO. 13 April 1999.

———. *Tax Administration: Implementation of the Restructuring Act's Personnel Flexibility Provisions* (GGD-00-81). Washington, DC: GAO. 28 April 2000.

———. *Tax Administration: Implementation of the Restructuring Act's Taxpayer Protection and Rights Provisions* (GGD-00-85). Washington, DC: GAO. 21 April 2000.

———. *Tax Administration: Innocent Spouse Program Performance Improved; Balanced Performance Measures Needed* (GAO-02-558). Washington, DC: GAO. 24 April 2002.

———. *Tax Administration: Innocent Spouse Relief* (GGD-98-77R). Washington, DC: GAO. 11 March 1998.

———. *Tax Administration: Interim Report on Advance Tax Refunds* (GAO-02-257). Washington, DC: GAO. 13 December 2001.

———. *Tax Administration: IRS and TIGTA Should Evaluate Their Processing of Employee Misconduct under Section 1203* (GAO-03-394). Washington, DC: GAO. 14 February 2003.

———. *Tax Administration: IRS Continues to Face Management Challenges in Its Business Practices and Modernization Efforts* (GAO-02-619T). Washington, DC: GAO. 15 April 2002.

———. *Tax Administration: IRS Faces Several Challenges As It Attempts to Better Serve Small Businesses* (GGD-00-166). Washington, DC: GAO. 10 August 2000.

———. *Tax Administration: IRS Should Evaluate the Changes to Its Offer in Compromise Program* (GAO-02-311). Washington, DC: GAO. 15 March 2002.

———. *Tax Administration: Problem-Solving Days* (GGD-99-1). Washington, DC: GAO. 16 October 1998.

———. *Tax Administration: Telephone Routing Interactive System May Not Meet Expectations* (GGD-98-152). Washington, DC: GAO. 13 July 1998.

———. *Tax Administration: Uses of and Problems with IRS' Non-Master File* (GGD-99-42). Washington, DC: GAO. 21 April 1999.

———. *Tax Systems Modernization: Assessment of IRS' Design Master Plan* (IMTEC-91-53BR). Washington, DC: GAO. 25 June 1991.

———. *Tax Systems Modernization: Challenge for the Twenty-First Century* (IMTEC-90-13). Washington, DC: GAO. 8 February 1990.

———. *Tax Systems Modernization: Imaging System's Performance Improving but Still Falls Short of Expectations* (GGD-97-29). Washington, DC: GAO. 16 January 1997.

———. *Tax Systems Modernization: IRS Needs to Resolve Certain Issues with Its Integrated Case Processing System* (GGD/AIMD-97-31). Washington, DC: GAO. 17 January 1997.

———. *Tax Systems Modernization: Issues Facing IRS* (T-IMTEC-91-18). Washington, DC: GAO. 9 July 1991.

———. *Tax Systems Modernization: Management and Technical Weaknesses Must Be Corrected If Modernization Is to Succeed* (AIMD-95-156). Washington, DC: GAO. 26 July 1995.

———. *Tax Systems Modernization: Progress in Achieving IRS' Business Vision* (T-GGD-96-123). Washington, DC: GAO. 9 May 1996.

———. *Tax Systems Modernization: Results of Review of IRS' Initial Expenditure Plan* (AIMD/GGD-99-206). Washington, DC: GAO. 15 June 1999.

———. *Tax Systems Modernization: Status of Planning and Technical Foundation* (T-AIMD/GGD-94-104). Washington, DC: GAO. 2 March 1994.

———. *Telephone Assistance: Limited Progress and Missed Opportunities to Analyze Performance in the 2001 Filing Season* (GAO-02-212). Washington, DC: GAO. 7 December 2001.

———. *Telephone Assistance: Opportunities to Improve Human Capital Management* (GAO-01-144). Washington, DC: GAO. 30 January 2001.

———. *Telephone Assistance: Quality of Service Mixed in the 2000 Filing Season and Below IRS' Long-Term Goal* (GAO-01-189). Washington, DC: GAO. 6 April 2001.

———. *Use of Enforcement Statistics in Employee Evaluations* (GGD-99-11). Washington, DC: GAO. 30 November 1998.

U.S. Senate Committee on Finance. *Hearings on IRS Oversight.* 105th Congress, Senate Hearing 105-598. 28 April to 1 May 1998.

———. *Hearings on IRS Restructuring.* 105th Congress, Senate Hearing 105-529. 28–29 January 1998.

———. *Hearings on the Practices and Procedures of the Internal Revenue Service.* 105th Congress, Senate Hearing 105-190. 23–25 September 1997.

———. *Nomination Hearing of Charles O. Rossotti, to Be Commissioner of the Internal Revenue Service.* 105th Congress. 23 October 1997. Moffitt Reporting Services, Washington, DC, 1997.

Vartabedian, Ralph. "IRS Pulls Plug on Its Electronic Tax-Filing System." *Los Angeles Times.* 11 September 1996.

———. "To an IRS Mired in the '60s, '90s Answers Prove Elusive." *Los Angeles Times.* 9 December 1996.

Warner, Margaret. Report on the IRS. *The News Hour with Jim Lehrer.* PBS. 24 September 1997.

Wells, Rob. "House Passes Broad Bill Overhauling IRS." *Chicago Sun-Times.* 26 June 1998.

———. "IRS Tries to Reform Itself as Congress Debates." Associated Press. 31 January 1998.

White, Ben. "Long-Term Capital Case Puts Tax Shelters on Trial." *Washington Post.* 23 July 2003.

Wilen, John. "Casino, Workers Beat IRS Over Tax on Meals." *Las Vegas Sun.* 13 May 1999.

———. "Court Overturns Tax on Casino Employee Meals." *Las Vegas Sun.* 12 May 1999.

———. "IRS May Not Budge on Casino Meal Tax." *Las Vegas Sun.* 22 January 1999.

———. "IRS Suspends Casino Meal Tax Work." *Las Vegas Sun.* 17 May 1999.

Williams, B. John. "The Office of Chief Counsel: A Renewed Commitment to Guidance." *Tax Executive.* March–April 2002.

Wiseman, Paul, et al. "Helpful IRS Attracts Thousands: Open Houses in Thirty-Three Cities Called Successful." *USA Today.* 17 November 1997.

Index